Understand Applied Psychology

D1546338

Teach Yourself

Understand
Applied Psychology
Nicky Hayes

For UK order enquiries: please contact Bookpoint Ltd,
130 Milton Park, Abingdon, Oxon OX14 4SB.
Telephone: +44 (0) 1235 827720. Fax: +44 (0) 1235 400454.
Lines are open 09.00–17.00, Monday to Saturday, with a 24-hour
message answering service. Details about our titles and how to
order are available at www.teachyourself.com

For USA order enquiries: please contact McGraw-Hill Customer
Services, PO Box 545, Blacklick, OH 43004-0545, USA.
Telephone: 1-800-722-4726. Fax: 1-614-755-5645.

For Canada order enquiries: please contact McGraw-Hill Ryerson
Ltd, 300 Water St, Whitby, Ontario L1N 9B6, Canada.
Telephone: 905 430 5000. Fax: 905 430 5020.

Long renowned as the authoritative source for self-guided
learning – with more than 50 million copies sold worldwide –
the **Teach Yourself** series includes over 500 titles in the fields of
languages, crafts, hobbies, business, computing and education.

British Library Cataloguing in Publication Data: a catalogue record
for this title is available from the British Library.

Library of Congress Catalog Card Number: on file.

First published in UK 2001 by Hodder Education, part of
Hachette UK, 338 Euston Road, London NW1 3BH.

First published in US 2001 by The McGraw-Hill Companies, Inc.

This edition published 2010.

Previously published as *Teach Yourself Applied Psychology*

The **Teach Yourself** name is a registered trade mark of Hodder
Headline.

Copyright © 2001, 2003, 2010 Nicky Hayes

Typeset by MPS Limited, A Macmillan Company.

Printed in Great Britain for Hodder Education, an Hachette UK
Company, 338 Euston Road, London NW1 3BH, by CPI Cox &
Wyman, Reading, Berkshire RG1 8EX.

The publisher has used its best endeavours to ensure that the URLs
for external websites referred to in this book are correct and active
at the time of going to press. However, the publisher and the
author have no responsibility for the websites and can make no
guarantee that a site will remain live or that the content will remain
relevant, decent or appropriate.

Hachette UK's policy is to use papers that are natural, renewable
and recyclable products and made from wood grown in sustainable
forests. The logging and manufacturing processes are expected to
conform to the environmental regulations of the country of origin.

Impression number   10 9 8 7 6 5 4 3 2 1
Year   2014 2013 2012 2011 2010

Contents

Meet the author

Welcome to *Understand Applied Psychology*!

As you'll know if you've read my sister book *Understand Psychology*, psychology, in general, is about ordinary people – how we think, act and make sense of our worlds. But psychology is also a profession, and professional psychologists use their knowledge in many different areas of everyday living. In this book, I have been exploring some of the many ways that psychologists contribute to our daily lives. Sometimes, this is about the work of highly trained professional psychologists. Educational, clinical and forensic psychologists, along with some others, are people who have undergone rigorous specialized training and work in clearly defined areas. But many other psychologists have applied psychological knowledge in different fields. Sometimes, they have been academic psychologists whose specialized knowledge has meant that they could contribute to a particular aspect of social practice. Sometimes they have been more general psychologists who have acted as consultants in particular areas.

Whatever their origins, I have always been fascinated by the sheer range of applications of psychology – and this book is only the tip of the iceberg. We are finding new ways to use psychological knowledge every day. And it is directly helpful, because just about everything we do has to do with other people in some way, and understanding other people better helps us to co-operate and interact in more positive ways. Not only that, but a lot of the insights which psychology has to offer just aren't obvious. Or, more importantly, they only become obvious once someone has pointed them out. Did you realize, for example, just how much a positive frame of mind can help people to deal with stress? Or how important belief is in recovering from strokes?

A better knowledge of psychology can help us to tackle any number of everyday problems. Even if it doesn't give us the answers, it can help us to go about asking the questions better, or dealing with the unknown so that it doesn't stress us as much. This book is only a sample of how psychological knowledge can help in this way, and I'm sure as you read it you'll think of other possibilities. I hope so, anyway, and I hope you enjoy reading it as much as I have enjoyed collecting all this information and bringing it together.

Happy reading!

Nicky Hayes, 2010

Only got a minute?

Psychology is about people – how our minds work, how we interact with other people, and how we cope with the challenges of day-to-day living.

People are 'natural' psychologists, in that we learn about other people almost from infancy. But people are complex, so psychology is complex too. There aren't any simple answers to understanding people, but a knowledge of psychological processes and mechanisms can give us a lot of insight.

Applied psychology is concerned with using the insights of psychology to understand different aspects of what human beings do. Psychology covers a great many different areas of human activity, and has a broad range of applications in everyday life. For example, insights from applied cognitive psychology can be used to improve memory, and applied bio-psychology helps people to deal with the effects of brain injuries or surgery. Clinical psychologists treat those whose life-problems have resulted in mental illness and forensic psychologists work with police and the judiciary to deal with psychological aspects of crime or criminal investigations.

These are just a few examples of how applied psychology is used to deal with everyday problems, often in quite unexpected ways.

5 Only got five minutes?

Historically, psychology has been applied almost since psychology first began.

As there are many areas of psychology, so there are many areas of applied psychology. Insights from applied cognitive psychology were used to improve the design of aircraft cockpits and radar installations during WWII, and have been applied in many other contexts, including improving memory. Social psychology has been applied in social skills training, and also in understanding and changing social prejudice. Applied bio-psychology tells us about the relationship between the body and the mind. Studies of people who have had surgery or injury to the brain allow bio-psychologists to understand more about its functioning, while our knowledge of emotion and anxiety enables development of better coping mechanisms. Developmental psychology is concerned with how people grow and develop throughout the lifespan.

Clinical, counselling and health psychologists all work mainly in the health system. Clinical psychologists work with other mental health personnel to help those whose life-problems has resulted in mental illness. Counselling psychologists work closely with other health professionals, and are generally concerned with assisting ordinary people to cope with their life-problems, rather than dealing with people who are mentally ill. Health psychologists aim to enhance aspects of health care, such as doctor-patient communication or health promotion schemes.

Some applied psychologists work in the judicial system. Forensic psychologists work with police, the courts, and the judiciary to deal with psychological aspects of crime or criminal investigations. Educational psychologists work with the courts to provide professional assessments, and also with schools to address special needs, underachievement, or school programmes like tackling bullying. Psychologists who specialize in the applied psychology of teaching and learning apply psychology to the learning and assessment process.

Occupational psychologists are particularly concerned with the individual at work, with considerable expertise in evaluation and assessment in different aspects of working life. Organizational psychologists work at the level of the organisation as a whole dealing with organizational change, teamworking or innovations, and organizational cultures. Engineering and design psychologists may specialize in ergonomics – that is, efficiency and effectiveness of design, or with the human–machine interface. Some applied psychologists have looked at how psychological processes are involved in interactive design. Space psychologists are mainly concerned with the social needs of astronauts, and coping with extended space missions.

Sport psychologists help athletes and ordinary competitors in maintaining motivation, in skill learning, and in achieving peak performance. Consumer psychologists are concerned with people's buying habits, and the choices which they make. Because of their expertise in handling data, consumer psychologists are also often involved in developing tools for market researchers. Environmental psychologists are interested in how people interact with their environments. They look at how people maintain territories and define spaces, at important psychological mechanisms such as self-efficacy or manageable goals for successful green living, and at strategies for reducing urban stress. Political psychologists apply psychological insights to various aspects of the political processes, such as how information is used in wartime, or how knowledge of social identity processes can help mediation and political reconciliation.

Each form of applied psychology has different training requirements. Some have clear training structures, while others, such as space psychology, do not. But whatever the area, becoming a qualified psychologist involves a recognized first degree in psychology, a relevant postgraduate qualification, and some period of supervised practice. In the UK, this is all overseen by the British Psychological Society, and more information can be obtained from their website at www.bps.org.uk.

10 Only got ten minutes?

As there are many areas of psychology, so there are many areas of applied psychology.

Cognitive psychology is the study of how the mind processes information, including attention and memory. Insights from applied cognitive psychology range from improving the design of aircraft cockpits and radar installations during World War II, to exploring the sources of everyday errors, which in normal life may be unimportant but which can sometimes lead to large-scale disasters such as explosions or major transport accidents.

Social psychology has been applied in a variety of contexts, since so much of what people do is social in origin. One of its first uses is social skills training, which can help people to recover from the social isolation resulting from inappropriate non-verbal behaviour. Applied social psychologists have also helped us to understand the roots of social prejudice.

Applied bio-psychology tells us about the relationship between the body and the mind. Applied psychologists working in this area have considerable knowledge of clinical neuropsychology – which bits of the brain are involved in which aspects of human activity or cognition. As a result, they are able to offer useful advice on recovery from strokes or specific brain injuries, and the effects of injuries such as closed head injuries. Another application of bio-psychology is concerned with how our emotions affect us physically, and this has helped us to develop better techniques for managing stress or anxiety.

Developmental psychology is concerned with how people grow and develop throughout life, but most of its applications to date have been to do with bringing up children. Applied developmental psychologists have investigated aspects of attachment and deprivation, and how these impact on the child, and at how socialization processes work. They have also investigated the psychology of effective discipline, showing how punishment is rarely effective as a means of controlling behaviour, and how the judicious use of reward, and also of positive social expectations, can have more effect.

Clinical, counselling and **health psychologists** all work mainly in the health system. **Clinical psychologists** work with other mental health personnel to help those whose life-problems have resulted in mental illness. **Counselling psychologists** work closely with other health professionals, but they are generally concerned with assisting ordinary people to cope with their life-problems, rather than dealing with people who are mentally ill. **Health psychologists** aim to enhance aspects of health care, for example in establishing good communication between patients and professionals, such as doctor–patient communication.

Some applied psychologists work in the judicial system. **Forensic psychologists** are particularly concerned with applying psychology to crime and the problems occurring around criminal activity. Some forensic psychologists work in the judicial system, dealing with psychological matters arising in the work of the courts or acting as expert witnesses in particular cases, while others work directly with the police to help to investigate crime, and to identify criminals and culpability.

Educational psychologists work in the educational system. One of their important roles is in evaluating special educational needs of particular children, and they are skilled at diagnosing educational problems such as dyslexia. Another important part of their work is in developing evaluation programmes for local authorities which look at specific learning strategies or the implementation of new aspects of curriculum delivery.

Psychologists who specialize in the applied psychology of **teaching and learning** are more closely focused on the learning process. One aspect of this is looking at how students can be encouraged to manage their learning effectively, and at the psychological processes taking place during study and in the classroom which either enhance or interfere with effective learning.

Both **occupational** and **organizational psychologists** are concerned with the world of work. **Occupational psychologists** are particularly concerned with the individual at work, using their expertise in job or promotional selection, to provide vocational guidance and to deal with individual work-related problems. **Organizational psychologists** work at the level of the organization as a whole; they may be concerned with introducing new practices, such as team-working, to the organization, or they may analyse resistance to change from the workforce; and some specialize in organizational cultures.

Engineering and **design psychologists** deal with how human beings work with machinery or other complex systems; their concerns include looking at ergonomics, human–machine interaction and the psychological factors which are involved in interactive exhibits and other programmes.

Space psychology is relatively new and really developed as a result of the Soviet space programme, which involved psychologists right from the start. The Russian psychological support teams would take care of the psychological needs of cosmonauts, particularly those on long-term missions at space stations, and help them to cope with the various demands of the experience – including readapting to earth gravity and to the social aspects of their return to earth.

Sport psychology has been in existence for a hundred years or so, and is one of the oldest branches of applied psychology. Sport psychologists assist both professional athletes and ordinary competitors in improving their sport performance, including helping people to maintain their motivation, contributing to training practices, and enabling people to develop and use psychological techniques which can help them to achieve peak performance on the day of a competition.

Consumer psychologists are concerned with people's buying habits, and the choices which they make. One important area is in the psychology of advertising, which draws on psychological knowledge to make sure that advertisements are distinctive and effective. Consumer psychologists also apply their psychological expertise to consumer decision making, looking at how mechanisms like anchoring and entrapment affect the decisions that people make.

Environmental psychologists are applied psychologists who are interested in how people interact with, and are influenced by, the settings in which they find themselves. They look at how people maintain territories, or define spaces as appropriate for certain uses, and apply this knowledge to help architects and others to design appropriate areas for human activity.

Political psychologists apply their psychological insights to various aspects of the political process, such as analysing the use of propaganda in wartime, aiding diplomats in mediating confrontations and bringing the various sides together to resolve conflicts, and helping to establish effective political reconciliation after open conflicts have ceased.

Each form of applied psychology has different training requirements. Established areas such as educational, clinical, occupational and forensic psychology have clear training structures, while others, such as space psychology, do not have explicit training systems. Whatever the area, though, becoming a qualified psychologist involves a recognized first degree in psychology, a relevant postgraduate qualification and some period of supervised practice. In the UK, this is overseen by the British Psychological Society, and more information about the work of professional psychologists and the training they are expected to complete can be obtained from their website at www.bps.org.uk.

1

Applying psychology

In this chapter you will learn:
- **the difference between applied and academic psychology**
- **about the historical beginnings of applied psychology**
- **to identify different areas and approaches of applied psychology.**

Psychology is the study of people – how they think, what they experience, why they act as they do and what motivates them. It's a fascinating subject, and a massive one.

We spend most of our conscious lives making sense of people, in one way or another. In fact, we begin from the moment we are tiny babies. Even the smallest infants arrive 'pre-tuned' to other people – ready to respond to human voices, faces and touch. A lot of our infancy and childhood is spent learning how to deal with social life, beginning with how to communicate effectively, and moving on to dealing with other family members, friends, school or work colleagues and eventually lovers and partners.

So we are all 'natural' psychologists in some ways, and lots of the time we are very good at it. But not always. People are enormously complicated, and even when we think we know someone really well they can still surprise us. We all have a lot of potential which doesn't show on the surface. So don't be fooled by anyone who tells you that people are easy to understand – they are not. There's much more to everyone than meets the eye.

And that's where psychology comes in. Psychologists look below the surface, to understand the underlying processes and mechanisms which produce human behaviour. They study how people interact, both in groups and in pairs, and what sorts of communication are likely to become effective. And they look at the different areas and functions of the human mind.

We looked at the main areas of psychology in the companion volume to this book: *Understand Psychology*. If you've read that, you'll have a pretty fair idea of what those are, and some of the kinds of knowledge which psychologists have developed. Or you might have read some other psychology books, which have also given you some knowledge of the discipline. There's quite a lot around. But you don't need to have read *Understand Psychology* to understand this book. They go together and complement one another, but they don't depend on each other.

Applying psychology

In this book, we are going to look at psychology from a slightly different angle – from the point of view of how psychology has been applied to some human questions and issues. Psychology has been used in many areas of life, ranging from how we bring up our children to how astronauts deal with weightlessness. Obviously, we won't be able to look at all of them. But we can take a look at some of the main areas of applied psychology, and that should give us a better understanding of some of the ways that psychology can contribute to our everyday lives.

Insight
Trying to define where psychology has been applied is a bit like catching water in a net. People are always finding new ways to apply psychology, because who we are and how we think affects just about everything we do.

Different sections of this book will be dealing with different aspects of applied psychology. We'll begin by looking at how knowledge obtained from traditional 'pure' psychological research has been applied. There have been quite a few spin-offs from academic research areas, so in the next four chapters we'll look at some of the applications of knowledge from social psychology, cognitive psychology, bio-psychology and developmental psychology.

Then we'll look at some of the areas which relate particularly to how psychologists work in the community as a whole. We'll begin with clinical psychology, since that is one of the oldest and most well-established areas of applied psychology. Then we'll go on to look at several other areas: health psychology, forensic psychology, educational psychology, and the applied psychology of teaching and learning.

The next group of chapters is concerned with how psychology has been applied to working life, or to particular vocations. They deal with occupational psychology, which has to do with working out the right types of work for different people; with organizational psychology, which is concerned with the human aspects of management; with engineering and design psychology, which is concerned with how people interact with objects and machines; and with space psychology, which as its name suggests is concerned with the psychological dimensions of space exploration.

This final group of chapters deals with some of the broader aspects of social living. We begin with sport psychology, an area of applied psychology which has existed for a long time and is becoming more and more important as our knowledge grows. The increasing professionalization of sport means that we could, of course, make a case for putting it with the previous set of chapters, but it can equally well link with the rest of the chapters in this set. We go on to look at consumer psychology, which includes the psychology of advertising and consumer behaviour – something that affects all of our lives. Then we look at environmental psychology, and how the environment we live in influences our experience, and then finally we will look at the increasingly important area of political psychology.

Naturally, that doesn't cover all of the areas of applied psychology. Psychology has relevance anywhere human beings are active and that, almost by definition, covers just about all aspects of social life. But this book ought to give you an idea of the range and scope of applied psychology – and perhaps some ideas for other areas where psychology could usefully contribute to our everyday lives.

Applied psychology – some history

Applied psychology is much older than a lot of people think. In fact, psychology has been applied from the moment that psychology became developed enough to make predictions. Those theories were brought into action to address small everyday problems, in much the same way that modern psychologists are often called on to help in the solving of small everyday issues. But that type of applied psychology is very informal, and doesn't tend to stay in the records.

Insight

Some (applied) psychologists have argued that actually, applied psychology came first and 'pure' psychology came later. Although academic psychology traces its academic roots in experimental philosophy, it has equally strong roots in clinical medicine and in the explanations of crowd psychology which were developed in the eighteenth and nineteenth centuries to explain social riots.

The applied psychology which has gone down in the history of the discipline began at the beginning of the last century, some say with the work of the French psychologist Alfred Binet. Binet had been observing children, and had particularly been looking at how they become able to tackle different problems at different ages. He was also mulling over a particular educational challenge. The French government was setting up special schooling to help those children who were what we would now call educationally challenged. These special schools were very advanced, and also provided full boarding for their children, so they were quite attractive to many poor families.

Binet needed to sort out a way of distinguishing between children who were genuinely 'slow', and children who were just pretending to be slow in order to get into the new schools. With a problem like this, you can't just judge it on how those children speak or what they look like (despite what some people think) because some very bright children speak quite slowly, and some children who find it hard to grasp new ideas seem perfectly ordinary on the surface.

Binet had observed that it wasn't a matter of such children being unable to learn. Instead, they just learned a bit more slowly than others. For example: a seven-year-old who fell into this category might be learning the kinds of things that an ordinary five-year-old would normally be tackling. So what Binet did was to use his research on children's problem-solving to put together the very first intelligence test. He assembled a series of puzzles of different kinds – some practical, some paper-and-pencil, and tried them out on a lot of children. The results let him see what ordinary children might be expected to do at different ages. That meant that he could use the test to form an idea of a child's mental age.

The idea of 'mental age' led on to a concept which has become everyday knowledge in our society – **IQ**, or the **intelligence quotient**. It's been through a lot of adjusting, but it originally came from Binet's formula:

$$IQ = \frac{\text{mental age}}{\text{chronological age}} \times 100$$

The way the formula works out is that someone whose mental age is lower than their chronological age – their actual age in years – will have an IQ below 100. The lower it is, the further behind they will be. Someone whose mental age is exactly the same as their chronological age – in other words, someone who is completely 'normal' in that respect – will end up with an IQ of 100. Someone whose mental age is higher than their chronological age – a precocious or advanced child – will end up with an IQ above 100.

The higher it is, the further ahead of other children of their age they will be.

This gave the French government a system for selecting children for special schooling – something which was very advanced social policy for its time. It meant that these children, rather than being rejected by society as a whole, could get the education they needed. It also meant that they could learn to become independent, participating members of society, because their education was paced at a speed that they could cope with. That was one of the very first systematic uses of applied psychology.

Like any other science, though, psychology can be abused, or used for negative purposes. Binet's work on intelligence testing was seized on and transformed by other psychologists (and by politicians in other societies), until it became completely different from the system which Binet had developed. In fact, it ended up being used in ways which were completely opposite to the ones which he had recommended. Eventually, those ideas were used (on the basis of some very dodgy science) to rationalize racist immigration policies and compulsory sterilization of imbeciles in the USA. Those policies in their turn were much admired by the German Nazis, and used as the basis for their social segregation of Jews, and ultimately as part of their rationalization of the Holocaust. (If you're interested, you can find out more about this in Steven Jay Gould's excellent book *The Mismeasure of Man*.)

Insight

The misuse of intelligence test results for ideological aims continued right through the twentieth century, and is sometimes used as the basis for racist propaganda even today. But it has no foundation in real science.

Any knowledge which works can be used for good or for evil. That's the nature of effective knowledge. Applied psychology isn't often abused so dramatically today, but any knowledge which has the potential to enrich people's lives also has the potential for abuse. A good understanding of non-verbal communication, for example, can be applied to help people to communicate with one another more effectively and to break down social prejudices. But it can also be applied to manipulate others so that they are more likely to act in ways that the manipulator wants them to act. Understanding how psychology can be, and has been, applied helps us to distinguish between manipulative and positive uses of that knowledge more effectively.

Academic and applied psychology

Academic psychology is largely concerned with developing psychological knowledge – exploring our understanding of human beings, mental processes, developing better ways of looking at human experience, and observing how physiological and developmental factors influence people. That knowledge, for the most part, is gathered for its own sake – it all helps us to understand more about people and what makes them 'tick'.

That knowledge often has implications for our everyday lives. Psychologists studying memory, for example, did so because it was an intrinsically interesting area of study. But the knowledge that they gathered can tell us a great deal about how we can improve our memories, or how we should go about preparing for exams if we want to remember the material effectively. It wasn't collected for applied reasons, but once it is there, it can be used.

A great deal of applied psychology is like that. Psychologists have brought together knowledge and insights that have been gleaned from academic psychology, and applied them to everyday life. For the most part, that works very well. But there are still some tensions between the two.

PROBABILITY AND CERTAINTY

One of the most important tensions relates to the question of certainty. If you look carefully at psychological reports – or indeed, at the research reports of any scientist – you will discover that their findings are always expressed tentatively, leaving room for alternative possibilities. Research scientists know that nothing can ever be definitively proven – there is always room for error or uncertainty even in the most promising of research findings.

An applied psychologist is interested in using knowledge in practice, though. So in applied psychology, a finding which implies a relationship between a cause and an effect is taken and used as if that relationship were fairly well established. It's a reasonable thing to do, partly because the ways that professional psychologists use knowledge always allows for alternative possibilities, and partly because academic knowledge is always expressed like that anyway. A scientist may express uncertainty about a finding even when they are 99 per cent, or 95 per cent confident of their results. In everyday living, we treat that as strong enough to act on, even though it isn't absolutely definite.

Applied psychologists have all been trained in research methodology, and are aware of those uncertainties. A psychology degree is broad-ranging, designed to give a would-be psychologist a good awareness across the discipline, and that's not accidental. Because people are so complex, we need to draw on a broad range of knowledge for any type of basic understanding. So the education of an applied psychologist includes that broad overview as well as the specialist knowledge covered in their higher-level professional training. It gives them a theoretical 'tool-kit' to gain a deeper understanding of the situations they are dealing with, but it also means that they have a good working awareness of the academic discipline from which their knowledge comes.

Insight

Applied psychology has sometimes been important for keeping psychology on the straight and narrow. Real-world researchers such as Lewin, Rogers and Bruner injected a note of realism into psychology when it might otherwise have become carried away by the formal reductionism of behaviourism or the intellectualized idealism of cognitivism.

RIFTS BETWEEN ACADEMIC AND APPLIED PSYCHOLOGY

For much of the twentieth century, applied psychology and academic psychology were quite separate. When the founder of behaviourist psychology, J.B. Watson, was asked to leave his university following the scandal of an affair with his secretary, he went into advertising, where he made a successful career applying the theory he had previously been developing. That was in the 1930s, and the general view within psychology was that his move into applied psychology was a complete break from academic work – the two had nothing to do with one another.

These rifts became wider and wider, particularly in the USA, until ultimately the US professional psychological association split into separate organizations. Other countries were a bit less extreme about it: what happened in the USA resulted in the deliberate forging of closer links between applied and academic psychology in the UK, so that the same thing wouldn't happen there, as people recognized the risks and disadvantages of that sort of separation.

The debates which resulted from this rift also enabled psychologists to recognize that the contribution wasn't just one way. Applied psychology feeds back into academic psychology, contributing insights and areas of exploration. The classic example here is sport psychology, which has always had a very productive two-way relationship between academic and applied research. It's not the only such area, and the dialogue between academic and applied psychologists means that new areas are being developed and explored all the time. So in many ways academic and applied psychology are coming back together.

....

Insight

In many respects, the distinction between academic and applied psychology is an artificial one. Academics are expected to state practical applications and social uses for their research when they are applying for research funding, and without good answers they wouldn't be likely to get it.

(Contd)

And applied psychologists are expected to show how their findings might contribute to wider general knowledge as well as the specific situations they have been studying.

So as you read through this book, you'll find some areas of applied psychology which are applications of theoretical knowledge that you might have come across in other reading. You'll find some areas of psychological knowledge which have been developed just by the psychologists working in that particular area. And you'll come across some areas of applied psychology which draw on knowledge obtained from research in other areas of applied psychology.

Wherever it comes from, though, it always has the same aim – to give us a better understanding of what is going on, so that we can help people to resolve problems, and use psychological knowledge to the benefit of society as a whole. That's really what applied psychology is all about – but I'll leave it to you to judge how effectively it has been able to achieve that goal!

10 THINGS TO REMEMBER

1 *Everyone is a 'natural' psychologist, but people are more complex than we realize.*

2 *Psychology helps us to identify underlying processes and mechanisms of the mind.*

3 *Just about all areas of psychology have relevance for the real world in some way.*

4 *Even traditionally academic areas of psychology have their real-world applications.*

5 *Many areas of applied psychology have specific qualification pathways and training.*

6 *Some areas of applied psychology have developed in new contexts and don't yet have recognized qualification pathways.*

7 *IQ testing was one of the earliest areas of applied psychology.*

8 *Academic psychologists do teaching and research; applied psychologists put psychological knowledge to work.*

9 *Academic and applied psychology have split in the USA, but not in most other parts of the world.*

10 *There is a healthy two-way relationship between academic and applied psychology.*

2

Applied cognitive psychology

In this chapter you will learn:
- *to describe three important factors which can improve sustained attention*
- *to see how we can use psychological knowledge to improve our memories*
- *why using mental imagery can improve memory.*

Cognitive psychologists study how the mind processes information: how we perceive the world, how we remember information, and how we think about and solve problems. Psychologists have been studying cognitive processes for over 140 years – ever since the beginning of psychology – and during that time they have learned a great deal. And applied cognitive psychology, as its name suggests, involves putting that knowledge to use.

Insight

Cognitive psychology is all about what the mind does – how we think, remember, analyse information, etc. So it could be argued that all cognitive psychology that connects with the real world is actually a form of applied psychology.

Although psychologists have studied some subjects, like memory, ever since the beginning of psychology, cognitive psychology as we know it actually only really developed after World War II. It began during the war itself, as psychologists were employed in military intelligence, and also worked in other military systems.

Psychologists were also involved in the code-breaking initiatives at Bletchley Park, which contributed so much to the eventual Allied victory. So we could say that applied cognitive psychology was really born during World War II.

One of the key psychologists involved in raising applied cognitive psychology to full maturity was Donald Broadbent, who applied a rigorous experimental approach to the study of complex problems. By doing this, he was able to study how the mind works in a precise, objective way: important in the post-war climate of scientific progress. Applied cognitive psychology grew rapidly, influencing developments from the design of aircraft cockpits to the introduction of postcodes and new coins. We don't have space to look at all of these in this book, so in this chapter we'll just look at three areas: attention, types of everyday error and their effects, and improving memory.

Insight

It is remarkable how much wars can drive the development of scientific knowledge. Chemistry, nutrition and metallurgy, as well as applied psychology, were all stimulated by World War II. And the period after the war, when so many demobbed servicemen went into universities to teach and study, is still regarded as the heyday of British universities.

Attention

Have you ever looked into an aircraft cockpit, or maybe seen one on TV? If you have, you may have noticed the sheer number of dials and indicators: anyone flying a plane has to deal with an enormous amount of information. They have to know what the internal systems of the plane are doing; how the controls are set and the capabilities of further adjustment that they offer; and about the external environment – wind speed, height above ground, and so on. All of these can be quite bewildering, but are vitally important. A mistake can be fatal, and in the case of early aircraft, often was.

So the first applied cognitive psychologists devoted a considerable amount of time to understanding attention – what catches our attention, how we choose what to notice from a large set of possibilities, and what factors can help us to keep our attention on something for long periods of time.

FOCUSING ATTENTION

Careful experimental research quickly established some fundamental principles about displays. One of them, for example, was that the most important information should be in the centre of the visual field, rather than towards the edges. Previously, indicator dials in aircraft had been placed rather haphazardly. But this meant that sometimes the most important indicators were right on the edge of the pilot's vision, while the ones right in the middle of the dashboard were less important. When they reorganized the dials following the psychologists' advice, it became apparent that the pilots were more comfortable with the arrangement and also made fewer errors.

There were other factors, such as the way that the size of letters or symbols should be larger when indicating more information, and colours should be deliberately used to help the important information to stand out. That's one of the ideas which sounds obvious when you think about it, but actually isn't obvious, because most people don't think about such things. A look around any town centre will show you countless examples where 'artistic' design has overcome the requirements of communicating information, so that the important information has become hidden or is easily missed.

Insight

Food labelling is a classic example of bad informational design. What people mostly want to know when they are reading food labels is what is actually in the food. But the ingredients list is often so completely overshadowed by other stuff, like the various energy and fat symbols or allergy warnings, that it can be quite hard to find.

The assumption, of course, is that people will seek out the information they want. But in a world in which people are surrounded by messages of one sort or another, it isn't practical to assume that they will always have the time and cognitive space to sift out the information they really need from the rest. If we want to communicate effectively, we have to take steps to attract attention towards the information that we want people to receive. Advertisers understand this very well, of course, but many public notices could do with applying this basic psychological knowledge more regularly. In situations where mistakes could have catastrophic consequences, it becomes even more important.

SELECTIVE ATTENTION

Selective attention is all about how we choose to pay attention to certain stimuli rather than others. An aircraft pilot, for example, receives auditory information through the headphones, as well as many different bits of visual information from the display. Often this is routine, but sometimes it contains crucial information which the pilot needs to pay particular attention to. So cognitive psychologists have spent a lot of time learning how people pick out relevant items of information from a lot of other stimuli.

There are other situations, too, where we need to pay particular attention to some stimuli and disregard others. If you are in a crowded pub or in a noisy shopping centre, you are often surrounded by the sounds of people talking. But you have no difficulty directing your attention so that you only hear the people you are listening to, and ignore all the rest. We do it so well, in fact, that it seems as though the people we are with are talking louder than other people – the sound of their voices seems to 'stand out' from the background of other voices. But if you were to make a tape recording of a conversation in the same situation, you would find that, actually, the background noise is so loud that it often drowns out the conversation itself.

This is known as the **cocktail party phenomenon**, because it was discovered in the 1950s when cocktail parties were very fashionable, but it happens in any situation where you have a lot of people talking to one another in the same place. Channelling our attention seems to exaggerate the strength of the signal. The visual cues – what we can see of the other person's face and body – help too. That's why it's often difficult to have telephone conversations with people who are phoning from crowded places.

Insight

We can really notice how much we use selective attention when we are trying to concentrate on something but keep being interrupted by other people or distracted by stimuli like TV or street noise. Most of the time we filter such things out quite easily.

The cocktail party phenomenon attracted a lot of attention from applied cognitive psychologists, because it was felt that understanding how it worked could help to cut out a lot of accidents. Broadbent's own model was somewhat simplistic – he believed that we attend mainly to the physical qualities of the message, such as which direction it is coming from, or what pitch and resonance the sound has, and filter out anything with the wrong physical qualities. As with most of our assumptions about human behaviour, though, researchers quickly found that it was more complicated than that, and later models of the filtering process were quite a lot more elaborate. That was partly because of another aspect of the cocktail party phenomenon. If you are in a crowded café or pub, as I said, you may be completely unaware of the conversations around you. But if someone nearby says your name, or the name of your football team, or something else which is particularly meaningful to you, then you hear it. Quite often, in fact, your attention is instantly diverted, and you begin to listen to that conversation instead of the one you are in.

Studying how we 'switch channels' like this led to a number of improvements in communication with people working in complex systems. Air traffic controllers, for example, always give the identifying call for the aircraft before they make announcements. They know that pilots monitor all of the messages, but are particularly 'keyed in' to the identifier for their own planes.

By giving the identifier first, they give the pilot time to 'change channel', as it were, which makes sure that they are fully focused on the information that they are about to receive. Research into selective attention has been applied in all sorts of ways, but mainly in the designing of systems which people can work with safely and effectively.

SUSTAINED ATTENTION

A third aspect of attention which applied cognitive psychologists investigated in some detail during and after World War II relates to sustained attention, or vigilance – how long we can keep on paying attention to things before we begin to make mistakes. In modern living, there are any number of complex systems which need constant watching, ranging from life-support systems in hospitals, to monitoring systems in nuclear power installations, to air traffic control systems, and even to the tracking and adjustment systems of astronomical telescopes.

Up until World War II, sustained attention wasn't really a very important topic. If you were watching something, you usually had enough time to let your attention wander a bit and still not miss anything important. But as technology developed and became more complicated, an increasing number of systems required people to remain absolutely attentive for long periods of time. Piloting fast machines or maintaining early-warning systems required constant attention and mistakes could have really serious consequences. Radar screens, for example, had to be monitored around the clock, so people had to be able to watch them constantly, and raise an alert whenever they detected an unusual signal.

Not surprisingly, as radar operators studied the screens for hours on end, they showed what the researchers called a **performance decrement** – in other words, the quality of their observation fell, and they began to make more and more errors. Since an error could be fatal, it was important for the psychologists to discover how accurately people could observe a screen, for how long, and which factors would help them to be more accurate. That led to a lot of experimental research, looking at different factors, and isolating each one to find out how important it was.

When Mackworth brought together the findings from these studies of sustained attention, in the 1950s, he showed how there were three sets of factors in reducing performance decrement – in other words, which could improve performance. The first set was associated with the task itself: people detected signals better if the signals were reasonably bright, lasted for a second or so rather than just occurring as a rapid flash, and occurred closer to the centre of the screen rather than out at the edges.

The second set of factors related to the people themselves. Introverts – that is, people who are content with their own company and don't particularly need others for stimulation – were found to be the best for sustained attention tasks. But even non-introverts could do better in certain situations. The researchers found that amphetamine drugs, for example, could improve performance, although later research showed that their unwanted side-effects make them unsuitable for use in this context. They also found that being told how well they were doing made a lot of difference to people. In fact, any kind of feedback (even if it wasn't accurate) helped people to keep up a steady rate of accurate signal detection.

Insight

The use of amphetamines to maintain performance and attention was very common in the first half of the twentieth century. But imagine the fuss there would be nowadays if we found out that the pilot of a plane we were travelling on was taking amphetamines!

The third set of factors which could help people doing what amounted to long, boring tasks which required constant vigilance were linked with the actual situation. Some of these were social – perhaps not surprisingly, people tended to do better if their boss or someone who was higher up in the organization was in the room. But also, interestingly enough, they did better if there was a certain amount of noise and activity. Not too much – excessive noise could make it hard for them to concentrate – but background conversations, telephones and that sort of noise actually helped them to concentrate. Perfectly quiet, still rooms are all right for short-term attention, but not if you need to attend to something for hours on end.

These findings were initially made in a military context, but they apply much more broadly in modern life. As we have seen, there are many situations where people need to monitor machinery for hours on end – in automated production plants, in traffic control centres, and in hospitals, to name just a few. So an understanding of how to organize their work in a way which will help to reduce errors and make it easier for them to keep paying attention is useful knowledge, which can be applied in many different contexts.

Everyday errors

An increasingly automated society means that people nowadays often deal with very complex systems – sometimes even to the point where a single human being can be monitoring a whole section of a factory, or several sets of intensive care machinery in a hospital. Even at a more mundane level, driving a car involves the operation of several complex systems, all of which need to be dealt with correctly.

The problem, of course, is that we didn't evolve with complex machinery. We evolved in a slower world, regulated by weather, terrain, and the occasional predator. We can cope with the complexity of the modern world because we can learn some things so well that they become **automatized**, and they don't need our conscious attention. When we become skilled drivers, we don't actually pay much attention to the actions we use when we are driving, although when we are first learning they are all-important to us. Learning skills is all about learning things so well that we do them more or less automatically.

But that has consequences too, and one of them is the fact that we can allow too much to slip into unconsciousness. Most regular car drivers have had the experience of taking a familiar route automatically, without really paying conscious attention to it. Either they don't remember actually getting to where they are, or they have followed the automatic route (usually to home), when really they wanted to go somewhere quite different. Similarly, most of us have had the experience of going into a room and forgetting what we went in for. Both of these are common examples of absent-mindedness, and neither of them is all that important.

Insight

Many people believe that we get more absent-minded as we grow older. But research findings have shown that younger people make just as many absent-minded errors as older people, if not more. Older people notice them more, because they are worried that it is a sign of their memory failing with age.

But the same type of error, in a different circumstance, can become extremely serious. There was a case a few years ago of a bus driver who took a familiar route instead of the new one he was supposed to be taking – exactly the same everyday error as many people make. But in this case, he was driving a double-decker instead of the single-decker bus he normally drove. It wouldn't fit under a low bridge, and the top deck was entirely destroyed. A simple slip of memory had dramatic consequences.

James Reason, an applied cognitive psychologist, looked at how human errors can produce massive effects. One of his first tasks was to identify the different types of error which people make. Some of his research was observational, some involved a method known as **protocol analysis,** in which people are asked to carry out a complex task while talking aloud about how they are doing it, and some were diary studies, in which people were asked to record all of the small errors or mistakes they made during a particular period of time.

The results of all this research allowed Reason to distinguish between three different types of error, which are listed in Table 2.1.

Table 2.1 Types of error	
Skill-based slips and lapses	Errors which come about because a set of actions have become so well learned that they are automatized, and we perform them without conscious thought.
Knowledge-based errors	Errors which happen either because we don't know enough, or because we know too much, and apply the wrong bit of knowledge to the situation.
Rule-based errors	Errors which come from trying to apply rules or sets of actions which we have used before in different circumstances.

Insight

Knowledge-based errors are surprisingly common, because of our natural tendency to assume that other people also know what we know. So it is often assumed that someone has had the relevant training or is in possession of the relevant information when really they are not.

A classic example of rule-based error occurred in 1986 with the disastrous decision to launch the Space Shuttle Challenger, even when the engineers warned against it. The decision was taken, against technical advice, because the management team concerned were applying rules which focused on building up public interest and attention. The fact that the Shuttle was about to carry the first civilian into space was an important part of that. Putting off the launch, they felt, would be bad PR, and might have adverse consequences on funding. As it happened, however, ignoring the engineers' warnings was even worse. It meant that the Shuttle exploded, killing everyone on board. The rule of avoiding bad PR whenever possible isn't a bad one, but in this case it was applied in exactly the wrong situation. And the negative consequences for the space programme as a whole, not to mention the families of those killed, were far more serious than a delayed launch would have been.

GROUPTHINK

There were other aspects to that decision too, of course. In 1991, Moorhead, Ference and Neck discussed how the whole decision-making process was a classic example of **groupthink** – the tendency for close groups to become insular and self-satisfied, so that they ignore unwelcome information coming from 'outsiders'. Sadly, groupthink is still a common type of error – the disastrous decisions made by the banking industry in the late 2000s is a more recent example – but it is more of an organizational problem, so we will look at it more closely in Chapter 13.

Reason produced a model of how everyday errors and lapses affect complex systems, which he called the GEMS (General Error Modelling System) model. The model has been extremely useful in highlighting design and management weaknesses in complex systems. It takes the form of a flowchart with steps for checking each type of error. It begins by checking the skill-based level, asking whether they are routine actions and whether there are built-in checks on how the action is progressing to prevent errors which have just come about by force of habit or absent-mindedness. Then it moves to the rule-based level, to look at whether the pattern of what needs to be done is familiar or not, in the context of other operations which the person may be undertaking in the course of their working day. Finally, it moves on to the knowledge-based level, analysing exactly what knowledge is required for accurate performance and whether that knowledge is being transmitted effectively. Reason showed how applying the model and identifying the scope for different types of error could prevent, or at least minimize, the opportunity for complex disasters in the modern world.

Insight
Computer-based models like the GEMS system have both strengths and weaknesses. One strength is the way they

can make sure that different parts of the system get proper attention. But a weakness is that they can make people feel too safe, and therefore vulnerable to completely unexpected problems which the model hasn't predicted.

Memory training

Another important area of applied cognitive psychology is in memory training. As you will know if you have read *Understand Psychology*, human memory is a very active process, and nothing like the factual recording which we imagine we possess. But we can all train our memories to work better. You will often see advertisements which claim to help people to improve or develop their memories. These work by applying the principles which cognitive psychologists have discovered about memory.

PROCESSING AND MEMORY STRUCTURES

Perhaps the most important of these principles concerns how memories are structured and stored. Most of our memory remains unconscious until we need it, and then it comes to the surface. This is necessary, of course – if we were always conscious of our memories we'd be completely overwhelmed by the sheer amount of information. But the brain keeps it dormant, and only brings memories to the surface when they become relevant in some way to what we are doing.

It does that by using **cues**, which link with relevant information and bring it back to the surface of our minds. Those cues may be information which reminds us of some other information; they may be sensory images of some kind; or they may be to do with the context in which the original memories were stored. By making these connections, we can associate what we have learned previously with what we are thinking about now, and use our memories of past situations to help us to understand or think about the current one.

Cues can only work when they link with information which has already been stored, and sleeping is an important part of how we store our memories. As we sleep, our brains organize the mass of information we have taken in during the day, and link it with other things that we already know, so that when we wake, that new information has become organized and properly stored. Most of this happens while we are dreaming: studies which have investigated what happens when people are allowed to sleep but stopped from dreaming (by being woken up whenever a dream starts) show that after a while they become extremely confused and unable to think clearly. If it goes on too long, it can even produce serious mental disturbance: we really need to get our experiences organized properly just to be able to survive.

Another aspect of storing memories has to do with processing the information so that it means something to us. We learn new information all the time, and we process most of it automatically, but if you are trying to learn something a bit different, it is quite important to be able to link it with things that you already know. Exam revision strategies which force the person to think about the meanings of the information and make sense of it in some way have been shown to be much more effective than ones which simply involve trying to learn the information by heart. There are lots of ways to do this – social ways, such as sharing your revision and developing quizzes; creative ways, such as changing the information into diagrams or images; or verbal ones such as rephrasing it or summarizing it in your own words. The important thing, though, is that they all involve getting to the meaning of the information in some way – processing the information rather than accepting it passively.

Insight
We remember information from other people better than anything else – it has to do with our evolutionary heritage as social animals. So it makes sense to get this working for us when we are revising for exams. Quizzes, making up songs and other social games are ways of doing this.

VISUALIZATION AND IMAGERY

Another principle concerns using **visualization** effectively. Memories are not just stored in words: we also store sensory images which can act as important cues to help us to remember information when we need it. Those images are sometimes visual – we see or imagine a 'picture' which links to the memory – but they can involve the other senses too. A familiar smell, an old song, or even the feel of a particular material can bring back a whole set of memories. All of our senses are involved in our experiences, and our sensory impressions are stored along with our memories. So we can improve our ability to retrieve memories by using sensory images as cues to bring those memories back.

The context in which a memory is laid down is also important – it gives us a whole set of cues which can help us to remember things. If you're trying to remember something which you have temporarily forgotten, the most practical way to go about it is to think back to the situation you were in at the time. The more thoroughly you recreate the context, the more the details will start to come back. This idea is the basis of the **cognitive interview** used by forensic psychologists, which we will be looking at in Chapter 9, which helps investigators to encourage eyewitnesses to remember the key details of crimes or other events.

We can construct images which will help us to remember things, as well. For example, there are well-known mnemonic (memory-improving) strategies which use imagery as cues to help people to remember lists. If you have a list or sequence of information that you need to remember in the right order, one way is to visualize a familiar walk or journey that you take regularly. Then you form mental images relating to the items on your list, and imagine them at different points along the walk. So if the walk was from your house to the nearest shop, for example, you might imagine the first item on the doorstep, the second at the gate, the third at the first corner of the street, and so on. This is known as the **method of loci**, and is a very well-known method of memorizing which dates right back to the ancient Greeks.

A friend of mine once used the method of loci to remember a sequence of complex chemicals for a biology exam. She couldn't visualize the complex chemicals, of course, but she converted the name of each one into a visual image based roughly on what it sounded like – for example, turning 'agglutinogen' into an image of a glue tin. By placing these images at different points along her imaginary walk, she gave herself cues which allowed her to remember the whole list. It was very successful, and the only problem, she told me, was that she had so many of these lists to remember that eventually she began to run out of walks and had to use journeys to further and further places!

THE ROLE OF PRACTICE

Another important principle of memory improvement is one which relates to all skills, whether they are cognitive or physical, and that is practice. The more you practise using cues to retrieve memories, the better you get at it. Practice means that the brain becomes more familiar with what you are asking it to do, and so it becomes able to do it more quickly and efficiently. That's the thinking behind many of the 'brain training' exercises which you can get for Nintendo or other computer systems, and it works.

Many applied cognitive psychologists believe that the reason it works is because of the way that our thinking involves pathways between different groups of nerve cells in the brain. When a message is passed from one nerve cell, or neurone, to another, the first neurone releases chemical 'messengers' which are picked up by the next one and converted into electrical signals. These pass along the neurone until they get to the next connection, at which point they stimulate that neurone to release its own chemicals, and so on. The more often these pathways are used, the easier it becomes for the nerve cells to release the relevant chemicals, and so the easier it becomes for us to think in this way.

There is some evidence that stimulating nerve pathways like this develops the brain even in adulthood. So practising using our memories and stimulating our brains to think is a helpful thing to do no matter what age we are. Practice is also the basis behind evacuation drills and refresher courses for people in work. We don't have any problem remembering skills or knowledge which we use every day, but we also need to be able to draw on skills and knowledge which we only need occasionally.

Insight

Revising for exams has two parts – learning and practice. Being able to summarize information and apply it quickly is another skill that needs practice. So practising exam answers is just as important as learning the stuff in the first place.

Applied cognitive psychology, then, has a great deal to contribute to our understanding of what happens as human beings and complex systems interact. This means that it is also very closely linked with other areas of applied psychology, such as human–machine interaction and ergonomics, which we will be looking at in Chapter 14. Applied cognitive psychologists study other aspects of how our cognitions influence our behaviour as well, such as the way that people make decisions. We will be looking at some of their findings in that area in Chapter 17, when we look at consumer psychology; we will also look at some aspects of decision making in groups, and in particular the phenomenon of groupthink, when we look at organizational psychology in Chapter 13.

10 THINGS TO REMEMBER

1 *Applied cognitive psychology received a major boost to its development from World War II.*

2 *People notice information best if it is in the centre of a display.*

3 *We adjust our attention all the time, and select the relevant bits that we want to notice.*

4 *The cocktail party phenomenon shows how we can attend to just one source of information and ignore others.*

5 *People are better at sustained attention if there is a little background noise but not too much.*

6 *Errors can be classified as skill-based, knowledge-based and rule-based.*

7 *Groupthink happens when groups become so convinced they are right that they ignore anyone with a different viewpoint.*

8 *Cues act like tags to link one memory with another.*

9 *Visualization and context are important parts of remembering.*

10 *The heart of skill learning is practice, which leads to the automatization of sequences of actions so they can be performed smoothly.*

3

....

Applied social psychology

In this chapter you will learn:
- *how training in social skills can help people become better at communication*
- *why it is important for people to feel they have an effect on their world*
- *ways in which prejudice can be reduced.*

Social psychology is the branch of psychology which deals with how we interact with, and understand, other people. Social psychologists can be interested in almost any facet of social living: some of them, for example, are mainly interested in social behaviour, and will conduct research which involves observing how people act in different circumstances and situations. Some social psychologists are interested in how we make sense of our social worlds – interpreting the social experiences that we have. And other social psychologists are interested in how our personal and social understanding shapes the psychological world that we live in, and the way that we deal with it.

Each of these aspects of social psychology has contributed to applied psychology in some way, but you'll probably be relieved to hear that we are not going to deal with them all in this chapter! That would need quite a large book in its own right. Some of them will appear later – for example, some social psychologists have conducted research into health beliefs, and this will come up when we look at health psychology in Chapter 8. In this chapter, we'll just be looking at three areas of applied social psychology: social skills training, challenging social prejudice, and enhancing public education.

Insight

Human beings are deeply social animals – in fact, some scientists believe that it is our sociability which caused us to develop such large brains and learning ability. It's actually quite hard to think of anything we do which hasn't been shaped by social influences in one way or another.

Social skills training

Social skills training began as a result of psychological research into the ways that people act and interact with one another. One of the most famous researchers in this field was Michael Argyle, who produced a number of books on the area. Psychologists call it **non-verbal communication**, because it includes all the different ways that we communicate without using words. By recording carefully how people behave in different social situations, and conducting a number of experiments, the psychologists working in this field have discovered a great deal about effective communication.

For example: they found that we are extremely sensitive to the signals which people make when they are in conversation with one another. There are precise rules about when we make eye-contact, how we time our responses to one another, the signals which indicate that one person has finished speaking and it is now the other person's 'turn', and so on. These rules are completely unconscious – we have learned them almost from the cradle, and hardly notice them at all. But we find it very disturbing if we are talking with someone who doesn't conform to them.

Argyle and others realized that some people don't automatically follow the right rules, for one reason or another. And those people tend to become very socially isolated, because they don't get much social contact. After all, if talking to someone makes you feel uncomfortable, after a while you'll tend to avoid them, won't you? That lack of social contact means that they often develop other emotional problems, through loneliness and isolation.

As a result, the psychologists working in this area developed a number of programmes for **social skills training**. These often took the form of workshops and training sessions, designed to sensitize people to appropriate social behaviours, and to teach them how to deal with others in a more socially skilled manner. They might, for example, teach someone how to make the right amount of eye-contact in a conversation – enough to signal that they were interested in what the person was saying, but not so much that the person began to feel uncomfortable.

Social skills workshops were initially used as therapy for disturbed people in the 1960s and early 1970s. But they rapidly began to become much more popular, as other people began to see the advantages of a good understanding of social behaviour. Social psychologists broadened their understanding of how people present themselves, and other organizations such as public relations firms began to put it to use. For example, when Margaret Thatcher became prime minister of the UK, she undertook training in self-presentation strategies in order to become a more effective communicator; these strategies included deepening her voice and developing verbal strategies for countering interruption or opposition.

The area of social skills training is broader than just aspects of non-verbal behaviour, of course. At the same time that Argyle and others were looking at social behaviour, and developing awareness of the actions which people use in communication, humanistic psychologists were investigating other aspects of social interaction, such as listening skills and team-building. Modern social skills training encompasses all of these, and is used in many different ways.

Insight

When most people are in conversation they spend more time thinking of what they are going to say next than they do

(Contd)

listening to what the other person is actually saying. That's why training in listening skills is necessary.

One way, for example, is for people who are working in the helping professions to receive some training in interpersonal skills. This training is surprisingly important. For example, we all tend to think that listening is an obvious and straightforward process. But really, it is astounding how little people actually hear of what others say. Instead, we tend to hear what we have expected them to say, and that's sometimes very different! A number of psychologists began exploring this area in the late 1960s, and they developed a range of exercises and techniques for sensitizing people in the helping professions to interpersonal information.

BODY LANGUAGE

Then there's the question of what has become known as **body language**. We give away a lot of information about ourselves quite unconsciously – in tones of voice, in small movements, in our posture and personal distance. Often, that information will indicate our emotional state, or how we feel about something. So being sensitive to these cues can be of real assistance to people in the helping professions.

Insight
The word 'attitude' originally meant body posture, or how we hold our bodies. It shows how powerful this is as a form of non-verbal communication that the word is now more commonly used to refer to our reaction to other people or social practices.

It can be of real assistance to those in other professions too. Police officers who need to question suspected criminals also receive social skills training. And they also often have equipment which helps them to monitor very subtle changes. The device known as a lie-detector, for example, is actually a **polygraph** which can measure the very tiny changes in the body which happen when someone is anxious about a particular question. Since lies are almost always accompanied by an anxious thought about whether the questioner will realize it's a lie, they can be fairly useful in that type of situation. We will be looking at how they work more closely in the next chapter. A voice-stress analyser performs a similar function: psychologists have shown that there are slight changes in how we use the voice when we are anxious, and these can be picked up by the right kind of sound analyser – even over the telephone.

Insight

Polygraphs and voice-stress analysers have become widely used as lie-detectors. But they can't actually distinguish between a lie and any other thing which makes people anxious. So criminals who can lie without anxiety can fool lie-detectors, and innocent but anxious people may appear to be lying.

Social skills training has become widespread in society. It is used in public relations training, as we've seen; in management training; and in marketing and sales training, as well as in training for those in the helping professions. Often, it is carried out by people who are not psychologists. But the specialist research in this field, and the development of new programmes, is still carried out by applied social psychologists, often working in the health or helping professions, or with the police. The knowledge which underpins the work in this area in the commercial sector is applied social psychology too, even though many people who use it are not aware of the fact. The basic knowledge and the new developments in the area have all come from social psychologists, exploring and applying their understanding of the mechanisms of social behaviour.

Challenging social prejudice

Prejudice is an area that social psychologists have been investigating since the 1920s, or possibly even before. As a result, we understand quite a lot about the mechanisms and processes which underlie racism, homophobia, sexism, and the other types of social prejudice which occur in society. This knowledge has been applied in a number of ways, through social interventions designed to combat or challenge prejudice in society. Most of the research into prejudice has tended to focus on racism, but the underlying mechanisms which lead to racism are very similar for other types of prejudice as well, and can be applied in very similar types of way.

THE AUTHORITARIAN PERSONALITY

One of the areas of research which was very popular in the middle of the last century involved looking for individual personality characteristics which might make someone more or less racist. We now know, of course, that individual personality is only a part of the story, and not enough to account for everything; but nonetheless there are some particular kinds of personality structure which do make people more likely to be racist or prejudiced against other social groups.

The most extreme of these personality structures has become known as the **authoritarian personality**, and was identified by Adorno *et al.* in 1950. Authoritarian personalities tend to be very rigid, have extremely black-and-white beliefs about society in general, and what counts as right or correct behaviour; and absolutely hate uncertainties or ambiguities in social living. They are also inclined to live their own lives by very rigid rules, and to dislike people having different lifestyles.

The authoritarian personality, Adorno showed, develops as a result of a very harsh, authoritarian upbringing. People who show this type of personality structure often have very rigid, unfeeling parents who insist on obedience at all costs, use a lot of physical punishment, and entirely disregard the emotional needs of their children. As a result, the child experiences a great deal of rage at the unfairness of the treatment, but daren't show it. That anger becomes bottled up inside, and when the child becomes older, it is expressed towards other targets instead.

The target which the authoritarian person chooses to dislike is generally one which is disliked by other people in their particular subculture too. In the first half of the twentieth century, it was Jews who tended to be singled out in Western society. Later on the focus changed to Afro-Caribbeans or Asians. So the culture in which the person is living shapes the prejudice, which means that we need to understand prejudice at wider levels as well: individual personalities aren't enough to explain it fully. But the authoritarian personality syndrome can tell us a lot about certain particular individuals and why their emotional reactions are so extreme.

Not every child who experiences this type of parenting becomes an authoritarian personality, of course. The authoritarian ones have channelled their anger and pain into hatred of others, and not everyone does that. Others who have experienced that type of parenting direct it inwards, and they have to work through their emotional problems differently. That can be hard without professional help. Many of them become very vulnerable to drug abuse and other types of self-destructive behaviour, because that is another way of expressing their pain. Fortunately, though, we are living in a society where it has become easier for people to obtain professional counselling or therapy, and the work of many clinical and counselling psychologists involves helping people to deal with the legacies of their childhood in this way, and so get on with living an emotionally healthy life.

SOCIAL DIMENSIONS OF PREJUDICE

The authoritarian personality is only one part of our understanding of social prejudice as a whole. Such people may become leaders or opinion shapers in a prejudiced community, but most prejudiced people are not particularly authoritarian. Instead, their opinions have been shaped by the social beliefs and discourse which is around them. So another area of intervention which has become common in combating racism in society is understanding and challenging the kinds of explanation and rationalization which racists use.

In recent years, it has become socially unacceptable in most communities to be overtly racist, but many racists use **discourse strategies** which express their prejudiced beliefs, while making it seem as if they are only being 'reasonable'. Van Dijk, in 1987, discussed some of the verbal strategies which racists use. One set involves techniques for making them seem especially credible or authoritative, such as claims to have special knowledge, or to be well informed about what they are saying. Another set of strategies involves singling out the other group for special attention when they are describing negative or illegal behaviour, as if all crime were conducted by members of that group.

A third set of verbal strategies identified by Van Dijk involved the person presenting themselves positively by claiming, for example, not to be racist, but then going on to give 'reasonable' reasons for disliking the minority group in question. I had a good example of this recently with someone who came to the door offering to clear some building refuse, saying 'I'm not racist, but I don't deal with Asians because I had one who didn't pay me what we had agreed.' The facts are that: (a) categorizing any ethnic group on the behaviour of one or two individuals is completely racist, and (b) this man had had white clients who had refused to pay him the full amount too, but he had taken that completely differently, as an individual problem. He was firmly informed that we didn't like racists in this area, and not given the work. But the verbal strategy he had used was precisely the one that Van Dijk described.

Insight

Increasing numbers of people are challenging 'everyday' racism by simply refusing to allow racist comments or implicitly racist remarks to pass by. Anyone can tackle racism like this, and because it is personal and face to face, it makes more of an impact than just about any other strategy.

Another psychological process underlying social prejudice is **scapegoating**. The term 'scapegoat' originally came from the practices of an early Middle Eastern culture, in which a goat was ritually 'blamed' for all the ills of the tribe, and sacrificed in order to make amends for them. That was making the whole process official, but it's a sad fact of human psychology that often, when things are going wrong, we look around for someone to blame. Too often, that means that we pick on someone who actually wasn't responsible at all.

Both psychologists and sociologists have shown how social prejudice tends to increase at times of economic hardship and depression. People who are unemployed, or struggling to make ends meet, are particularly vulnerable to the discourse used by racists, who deliberately make it appear that economic and other problems have been caused by the particular group they dislike. So unemployment may be blamed on a particular ethnic group 'taking all our jobs', even when the economic indicators show that the group in question has actually created more jobs in the community. Blaming ethnic minority members provides racists with an easy set of scapegoats, and lets them avoid facing up to social and economic realities.

Insight

Economic recession almost always produces a rise in fascists or extreme right-wing groups, because they seize the opportunity to scapegoat the groups they particularly dislike. But more and more people are becoming aware of this process, so it is easier to challenge.

Scapegoating is made particularly easy by the natural tendency which all human beings have to see the world in terms of 'them' and 'us'. That process is known as **social identification** and there has been quite a lot of research into how it operates. Effectively, we live in a social world in which people are categorized into different groups: adults and children, men and women, drivers and pedestrians, students and working people, and so on. We tend to identify with the groups to which we belong, and like to be able to be proud of belonging to them. So it is very easy for us to slip into thinking that 'our' group is better than 'their' group.

It isn't inevitable, though. Early research into social identification seemed to imply that groups will always compete with one another, but more recent research shows that this only happens when they see themselves as being in competition for resources of some kind. So if a racist can convince others that members of an ethnic group are taking up jobs, that makes it seem as if there is competition for resources, and makes people more likely to become hostile to the other group. It's a strategy which has been used by many politicians, for example, in the Balkans and other places, and sadly it can be very effective. In Chapter 19, we will be exploring how a knowledge of social identity processes can help diplomats in their efforts to reconcile social conflicts of this kind.

But belonging to different social groups doesn't always result in prejudice. A better understanding of how society works makes us far less likely to engage in scapegoating, which is why social prejudice is more common among people who are less well informed. Also, we all belong to many different social groups and have a number of different social identities. Other group memberships – such as belonging to the same profession, or playing the same sports, or living on the same estate – can easily become much more important than the colour of someone's skin or their sexual preferences.

Insight

'Them-and-us' is very deeply built into our thinking. But it only leads to conflict when 'they' are seen as in direct competition with 'us' for limited resources. Otherwise, we are more inclined to co-operate peacefully with other groups, and even to involve them to create a larger 'us'.

All of this knowledge about prejudice has been put into use by applied social psychologists, and others. Intervention strategies to reduce social prejudice have emphasized building social contact between different ethnic groups within particular communities, so that people can see what they have in common. They have also emphasized the importance of role models for young people, to encourage positive social identifications. And they have brought to the surface and challenged racist discourse, so that it can be recognized for what it is. The 'hard-core' authoritarian personalities will always find people to dislike, of course. They can be helped by therapy, but in the meantime a better understanding of how social prejudice works can help us to make sure that the social environment doesn't support and encourage their unpleasant opinions.

Enhancing public education

Another area of applied social psychology focuses on applying our knowledge of **social cognition** – how individuals make sense of social knowledge, and how that affects what they do. It can be applied to a number of different situations. We will just take one example here: that of looking at how applied social cognitive research has helped to enhance public education.

The first thing which applied social psychologists working in this area have to investigate is how people make sense of the information that they have been given. That isn't as straightforward as it sounds, because we all make sense of information in different ways. It depends on our own experience, our likes and dislikes, our motivations, and all sorts of other factors. People don't just accept factual information – they make their own versions of it, known as **social representations**. Applied social cognitive psychology involves looking at these representations, and at how people behave, and seeing which types of representation go with the more positive types of behaviour.

Social representations are the common shared explanations which people use to make sense of what is going on. They are the explanations which come up in conversation, over and over again, and become treated as 'common sense'. Social representations may be widely believed, and they often sound plausible to people who don't really think very hard about what is going on, but they are not necessarily reasonable or sensible. And sometimes, as in the case of ascribing economic problems to members of minority groups, or expecting terrorist attacks in quiet country villages with no political importance, they can be downright illogical.

We don't just accept social representations passively. Instead, we negotiate and adapt them, usually through conversations, until they fit with our own world-views and existing opinions. This means that social representations are adjusted all the time, although they often have a central 'core' that remains stable.

Once researchers can identify factors like social representations, they can use them to develop training packages which will help health educators to get their messages across more effectively. That takes testing, of course, and they have to carry out experiments to see which ways of communicating are most likely to produce the effects that they want. But the end result is a deeper understanding of what will, and what won't, be more effective.

Perhaps the clearest example of this is one that Abraham and Hampson (1996) used when they were looking at ways of persuading people to stick to medical advice when it comes to taking medicines. When they looked at the representations which people had of this area, they found that some people had much higher **self-efficacy beliefs** than others – in other words, they felt that they were able to act effectively, and to take positive action for themselves. It was those people who were more likely to stick to the medical advice that they were given.

As a result of this discovery, the researchers began to develop different ways of communicating information which would enhance people's sense of self-efficacy. They carried out tests of different approaches, and evaluated them carefully. The end result was that they were able to make some clear recommendations about the best ways to get these messages across, and how to use social influence to the most positive effect.

I adopted a similar approach when I was looking at the psychology involved in interactive exhibit design (Hayes, 1999). Interactive exhibits are the 'hands-on' activities we find in science centres and other places, which encourage people to participate actively in learning about the topic which is being displayed. People enjoy them, and they are becoming increasingly popular. So the psychological research which I was doing involved identifying the psychological mechanisms which are involved as people play with the exhibits, and looking at how different design features of the exhibits encouraged different types of outcome.

Like Abraham and Hampson, I found that self-efficacy beliefs were an important part of the process. Interactive exhibits encourage people to feel effective and capable, which helps to make them ready to learn about the scientific processes they are playing with. Social identification is also part of it: exhibits are particularly popular if people can relate to them. So, for example, an interactive exhibit at the London Science Museum which is all about sound technology, and lets people experiment mixing music tracks, is particularly popular with teenagers. We'll be looking at this in more detail in Chapter 14.

Insight

Self-efficacy beliefs are all to do with how competent and in control we feel ourselves to be. Knowing we can act effectively if we want to helps us to relax and be more accepting of new information or unexpected behaviour.

As I said, there are many other types of applied social psychology, and we will be coming across some of them in other chapters of this book. There's always a lot of overlap between areas – the medical advice example could just as well have gone into Chapter 8 (health psychology), and we will look again at the psychology of interactive exhibits in Chapter 14, when we look at engineering and design psychology.

Similarly, in the next chapter, we will be looking at some of the ways that biological psychology has been applied. Biological, or physiological psychology as it is sometimes called, investigates another aspect of our psychology, which is how our physical selves – our bodies and brains – affect our experience. Applied bio-psychology is all about how we can use this knowledge to improve our understanding of everyday life.

10 THINGS TO REMEMBER

1 *Social psychology is concerned with how we interact with and are influenced by other people.*

2 *A lot of communication is non-verbal – that is, it doesn't need words.*

3 *Social skills training can help people to 'fit in' socially.*

4 *Both professionals and others have benefited from listening skills training.*

5 *We communicate quite a lot with our body language.*

6 *Authoritarian personalities are rigid, prejudiced and often very right-wing.*

7 *Scapegoating minority groups for bad economic conditions is a common form of prejudice.*

8 *Belonging to different social groups does not always lead to prejudice.*

9 *Social representations shape the ways people explain what is going on around them.*

10 *Self-efficacy beliefs are important in many aspects of applied psychology.*

4

Applied bio-psychology

In this chapter you will learn:
- *about the consequences of head injuries*
- *how the two halves of the brain work*
- *how an active imagination can help a person control their anger.*

Like applied cognitive psychology and applied social psychology, applied bio-psychology is concerned with applying the insights and understanding gained from a specific area of academic psychology to everyday living and the real world. The term 'bio-psychology' is relatively recent, and it means all of those areas of psychology which are concerned with how our biology directly influences our experience. It was originally known as physiological psychology, because it was particularly concerned with studying the workings and effects of the brain, nervous system and hormones in the body. However, the term 'bio-psychology' is more popular now because it includes broader aspects of biological influence, such as the impact of our evolutionary and genetic history, or biological drives and motives.

Bio-psychology is a massive area, and we will come across several of its insights when we look at other areas of applied psychology. But in this chapter, we will look at just three areas: how clinical neuropsychologists deal with recovery from head injury; the research which shows how the two halves of the brain act differently; and how a knowledge of physiological processes can help us in coping with anxiety, anger and stress.

Clinical neuropsychology

The area of applied bio-psychology known as **clinical neuropsychology** is really a whole section of psychology in its own right. Neuropsychologists are interested in how the brain and nervous system work – which parts of the brain do what, and how they all interconnect. Clinical neuropsychologists put that knowledge to use, helping people who have neural diseases or who have suffered from head injuries, or similar kinds of problem. In fact, a great deal of what we know about how the nervous system works has been discovered from injuries of one sort or another. For example, when somebody suffers a stroke, or a specific type of head injury, it is often possible to detect from their symptoms exactly where the injury has taken place. And from that, we can deduce a lot of things about how the brain works.

Actually, when we talk about the 'brain' in this context, we don't usually mean the whole of the human brain. The whole brain is a highly complex structure, consisting of a lot of different parts. Most of the interest in clinical neuropsychology – or at least the research which we will be looking at in this chapter – is actually concerned with the largest part of the human brain, which comprises the two structures known as the cerebral hemispheres. They are so big that they cover all the other parts of the brain, and they are also the parts of the brain that we think with consciously.

STROKES AND BRAIN DAMAGE

A 'stroke' is an interruption of the blood supply to a particular part of the brain, which causes some brain cells to die because they are not receiving the necessary nutrients from the blood vessels. Strokes happen in different places, and can produce some very specific effects. For example, one woman who experienced a stroke found that she became unable to detect movement – things appeared to be completely still, and just changed from time to time, like a series of photographs. It was a big problem, because she found it impossible to do everyday things such as pouring out a cup of tea, or crossing the road, because she couldn't judge how full a cup was becoming or how close a car was. But the rest of her vision worked perfectly well.

Other people with similar strokes may experience different problems. For example, one person was fine at detecting movement, but had difficulty seeing shapes, while another became unable to see colours. Some people have problems recognizing familiar faces, while others find it impossible to recognize unfamiliar ones which they have been shown only a few minutes before. What these injuries tell researchers is that our brain functioning involves several different sets of mechanisms, even in systems which seem to work as a single process, such as vision.

Some strokes, of course, are much more severe than that, and can result in paralysis or near paralysis. But clinical neuropsychologists, working with physiotherapists and others, have shown that it is possible for people to recover a very large amount of their functioning from this type of stroke. What's important is having the motivation to do it, because it does involve perseverance and effort. But many people who are nearly paralysed by a stroke become able to walk again and even look after themselves, if they put the time and effort into forcing their bodies to recover.

It used to be thought that brain and nerve cells never recover from injury, but nowadays, we know that they often do, as long as enough effort is put into forcing the brain to provide the relevant stimulation. But only the person themselves can do that – nobody else can do it for them. And it is a lot of hard work.

Insight

Personal belief can be the strongest factor of all in recovery from stroke. It doesn't happen without considerable effort, and unless the person feels that it is possible, they won't put in the hard work to force their brain cells to recover.

Even where they are too badly damaged to recover, neighbouring groups of cells are sometimes able to take over those functions so that the person is able to relearn the ability they thought they had lost. This type of recovery particularly applies when it is control of movement which has become impaired. We know much less about the potential for recovery from other forms of brain damage, perhaps because it is much less apparent when someone puts effort into recovery from more subtle problems. With movement, we receive clear feedback about small achievements. If we are unable to move an arm, for example, and concerted effort allows us to produce a very slight jerk, we are aware of what we have done and feel pleased with the achievement. It tells us that our efforts are worthwhile, and encourages us to continue to try hard.

It's difficult to work out a similar rehabilitation process for a problem like being unable to perceive movement. Because we take that kind of functioning for granted, we are not so aware of 'mental exercises' which might be useful, and it is also difficult to see how we could get feedback. The therapeutic work of clinical neuropsychologists usually focuses on exploring the deficit so that the person has a clear understanding of what they can and can't do, and developing strategies which will help them to lead their lives more effectively. On the other hand, our knowledge of the nervous system is continually improving, and 50 years ago everyone agreed that it was impossible to recover from neural paralysis. Anything is possible.

CLOSED HEAD INJURY

Closed head injuries are injuries which happen as a result of an impact of some kind. They are called 'closed' because they happen inside the skull – the brain casing is not broken open. Most closed head injuries happen among people aged under 30, mainly as a result of car accidents, but also sometimes because of fights or falls, or other kinds of accident. Alcohol plays a very large part in that type of incident. A high proportion of people suffering closed head injury severe enough to need hospitalization also have high levels of intoxication at the time.

Closed head injuries can have surprisingly long-term effects. Often, the only sign at the time is a slight swelling. But the twisting and shearing of the nerve cells inside the brain itself can damage neural pathways, producing effects which only become fully apparent several months, or even a couple of years, later. The most important sign in detecting the seriousness of a closed head injury is whether the person lost consciousness at the time of the injury, and if so, for how long. Even a small loss of consciousness, lasting for only a few seconds, can signal an injury which may produce lasting damage, and one where the person is knocked unconscious for as much as a minute can be very serious indeed. Loss of vision is also a sign that the person may be suffering a severe concussion.

Insight

Many closed head injuries go unreported, with people just accepting that accidents happen and assuming that there is little that can be done. But serious ones involving concussion or loss of vision should always be reported, because there are often specialized treatments which can offset their effects.

Head injuries of this kind tend to be accompanied by a small loss of memory, and the greater the injury, the more the memory loss. People generally lose memory for the events which happened just before the accident. This is known as **retrograde amnesia** (amnesia means loss of memory). It doesn't set in immediately, though. Yarnell and Lynch (1973) found that if they questioned American football players immediately after a concussion, they could recall what was going on just before their accident, but those memories vanished within a few minutes and never came back.

Often, too, there is some **post-traumatic amnesia**, which means that people have problems remembering new or ongoing information. This is temporary, and most people recover from it within a few weeks. Severe injuries, though, can produce more subtle forms of memory impairment. Richardson (1990) showed that the impairment often involves a disturbance in mental imagery, which can have knock-on effects for a number of separate memorizing abilities. There are also problems with attention, and with some general mental skills, although not usually with language.

As Richardson showed, even a single closed head injury can sometimes cause lasting effects, and people who are exposed to repeated head injuries of this kind, like boxers or some other kinds of sportspeople, can suffer even more serious effects. There is a disorder which used to be known as *dementia pugilistic*, which begins after the end of a boxing career, and shows itself in muscle tremors and difficulties in speaking. The great boxer and human-rights campaigner Muhammad Ali showed some of these symptoms in later life. The effects of the broken and sheared nerve cells build up, and are no longer held in check by the rigorous daily training workouts of the professional boxer.

Closed head injuries, then, can be a major problem, with lasting effects. Sometimes, these effects are very subtle, and only become apparent when the person is trying to do a particularly complex task, but sometimes they are more extreme. Clinical neuropsychologists often work very closely with people suffering from closed head injuries, diagnosing the specific location of the injury in the brain, identifying its precise effects, and also helping the person learn better ways of dealing with them. But sadly, a great many closed head injuries need never have happened at all, and have only come about because of stupidity or thoughtlessness. Table 4.1 lists four ways that the risk of head injury can be minimized. It's worth following them, because the consequences can last for the rest of your life!

> **Table 4.1 Minimizing the risk of head injury**
>
> 1 *Consume alcohol responsibly, and avoid extreme intoxication which might encourage you to do silly things.*
> 2 *Use seat belts and cars equipped with air bags, which prevent heads from hitting windscreens.*
> 3 *Wear protective headgear when riding any two-wheeled transport or engaging in wheeled sports like skateboarding.*
> 4 *Wear protective headgear when playing sports with any risk of head impact.*

Split-brain studies

What we know about the two halves of the brain and how they work first started when surgeons and neuropsychologists tried out a new treatment for severe epilepsy. Epilepsy involves a sudden burst of electrical activity in the brain, when lots of brain cells all fire at once. There are many different kinds of epilepsy, and some of them are relatively localized – that is to say, the electrical activity happens only in a relatively small part of the brain. Even so, it can mean that the person becomes disoriented and forgetful, and it can interfere with their ability to concentrate.

A few particularly unfortunate people suffer from *'grand mal'* epilepsy, in which the electrical activity begins on one side of the brain but then spreads across it. This means that it interferes with the parts of the brain that co-ordinate body movement. The person falls down and has a 'fit', or seizure, as their muscles shake and spasm in response to the random messages being sent to them from the brain. When the seizure is over, they are usually very confused and can take some time to come back to reality.

Insight

Until the electrical activity of the brain was discovered, epilepsy was a mysterious illness which seemed completely

(Contd)

unpredictable. In some societies, it was considered to be a religious experience, or evidence of demonic possession. Our clearer understanding of what is going on has helped many epileptics to lead easier lives.

In the 1960s, a pioneering operation was developed in an attempt to control epilepsy in a few patients who were experiencing *grand mal* seizures so often that they couldn't get on with their lives at all. The top part of the human brain is divided into two halves, or hemispheres, which control movement and thinking, and these are joined by a membrane called the corpus callosum. The surgeons decided to cut through the corpus callosum, severing the connections between the two halves of the brain. By doing this, they reasoned, the seizure would affect only one side of the brain, so even if the patient had a *grand mal* seizure, they should be able to keep control of one side of the body.

THE TWO HALVES OF THE BRAIN

In fact, carrying out the operation seemed to reduce the fits much more than that. The patients concerned experienced much milder forms of epilepsy, and became able to live normal lives again. But when the neuropsychologists carried out their tests, they found that the two halves of the brain seemed to be able to act quite independently, as if each were a separate brain in its own right.

One patient, for example, reported how she would sometimes decide to wear a particular dress and would go to her wardrobe to take it out with her right hand, only to find that her left hand would pick out something entirely different for her to wear. Since the right side of the brain controls the left side of the body, and the left side of the brain controls the right side of the body, the action implied that the two halves of the brain had different ideas about what she ought to be wearing that day!

It has been known for a long time that our ability to use language is controlled by a few areas on the left side of the brain. By using a special screen, the neuropsychologist Sperry showed that split-brain people could easily name an object that was shown to the left side of the eye, because that meant that the image was interpreted by the left side of the brain. But if the right side of the eye was shown something that the left side couldn't see, the person couldn't say what it was.

That didn't mean, though, that they couldn't recognize it. They could point to a picture of it, using the left hand (which is controlled by the right side of the brain). And they could pick it out by touch from a tray of other objects. They just couldn't name it, because the image had been passed to the right side of the brain, and the right side of the brain does not control language.

Figure 4.1 A split-brain study.

HEMISPHERE DIFFERENCES

By doing more tests of this kind, Sperry found that the two cerebral hemispheres seemed to have different abilities. As we have seen, the left side of the brain handles language and it also seems to be concerned with mathematical problems and arithmetic. The right side of the brain, though, is better at geometric or spatial puzzles, and seems to be particularly good at interpreting drawings. We understand speech with the left side of the brain, but most of us (apart from trained musicians) understand music with the right side.

These findings are interesting, but it is important to realize that we are talking only about how some kinds of information are processed. In fact, later research showed that each side does have the basic rudiments of the other side's abilities, even though they aren't very highly developed. The right hemisphere can sometimes cope with very simple language, while the left hemisphere can deal with simple drawings. And if a child under 12 suffers some kind of serious brain damage, the other side usually takes over the damaged side's functions as well as its own. That can happen with adults too, but it takes longer and needs a lot more effort from the person with the injury. Similarly, learning and experience have an effect: trained musicians perceive music with their left hemispheres as well as their right, because they are able to analyse the music, and analytical skills are located mainly on the left. But this has been something they have learned – it isn't some magical ability, inborn from birth.

Insight

There's a lot of nonsense talked about 'left-brained' and 'right-brained' people. Some mystics have claimed that the right side of the brain contains all of the creative and spiritual side of being, while the left side is purely logical and mechanistic. But really there isn't actually any psychological evidence to support this. Actually, both halves of the brain can do both sets of functions, it's just that they do their preferred functions better, because they've had more practice and the brain pathways are better developed.

ALERTNESS AND ATTENTION

If something unexpected catches our attention, we become instantly alert. This involves a set of reactions which are very similar to the arousal response discussed below, although not quite as extreme. For example, the blood pressure goes up slightly and our heart rate increases. We also turn towards the source of the unexpected stimulus, keeping muscle movement to a minimum so that we can catch any slight sounds, and keeping our eyes open so that we can see anything there is to see. All this is known as the **orientation response** and it is partly controlled by a part of the brain known as the reticular formation.

The reticular formation is located above the top of the spine, just above the part of the brain that controls basic, essential activities like breathing and digestion. It seems to act as a general switching mechanism for the cerebral hemispheres, switching them on if we need to be awake, nudging them into greater activity if we need to pay attention to an unexpected stimulus, and damping them down when it is time to sleep.

Insight

The development of EEGs allowed us to measure the general activity of the cerebral cortex, which showed up general states like sleeping, waking and alertness. But until the development of more specialized forms of scanning, it was all a bit like standing outside a factory and trying to work out what was going on by listening to the noises coming through the window!

In one set of studies, the neuropsychologist French showed how gentle electrical stimulation to a particular part of the reticular formation would rouse a sleeping cat. The cat would wake up in the same way as it did naturally, which suggested that electrical activity in this part of the brain might be the normal way that mammals – including humans – change from sleep to wakefulness. French also found that cats who had the reticular formation removed would sink into a deep coma, from which they could not be woken up. It seems likely that coma in human beings, too, may sometimes happen as a result of damage to the reticular formation. But we should be careful about making too many generalizations, though, because French also found that stimulating the same area in rats produced an aggressive response rather than sleeping.

Arousal, anxiety and anger

Another significant area of applied bio-psychology is our understanding of how to deal with extreme emotions. We often think of emotional experiences as being mainly to do with the mind: that is, coming from how we understand the situation, and how we feel about what has been happening lately. And that's partly true. But it isn't by any means the whole story. As you will know if you have read *Understand Psychology*, our physiological reactions can make a great deal of difference to the emotions that we feel, and understanding how they work can tell us a great deal about effective coping.

Perhaps the most useful place to begin here is by looking at anxiety. Anxiety is the unpleasant emotion that we feel when we are anticipating something that we believe will be unpleasant – like a driving test, or perhaps a visit to the dentist. It isn't caused by the experiences themselves – we have a much more direct reaction to those. It's caused by thinking about those things before they happen, and anticipating that they will be absolutely awful.

THE FIGHT OR FLIGHT RESPONSE

Our anticipation is cognitive – it's in the mind. But the reaction which it causes is physical. It has to do with some ancient responses in the body, which are a direct inheritance from our evolutionary past, when we might have had to defend ourselves against dangerous predators. If we perceive a threat, the body begins a set of reactions which are all designed to give us as much energy as possible. It's called the **fight or flight response**, because, depending on the threat, we might need to run away as fast as possible, or we might need to fight. And in either case, we'd need as much energy as possible. There's no point holding anything back if you're not alive to use it later!

All mammals have this reaction – as I said, it's an ancient one. It involves a whole section of the nervous system, known as the **autonomic nervous system** (or ANS for short), which has nerve connections running to the heart, the lungs, the adrenal glands, the skin, the stomach, and other internal organs. The ANS has two ways of working. One way activates everything, releasing stored energy and getting us ready for action. Blood provides the fuel for muscles to work, in the form of oxygen and glucose. So the heart beats faster to pump blood to the muscles more effectively, the lungs take in more oxygen, stored glucose is released into the bloodstream and the blood vessels dilate so that they can carry more. Other changes happen too: we sweat more, and the adrenal glands release the hormone adrenaline, which keeps all these changes working. Table 4.2 lists some of these changes. We refer to them collectively as **arousal**.

Table 4.2 Characteristics of arousal

▶ *Breathing becomes deeper to bring more oxygen into the lungs.*
▶ *The spleen releases stored red blood cells to carry extra oxygen to the muscles.*
▶ *Stored glucose is released for additional energy.*
▶ *Extra blood platelets are released into the bloodstream, which helps the blood to clot.*
▶ *The brain produces endorphins – neurotransmitters which block out immediate feelings of pain.*
▶ *The pupils of the eyes dilate and become more receptive to external stimuli.*
▶ *Digestion is suppressed apart from the rapid metabolism of sugars for instant energy.*
▶ *An increase in the rate of sweating helps the body deal with heat from active muscles.*

(Contd)

> ▶ *Long-term immune system activity is suppressed.*
> ▶ *Blood is diverted from the skin to the vital organs and muscles.*
> ▶ *Stored hormones (adrenaline and noradrenaline) are released into the bloodstream to maintain levels of arousal.*

That's the physical side of anxiety. When we are anxious about something, our imagination keeps rehearsing it, and it always tends to dwell on the most threatening part. So the mind ends up perceiving threats all the time, and each time it does, it activates the arousal reaction. Lie-detectors work from this principle: they detect the slight changes in sweating, heart rate and so on which happen when somebody tells a lie, and those changes come from the fact that we are always a little more anxious when we are lying than when we are telling the truth. Sometimes we can't detect the changes ourselves, so we think we are completely relaxed, but the machine is much more sensitive and so can pick them up.

So even a small thought can have an effect, and when we are anxious, we have a lot of worrying thoughts. If it goes on long enough, we call it **stress** and it can become very damaging – we'll be looking at that in Chapter 7, and at how counselling psychologists can help people to cope with it. But even in the short term, it's pretty unpleasant.

Insight

Recognizing that even small anxious thoughts have a physiological effect can help us to understand why positive thinking can be so good for physical health. A worrier is continually using energy as the body copes with all of their worrying thoughts. An optimist is much more likely to allow their bodies time to relax and bring its recovery and repair mechanisms into action.

REDUCING AROUSAL

There is, though, quite a lot that people can do to reduce anxiety, and applied bio-psychologists have been involved in teaching people how to do this. One approach, for example, is to tackle it on a purely physical level. I mentioned before that the autonomic nervous system has two ways of working, and that one of them is to activate arousal. That part of the ANS is known as the sympathetic division, which is a little odd, because it isn't. If anything, it's about anger and attack rather than sympathy! Anyway, the other way is how the ANS works when we are not experiencing any threats, either real or imaginary. That part of the ANS is known as the parasympathetic division, and it is involved in calming the body down, storing energy for future use, and so on.

You might have noticed that if you play sport or do something else which involves sustained energetic activity, like swimming or a workout in the gym, that afterwards you feel very relaxed and calm. That's because the parasympathetic division has become active. The sympathetic division was active while you were exercising, and generating lots of adrenaline, but afterwards, the body goes into a different mode. It's particularly obvious if you eat a meal afterwards: you generally feel really good, as your body calms right down.

That's one of the things which applied bio-psychologists use to help people to control their anxiety. While people are anxious, their bodies are generating masses of energy because of the fight or flight reaction, but in the modern world we just don't use it. So it makes us fidgety and nervous, and that makes the anxiety worse. Doing vigorous exercise helps us to use the energy we have generated and, more importantly, it allows the other part of the ANS to come into play afterwards, so we manage our anxiety better.

I use this if I have to have a filling at the dentist. Modern dentists are very good and pain-free, but when I was young I had some bad experiences, so I'm always a bit anxious. But the dentist's chair is the last place you would want to be twitchy, and I need to control my feelings. So if I have an appointment for a filling, or for anything which is more than a routine check-up, I make a point of going to the gym beforehand and having a good workout. That way, my body is much calmer when I'm in the dentist's chair, and I can control my anxiety better.

There are other ways of controlling anxiety too. Some drugs, for example, actually stimulate arousal mechanisms, and caffeine is one of the worst. Carbohydrates, on the other hand, help the parasympathetic division to work better – they are 'comfort foods'. So applied bio-psychologists often advise people to be careful about their diet. Avoiding or cutting down caffeine, particularly in coffee (cup for cup, there's much less in tea) is a good idea, and so is eating foods which give long-term energy such as pasta or potatoes, rather than foods which give an instant 'hype', like sugary things. Milk is particularly good, because it contains naturally occurring morphine-like substances which help the body to calm down. If you've a stressful time coming up, try drinking milk instead of coffee throughout the day. You'll be surprised at how much of a difference it makes!

Insight

Eating for calmness is a real possibility, and if you're going through a stressful time you might like to try it. Avoid stressors like caffeine and sugar, and eat lots of comfort foods like milk, mashed potato, fish and raw vegetables. Try it for three days, and see how you feel.

ANGER MANAGEMENT

Understanding the physiological basis of the reaction, then, means that we can learn how to control it on a physical level. But the physical level isn't all there is. Both stress and anger management training use a combination of physical and cognitive exercises. The physical ones work on the same principles we have been looking at with anxiety: using constructive exercise to 'work off' the frustrations. The cognitive techniques use mental exercises, some of which aim to calm the person down, and some which just aim to reduce the number of times they get aroused.

As we've seen, even a single thought produces a physical reaction. But it works both ways: being in an aroused state also makes us more likely to have negative thoughts. So if we're not careful, we end up in a kind of vicious circle, thinking angry thoughts, which make us more angry, which make us more likely to think even more angry thoughts. Calming ourselves down physically is one of the best ways of breaking that cycle, but we also need to learn to control how much we think angry thoughts.

One of the ways we can begin to do it is through distraction – deliberately thinking about other things, rather than rehearsing the thing which has made us angry over and over again. Applied psychologists who are training people in anger management teach them mental strategies to interrupt their thinking so they can deliberately learn to think about something else – something positive, which they enjoy, and which has nothing at all to do with the immediate situation.

People who read for pleasure have a great advantage here, because many books encourage the imagination to take the person off into another world – ideally a much nicer one. That type of distraction doesn't solve any long-term problems, of course, but it can do a great deal to help coping in the short-term, and to break the mental–physical cycle. By giving the person a bit of mental 'rest', it allows them to see things in better perspective.

Distraction, though, is only part of the process. Psychologists training people in anger management also have to teach them more positive ways of expressing anger or frustration. It's for those reasons that so many psychologists are deeply concerned about the use of physical punishment for children. What it teaches them is that, when all else has failed, adults resort to violence, and that is a very dangerous lesson for a human being to learn. There are many other ways of disciplining children, which are also much more effective, and we'll be looking at some of these issues in the next chapter. But adults, too, need to find ways of expressing their anger and frustration without resorting to violence.

Some ways of doing this are by diverting the massive amounts of energy generated by emotional arousal into some other activity – a 'cooling off' walk around the block, or a difficult physical challenge. That's really the same technique as I talked about before, and it works for the same reason – once the energy has been worked off, the calming parasympathetic division is able to come into play.

Often, though, the problem builds up because people are unable to talk about their feelings, so encouraging them to do that helps a great deal. It is at this point that applied bio-psychology shades over into counselling, and there are a number of techniques used by counselling psychologists to help people to learn new ways of living. We'll be looking at some of these more closely in Chapter 7.

Insight

Anger management is one of the psychological tools most needed in modern society. Life can be full of stressors, and our perceptions of how to deal with them are not helped by the negative anger scripts we see on TV, particularly in soap operas. So it's not surprising that incidents of 'road rage' and other anger-related problems are increasing.

In this chapter, then, we have seen something of how the work of applied bio-psychologists helps us to understand quite a range of different experiences. There is much more, of course – these chapters can only discuss a few aspects of each area of applied psychology – but understanding the effects of head injuries, emotional arousal, anger and anxiety shows us how useful this area of applied psychology can be. In the next chapter, we will look at that area of applied psychology which is particularly concerned with bringing up children.

10 THINGS TO REMEMBER

1 *Applied bio-psychology is our knowledge of how the workings of the human body affect our minds.*

2 *Strokes are caused by interruption of the blood flow to parts of the brain. They can be ameliorated by rapid action and sustained effort.*

3 *Closed head injuries, particularly involving concussion, can have lasting effects.*

4 *The two halves of the cerebrum can act like separate brains if the connection between them has been severed.*

5 *Different sides of the cerebrum control different functions.*

6 *Alertness and attention are mediated by older structures in the brain.*

7 *The sympathetic division of the autonomic system is activated when we are anxious, upset, or angry.*

8 *'Fight or flight' mechanisms all act to give the body more energy and a better chance of recovery from injury.*

9 *Exercise is one of the best ways of reducing the harmful effects of long-term stress.*

10 *Distraction, diversion and communication are all good techniques in anger management.*

5

Applied developmental psychology

In this chapter you will learn:
- *how attitudes towards the behaviour of children have changed over time*
- *safe and effective methods for disciplining children*
- *the importance of being sociable with babies.*

Applied developmental psychology, as its name suggests, is all about development. Psychologists have been involved in applied developmental psychology for over a hundred years. Ever since the beginning of psychology as a discipline, there has been professional as well as popular interest in how children develop, and what types of influence produce healthy, morally sound and intelligent children. In recent years, developmental psychology has extended its scope of interest too, to include the way that we develop throughout our lifespan. But most applied developmental psychologists tended to focus on children and teenagers.

Approaches to child development

Ideas about how children develop psychologically have changed a great deal during the past hundred years. At the beginning of the twentieth century, there was a strong trend to say that just about everything to do with development happened as a result of genetic influences and there was virtually nothing that anyone could do about it. This trend arose partly as the traditional divisions in society were eroded, and the idea that you had your place in society because of the family you were born into was gradually replaced by the idea that you earned your place in society, through your personal merits and hard work. A genetic explanation for development provided a convenient rationalization for why, nonetheless, some families continued to be more wealthy, successful and influential than others. So it had a great deal of coverage, and became the dominant way of thinking about development at that time.

The psychologists who believed that development arose from genetic influences were sometimes very insistent about it. For example, the Gesell Institute for the Study of Child Development in the USA produced a handbook on child behaviour which said:

> *'First of all, recognize your child's individuality for what it is, and give up the notion that you either produce it (except through inheritance), or that you can basically change it.'*

So applied developmental psychologists of that time tended to focus on advice to parents which was all about bringing out the child's 'natural' tendencies. That was a big contrast to the strict Victorian pattern of upbringing which had been common in Western society only a few years before, and it emphasized the idea that children were precious, and to be valued. That doesn't mean, however, that it was a case of 'anything goes' – by contrast with modern society, we would think that it was still moderately strict. But it was much more positive, and less punitive, than the child-rearing practices which had gone before.

Insight

Theoretical models of child development all reflect the 'common sense' of their time. To us it is obvious that parental encouragement and support will help children learn. But to a Victorian it was equally obvious that the child needed to learn to suppress the wildness and savagery in its nature in order to take part in civilized society, and that this could only be done by strict discipline.

Nowadays, of course, we recognize that such extreme ideas are completely mistaken. Genetic factors are there, of course, but parents and others have a great deal of influence on how children develop. But in the first 30 or so years of the last century, it was a very popular idea. So child psychologists at that time concentrated their efforts on conducting careful observations of how babies and young children developed. They identified sequences of physical development, categories of play, and stages in the development of thinking. Many of their ideas have left their traces in ideas about child development today, although the emphasis on genetic influence as the only important factor in development has almost completely disappeared.

The social changes which occurred after World War I, however, produced a gradual change in applied developmental psychology. This was partly influenced by the work of the behaviourist psychologists who were becoming more and more influential in psychology as a whole. The behaviourists took entirely the opposite view about development – they thought the child was born as a completely blank slate, ready to learn from all its new experiences, and capable of being moulded in any way that society wanted. Through trial and error learning, and also through basic conditioning – avoiding pain, for example – children gradually acquired knowledge about their worlds, and learned ways to behave.

The behaviourists were just as extreme in their views as the genetic psychologists, but they completely disregarded any influence from heredity at all. J.B. Watson, who is known as the 'father' of behaviourism, said in 1924:

> *'Give me a dozen healthy infants ... and my own specified world to bring them up in, and I'll guarantee to take any one at random and train him to become any type of specialist I might select – doctor, lawyer ... and yes, even beggarman and thief, regardless of talents, penchants, tendencies, abilities, vocations, and the race of his ancestors.'*

This view was almost as unrealistic in its own way as the genetic one. However, it was very popular during the middle decades of the twentieth century, because it fitted so well with the ideas about building a new, fairer society which were so common in the UK and the USA at the time. The problem, though, was that the behaviourists saw learning as a very mechanical process, arising simply from reactions to different forms of stimulus in the environment. They thought that it made no difference whether the child's experience came from physical surroundings or other people – it was all just stimuli of one sort or another, and the learning all worked in the same way.

Applied developmental psychology at this time, therefore, tended to concentrate on the types of learning which the child was experiencing. Developmental psychologists, though, were generally less mechanistic than the strict behaviourists – perhaps because they were dealing with real children. They included other forms of learning such as imitation and identification, and tended to look at how children learned from parental influences – the effects of different types of punishment, of reward, and of styles of authority. There were some useful studies of parenting and even leadership at this time which still have relevance today.

Insight

If there's one thing we can learn from all these different theories of child development and their applications, it's how resilient children are. As long as they have people to interact with, they seem to be able to deal easily with most patterns of child-rearing. It's further evidence of the adaptability of human beings as a species.

In the 1960s and 1970s, another approach became popular. This saw development as a combination of genetic influences and learning, and was expressed most clearly in the work of Jean Piaget. Piaget produced a grand theory of child development, which saw the child's psychological development as following established sequences which were shaped and developed as a result of the child's learning. The sequences of development and how the child went about learning were genetic in origin, but what the child actually learned and how it put its knowledge together to make sense of the world happened as a result of experience.

Applied developmental psychologists of that time, therefore, devoted a lot of attention to the idea of developmental stages, and the concept of 'readiness' – whether the child had reached a stage where it was ready to acquire a certain type of learning. Advice to parents was often concerned with types of experience which they could provide which might help a child to develop in this way, or giving them a general overview which would allow them to see their child's behaviour in context, and learn ways of dealing with specific problems which were apparent as a result.

This mixture of what had come to be known as 'nature' and 'nurture' was very popular at the time, but it too had its weaknesses. Although Piaget was able to show how both types of influence might work together in development, the theory still tended to focus purely on the individual, without seeing the child in its social context. When researchers came to re-evaluate Piaget's work with this in mind, they found that the child's mental abilities had been seriously downplayed – children were much more socially sophisticated, and more able to grasp complex ideas, than had been thought. It was just that those ideas needed to be expressed in a context which made sense to the child in the first place.

This set the groundwork for the next phase in applied developmental psychology, which is roughly the one we are in today. Modern ideas are perhaps best expressed in the theoretical work of Vygotsky, which is interesting because, like Piaget, he developed his ideas a long time ago. But his work was only translated from Russian into English in 1962, and it gradually gathered influence, until by the end of the twentieth century it had become the approach which best expresses the way that modern developmental psychologists see child development.

Vygotsky didn't deny either genetic or environmental influences on the child's development. But what he was particularly interested in was the way that the child responds to other people (see *Understand Psychology*). Children are particularly strongly set to respond to other people, even from their very earliest days. Vygotsky showed how social influences from others provide the child with structures, so that it can build and shape its growing knowledge of the world. The learning that the child does from other people is different, and much stronger, than the learning it acquires from other features of the environment.

J.S. Bruner, a famous psychologist who was very strongly influenced by Vygotsky's ideas, described what the adult provides as **scaffolding** – a kind of supporting framework helping the child to build and shape its growing knowledge. Applied developmental psychologists following this framework are often concerned with teaching parents how they can help and support their child's development, and shape its learning, so that it is able to acquire the values and abilities it will need to become a competent, strong and responsible adult.

Every child is different, because children have different genetic predispositions and different experiences, so the shaping process can't happen by a simple formula. But the learning which a child acquires from the other people around it is vitally important in shaping that child's character, mental skills and personality.

Insight

Topics like child development are both politically and socially sensitive, as they link with their society's core social representations. We see clearly how the ideology of that particular age influences the research and theories considered acceptable at that time. The question is, can we see the influences on our current research just as clearly?

So another important area of modern applied developmental psychology is concerned with how the young child comes to relate to the other people around it, and the relationships which it forms with others. A great deal of research in developmental psychology has been concerned with this area. Applied developmental psychologists use the knowledge we have gained from this research to understand, and also sometimes to help, family relationships.

Attachment, deprivation and socialization

Ideas about attachment, or 'bonding', between mothers and infants have sometimes achieved a kind of mystical status – the attachment is seen as something magical and mysterious. But psychologists have spent decades studying how infants develop attachments to, and with, the people who look after them. As a result, we have a much deeper understanding of what is actually going on.

The idea that 'bonding' happens in an instant, magical way actually came about because of a set of animal studies which took place in the 1950s and 1960s. These studies showed how small ducklings, goslings, foals, and lambs develop a unique, special attachment to their mothers, very quickly after being born, as a result of a special learning process called imprinting. Several researchers of the time thought that this was the basic mechanism for all attachments, and began to talk about the idea of human mothers and infants 'bonding' soon after birth.

The reality is a little different. Those animals that showed imprinting were all ones which could move around independently soon after birth. Their rapid attachment was a special, genetically programmed system which made sure that the young animals, which didn't know anything about their world and its dangers, stayed close to their mothers and didn't stray away. But species which are more helpless when they are born – including human beings – take much longer to develop their attachments.

Insight

Ideas about the importance of social factors in child development had to be fitted in with the powerful biological/genetic theories which dominated thinking at the time. Imprinting was a sort of half way house, showing social factors having influence in a genetically determined context.

Studies of human infants show that what appears to be the most important factor in developing attachments is what Schaffer and

Emerson (1964) called 'sensitive responsiveness'. Even very young babies respond to other people: they often smile, or quieten down, at the sound of a familiar voice; they look particularly closely at people's faces, turn their heads when they hear a human voice, and so on. When they are interacting with people, they give out their own little behavioural cues which show when they are interested, enjoying what is happening, or becoming uncomfortable or distressed. And they are most likely to develop attachments to the people who respond most sensitively to those little cues, and pattern their interaction accordingly.

The mother or person who looks after the child most of the time is usually one of these people, of course, since they have most opportunity to play with their babies, but that isn't always the case. Sometimes, babies form very strong attachments with people who are only with them for a couple of hours a day. And it is very common for them to develop attachments to more than one person. But the attachment develops gradually, as the infant learns who is particularly 'special' in its social environment.

Babies develop attachments gradually, but for mothers it can be much more rapid. Most mothers experience a very strong attachment, or bonding, towards their infant when it is born. It comes partly from their emotional reaction to the birth, partly from the amount of hard work which the mother has put into carrying and giving birth to the child, partly from the expectations which have built up over time, and partly from the delight and gratification involved in producing a new, special human being. Some mothers, though, don't have the same experience. They feel fairly neutral towards their infant when it is first born, but their loving attachment with the child builds up gradually as they and the infant interact, and as the child grows.

DEPRIVATION

In the middle of the last century, there was a considerable amount of research which investigated the effects of deprivation on the young child. It was partly stimulated by the devastation of the war years, which had left many children orphaned and growing up in institutions, and partly by the work of J.S. Bowlby, who published an influential report for the World Health Organization in 1951 which asserted that what he called 'maternal deprivation' could produce serious, long-term social and emotional damage, leading to juvenile delinquency and a number of other problems.

Insight

The devastation caused by World War II raised many questions about social deprivation and its impact, but at the same time there was pressure for women to stop the work they had been doing during the war years, to free those jobs for returning soldiers. It was this which caused many of the ideas about maternal deprivation to become exaggerated.

Bowlby's original view of 'maternal deprivation' had been based on animal studies of imprinting, which seemed to imply that the attachment to the mother was distinctive, special and irreplaceable. In later years, he modified his approach, acknowledging other research in the area and recognizing that children's attachments were more complex than they had at first appeared.

Bowlby's early work also caused controversy as he listed 'mother working full-time' as one of the conditions in which children could become emotionally damaged. This produced a social debate which is still going on in the present day: but it also stimulated a great deal of research which showed that what is important is, as we have seen, the quality of the social interaction which the child receives. A mother who is working full-time and enjoying her work may provide a child with a better quality of interaction than one who is at home, but bored and under-stimulated.

Other people are by far the most important part of a young child's life and being deprived of them, whether in an institution or from a particularly unsocial environment at home, does affect children considerably. Some studies have investigated so-called 'feral children' – that is, children who appear to have grown up without any social contact – and have shown just how restricted these children are.

But time and again, these studies also show how much improvement the children make when they are discovered and put into contact with other human beings who interact with them and care for them. The quality of care they receive affects how much they improve, and such children almost always show a dramatic improvement when they find themselves in a secure and loving environment.

Other applied developmental psychologists have focused on children who have experienced different kinds of deprivation – generally, the deprivation of family interactions and everyday loving which can happen to children who grow up in institutions. Such children can suffer physical symptoms, such as **dwarfism**, which appear to happen as a response to emotional stress, and they can also suffer more serious emotional consequences, which make it difficult for them to form relationships with others. As with the feral children, though, psychologists have found that a stable, loving family environment can do a great deal to repair this type of damage, even with older children and sometimes even with adults.

SOCIALIZATION

Being in a family, whether that is with a natural family, an adoptive family, or a foster family, allows a child to learn the kinds of rules of everyday behaviour which most people take for granted. But it also gives the child the opportunity for the kind of sustained, reliable interaction which forms the basis for attachments in human beings. Infants can take anything up to seven or eight months before they begin to form attachments with other people, even though they might recognize other people before that; but those seven months are spent interacting with others and learning basic social skills, such as turn-taking and communicating.

Similarly, older children who have spent their early years in institutions often have a great deal to learn about communication and social interaction. They are ready to learn, as the infants are, but their previous experience has not given them the practice which they need to build up their skills. Stratton (1983) argued that infants and children build up social skills, and also their wider knowledge of the world, partly through **contingencies**: that is, by learning about what is likely to happen as a result of a particular action or activity. Contingencies help infants, and older children too, gain some kind of sense of themselves as active agents who can make things happen, and this helps them to explore and develop their knowledge of their social world.

> **Insight**
>
> The inherently social nature of babies and toddlers shows in how much they enjoy repetitive transactions, such as 'peek-a-boo' or 'pick up teddy'. Taking turns is fundamental to every social interaction, and we learn it very early in life.

Apart from contingencies, children and infants also learn through **transactions** – exchanges between two people, when one person does something as a result of the other person's **actions**. A transaction can be as simple as getting a positive response to a 'please' or 'thank you'; and social life is full of them. Everyday interactions in the family allow children the experience of everyday transactions, which helps them to learn about social living and getting on with other people.

One of the important tasks which is often undertaken by applied developmental psychologists, therefore, is teaching people how to recognize and enhance the contingencies and transactions experienced by their young children. As the child explores its environment, it develops a sense of mastery and competence, which forms the basis for further learning; and parents can be very important agents in helping children to achieve this. Their use of rewards, encouragement and attention helps the child to learn more effectively, and to develop its social skills and competences.

> **Insight**
>
> There is a growing trend, at least in the UK, to have children cared for in nursery schools and playgroups from an ever-younger age. Some researchers believe that early schooling helps build social resilience and social skills; others believe that keeping such experiences for a later age – for example,

in Norway children don't go to school until they are seven – promotes independence and self-confidence.

Discipline, reward and punishment

The explicit training provided by parents about which types of behaviour are acceptable and which aren't is an important part of child-rearing. Developmental psychologists have carried out a great deal of research into parenting, and how children's development can be helped by the adults around them. Many applied developmental psychologists work directly with families who have problem children, to help parents to learn more effective ways of dealing with them.

DISCIPLINE AND REWARD

In recent years there have been some hot debates about the forms of punishment which are appropriate when bringing up children – mainly centred around the acceptability or otherwise of physical punishments such as smacking or slapping children. Applied developmental psychology has a great deal to contribute to this debate, not least because psychological research into the effectiveness (or otherwise) of punishment has been going on for several decades.

One of the most fundamental findings of researchers in this area is that, by and large, punishment is a fairly inefficient way of controlling children's behaviour. Since the only aim of punishment is to suppress unwanted behaviour, it is always specific to a particular activity. But being punished for one thing doesn't stop the child from going and finding something else to do that is equally undesirable. So parents who attempt to control their children's behaviour through punishment can easily find themselves in a never-ending chain of punishments and reprimands.

The alternative is to attempt to step out of the punishment trap altogether, at least when it regards ordinary day-to-day behaviours.

It is much more efficient to focus on rewarding appropriate behaviour from the child. That way, the child learns what it should be doing instead of what it shouldn't. Changing from punishment to reward can be difficult for parents who have become used to using punishment, or whose children are particularly badly behaved, so many applied developmental psychologists work with parents to show them how it can be done.

Insight

Our inherent sociability is reflected in the way that psychological forms of punishment are so much more effective than physical ones. Being shamed, embarrassed or made to feel guilty are far more effective than being fined or confined. But encouragement and reward are more effective still.

Rewarding doesn't have to mean giving a child sweets or money. For children, the most valuable reward of all is attention – and indeed, some children become badly behaved purely because that is the only way that they can get their parents' attention. So one of the things developmental psychologists can help parents to do is to notice and show approval when their child is behaving well. That seems obvious, and some parents do it without thinking; but for many parents who have a lot of other stresses or demands on their attention, it is quite hard to learn. When they do learn how to do it, though, they find that the extra effort which they have to expend is more than paid back by the improvement in their child's behaviour.

Rewarding good behaviour, though, doesn't replace everyday discipline. Children also need to know their limits, and it is through parents being firm about what is acceptable and what isn't that the child eventually learns self-discipline. One useful analogy is with muscle development: muscles grow strong as a result of pushing against resistance. In the same way, 'mental muscles' such as self-control grow stronger as the child learns what it can and can't do. Toddlers, as all parents discover, are incredibly self-willed; but giving in to tantrums doesn't help a child to deal with later life. The parent needs to be firm and to resist the pressure which the young child exerts. It isn't cruelty – it's helping the child to become more socially skilled, in the long run.

The short run, though, can be difficult, and again many parents have found the guidance provided by psychologists to be helpful in showing them strategies for dealing with a wilful child without resorting to physical punishment. Some of these strategies, such as 'time out' in another room have become widely known in recent years, as parents discover how effective they can be. The use of distraction (as opposed to bribery) is also a skill that many parents learn; and so is recognizing how to be consistent and whether to give in to the child or not.

Insight

The interactions children have with older and younger siblings can be just as important as those they have with adults. Most family play happens between older and younger children, or between adults and children, and children can develop their own ways of sanctioning and curbing one another's behaviour.

USING PUNISHMENT

There are occasions, of course, when some kind of punishment is unavoidable. Children, particularly as they grow older, sometimes deliberately do things that they know to be wrong. But even then, there are effective and ineffective forms of punishment. Slapping or spanking rarely has much effect. They are over quickly, and all they really teach a child is to resort to violence when they can't think of any other way to communicate. There are other ways of punishing children which are much more effective.

Table 5.1 lists the four characteristics of effective punishment for children. The first is that such punishment is applicable to the situation – for instance, a teenager coming in late might be punished by being unable to go out the next evening. The second is that the punishment includes explanation – of exactly why the action was wrong, how it might have hurt others, or involved excessive risk, or whatever reason it was. Children need to understand why they are being punished and what exactly they are being punished for, and it is important that this isn't taken for granted.

> **Table 5.1 Characteristics of effective punishment**
>
> 1 *The punishment should be appropriate to the offence.*
> 2 *The punishment must be accompanied by explanation.*
> 3 *The punishment should include some kind of act of atonement.*
> 4 *The punishment should take place immediately or reasonably soon after the offence.*

Too often, parents assume that it is obvious to the child why a particular action was wrong, yet the child really doesn't perceive what the parent is upset about. A teenager coming in long after the agreed time, for example, may simply not understand why a parent needs to know when to expect them home. Not many of us are good at obeying rules we think are irrational, so teenagers sometimes disregard such rules because they don't see any need for them. But teenagers do know about the dangers of rapists or serial killers, and if the reason is explained to them in terms of a parent knowing at what point they should initiate searching or contacting the police, they can see more clearly where the problem lies and why compliance to the rule matters.

A third characteristic of effective punishment is that it should provide the opportunity for some kind of act of atonement, such as doing something to 'make up' for the behaviour, or apologising to everyone affected by it. This isn't just invented to humiliate the wrong-doer – research shows that these acts of atonement help a child to make sense of their action in terms of its social context and how it affects other people.

The fourth characteristic of effective punishment has to do with its timing. It needs to be closely linked in time to the offending action. Children's sense of time varies at different ages, so a young child needs to see the consequences of its actions pretty well immediately, while an older child can wait longer, and a teenager longer still. There's not much point punishing a five-year-old who is misbehaving in the morning by sending it to bed early that evening. By that time the child has totally forgotten the morning incident, and it no longer has any relevance. Teenagers, on the other hand, have a more highly developed sense of past, present and future, so a teenager who is very late home one evening might be effectively punished by having to stay in for the next few evenings, or even perhaps the next weekend.

Insight

As with most other areas of child development, widely different approaches can all seem to produce psychologically healthy, happy adults. Whatever discipline framework is used, the crucial factors seem to come down to three basic principles: high expectations, reasonably consistent sanctions, and fairness.

For some parents, the kind of applied developmental psychology I have been talking about in this chapter won't seem particularly special – it will just seem like common sense. That is because developmental psychology has, over the past half-century, contributed so much to our everyday knowledge of children and child development that we take those ideas for granted. For other parents, though, it is something that they haven't particularly thought about, and applied developmental psychologists have often found that helping parents to understand the principles in this way can really allow them to sort out their family problems. What counts as 'common sense' isn't always common, and can vary quite a lot from one family to another. It also varies over time: the kinds of discipline and punishment adopted by parents a hundred years ago, and assumed to be 'common sense' then were very different from modern child-rearing.

Children are still brought up in many different ways, though, and applied developmental psychologists often work with parents who find their children particularly difficult. But this, of course, is not the whole scope of applied developmental psychology. In the next chapter, we will be looking at the work of family therapists, who also use applied developmental psychology as part of their strategies for helping troubled families, and in later chapters we will be looking at the work of educational and school psychologists, who are concerned with how children learn and related aspects of their development. There are many other areas of applied developmental psychology too, but not enough space to deal with them in this book. Nonetheless, I hope this chapter will have given you a reasonable idea of this area of applied psychology.

10 THINGS TO REMEMBER

1 *Ideas about child psychology have changed considerably during the past 150 years.*

2 *Behaviourists argued that development happened through learning and environmental influences alone.*

3 *Piaget believed that children passed through stages of biological readiness to learn certain types of knowledge at certain times.*

4 *Vygotsky emphasized the importance of social guidance and structuring from adults in the child's cognitive development.*

5 *Human infant attachments develop through social interaction and sensitivity.*

6 *Children deprived of human relationships can suffer physical as well as emotional damage.*

7 *Infants are particularly ready to learn through contingencies and transactions.*

8 *Transactions between infants and adults often mirror the later 'give and take' of conversation.*

9 *Reward is more effective than punishment in controlling a child's behaviour.*

10 *Effective punishment always has to include an act of atonement as well as explanation.*

6

Clinical psychology

In this chapter you will learn:
- *the types of problem usually addressed by clinical psychologists*
- *the major methods in clinical psychology*
- *five different approaches to psychological therapy.*

Clinical psychology is one of the oldest and most highly developed areas of applied psychology. It is the one that people most often think of when they think of the work that psychologists do – they think of counselling, therapy, helping people to recover from traumas or disasters, and so on. All of which are good reflections of the type of work that clinical psychologists are able to do.

The scope of clinical psychology

Clinical psychologists, as their name suggests, are trained to work with clinical problems: that is, psychological problems which have become so acute that they interfere with people conducting their day-to-day lives. Some clinical psychologists work in psychiatric hospitals, working closely with psychiatrists to help people who are suffering from a 'mental illness', or some other kind of severe problem in living. Some clinical psychologists work with other medical practitioners. It is becoming increasingly common, for example, for a clinical psychologist to work in a general medical practice, dealing with the type of problems which people bring to their doctor, but which are psychological in origin and better dealt with by a specialist in psychological matters.

Insight

People often do distinguish between psychologists and psychiatrists, but really they are quite different. A psychologist specializes in understanding the human mind, in both normal and abnormal conditions. A psychiatrist is a medical doctor who specializes in illnesses and disorders.

Others work with specialist treatment units of one kind or another. Paediatric clinics, for example, have clinical psychologists among the team members, who are able to provide psychological evaluations, guidance for parents, and therapy for children who need it. Some clinical psychologists work in community contexts, contributing their skills to teams which deal with a wide range of issues such as the problems of homelessness and street drinkers, or the challenges created by lack of institutional care for severe schizophrenics.

In addition to this, clinical psychologists often contribute their skills to emergency relief. They work closely with counselling psychologists and other professionals to help to relieve the psychological consequences of disasters or traumas. This often involves dealing with the common problem of **post-traumatic stress disorder** – a series of psychological problems that people experience after they have been involved in some particularly disturbing or traumatic situation.

Clinical psychologists bring a number of skills to these contexts. Because of the intensive training they have undergone (it takes at least eight years to become a fully qualified clinical psychologist), a clinical psychologist is trained in evaluating and diagnosing psychological problems, in techniques for **ameliorating** them – making them more bearable or less severe – and also in a number of different approaches to therapy. Although most clinical psychologists tend to develop preferred ways of working, their training is deliberately **eclectic**: that is, it covers different approaches and frameworks, and explores how they can each be used in practice. It is their depth of knowledge of so many different approaches that makes professional clinical psychologists so effective.

EVALUATING PSYCHOLOGICAL PROBLEMS

When a clinical psychologist is dealing with a new client, for instance, they don't adopt just one single approach. Instead, their evaluation of the problem will draw on elements from a number of different approaches. If it is someone with a recurrent anxiety problem, for example, they might gather information about their childhood experience and family relationships, in the way that a psychoanalyst might. But they would also be likely to gather information about that person's daily habits, and the environmental stimuli which provoke anxiety attacks, as a behaviourist would. And they will learn about how the person understands their own problem, and the kinds of thinking styles that they commonly adopt, so that they can bring in insights from cognitive therapies. By combining these, and many other different sources of information, they can make use of the best insights from a wide range of approaches, which will help them to see what is best for that particular person.

All this means that one of the most important tools of the clinical psychologist is the **clinical interview**. Clinical psychologists need to be able to interview people in such a way that they can listen carefully to, and learn from, what that person is saying. This means that they need to be trained in **listening skills**, and in ways of encouraging the person to feel able to talk freely without imposing their own views and ideas on the conversation. That might seem easy, but actually it's a very difficult skill to learn. Counselling psychologists need to learn it too, in order to work effectively, and many professional clinical psychologists become involved in teaching counsellors and nurses these types of skill.

Clinical psychologists are also trained in the use of **psychometric tests**. Psychometric tests are sets of carefully developed questions or tasks, which give an insight into particular psychological issues. Some psychometric tests look just like questionnaires on the surface, but actually they are very different. Each item on a psychometric test has been through a rigorous process of development, being tested, retested, standardized on different populations, and carefully balanced with all the other test items to produce an exact result.

Psychometric tests are useful in a variety of contexts. Some tests are diagnostic – that is, they are able to alert the professional administering the test to particular types of problem. For example, there are different diagnostic tests which can identify specific forms of brain damage, such as the exact consequences of a stroke. Other tests don't diagnose problems as such, but they are used to assess how skilled someone is, or how severe a particular problem is. Some tests, by contrast, are used to give a general picture of what that particular person is like, such as personality or general intelligence tests.

Clinical psychologists have to know how to use all of these types of test, and many of the more powerful diagnostic tests can only be used by people who have had the appropriate clinical training. This is because they can give very misleading results if they are administered in the wrong way, or if someone who doesn't really know what they are doing is trying to interpret the test outcomes.

But testing is only one small part of the clinical psychologist's repertoire. As we saw earlier, they are also required to have a detailed knowledge of different types of psychological therapy.

In a book like this, of course, there really isn't enough space to deal with these to any detailed extent, but in the next part of this chapter we will look very briefly at some of the main approaches to psychological therapy, and the underlying theories on which they are based.

Approaches to psychological therapy

A clinical psychologist, as we have seen, will use a number of different approaches in their work. There are many different types of therapy, all with different assumptions, but they can be roughly grouped into psychoanalytic, behavioural, humanistic and cognitive approaches. So we will use these groupings to look at some of the principles underlying psychological therapy, bearing in mind that this is only a general overview, and not by any means a detailed account. Clinical psychologists have far more specialized knowledge of these approaches, and are able to combine and apply insights from several of them in their work.

THE PSYCHOANALYTIC APPROACH

Some of the earliest forms of clinical psychology were based on the **psychoanalytic** approach. This is the approach to therapy which was pioneered by Freud, and developed in other forms by Jung, Adler and many others. It began when Freud, as a young doctor in Vienna, began investigating what were then referred to as hysterical disorders. (In the medical language of the day, 'hysterical' meant 'coming from the womb', and was used to describe problems suffered by women which were real enough – such as a paralysed arm – but didn't appear to have a physical cause.)

Using hypnosis, word-association, and close investigations of the patient's personal memories, Freud came to the conclusion that these disorders were **psychosomatic**: that is, they were real physical disorders of the body ('somatic'), but their origins were in the person's mind (the 'psyche'). There seems to be an unconscious dimension to the mind, which sometimes appears to take control of the body and to produce these physical symptoms.

Freud explored this unconscious dimension further, and found that it appeared to be able to influence all sorts of aspects of living, including how people talked, the decisions they made, the ways they reacted to events and people, and the emotions that they felt. Moreover, parts of this unconscious mind were elemental, primitive and demanding – quite different from the rational, balanced mentality expected of adults in middle-class nineteenth-century European society.

The idea of the unconscious mind doesn't seem like such a surprising idea to us now, because we have all grown up in a society which accepts Freudian thinking, or that part of it, anyway. But in nineteenth-century Vienna, it was astounding. The social representations of the day assumed that the mind was conscious and rational, and that the body was essentially a machine, functioning automatically and carrying out conscious commands when required. The idea that there might be some buried part of the human mind of which people were unaware, but which could influence how we behaved, was quite radical.

Freud developed an extensive theory of how the mind developed, in which he emphasized the importance of sexuality and sexual energies. But that wasn't the only approach. Other psychoanalysts who worked with Freud believed that different types of energy were important. Jung was concerned with the mystical and symbolic aspects of unconscious experience, for example, while Adler focused on the feelings of inferiority experienced by the young child in the adult world. There are many other approaches to psychoanalysis, but they have in common the idea of the unconscious mind underlying, and influencing, our everyday experience.

Insight

The idea of an unconscious mind, which can influence us without our being aware of it, is probably the greatest single contribution that the psychoanalytic approach has made to psychological understanding.

According to the Freudian approach, the conscious, rational part of the mind (the ego) is constantly keeping the balance between the unconscious, unreasonable demands of the id, and the equally unconscious and equally unreasonable demands of the superego. But what is more important for psychoanalysts is the idea that the unconscious parts of the mind reflect buried conflicts and traumas from infancy and childhood. The idea is that the ego is usually able to maintain a satisfactory, dynamic balance between the demands of the id and superego, but in cases where childhood trauma was very powerful, or created a lot of unresolved conflicts, it would be unable to do so. Clinical problems such as neurosis or obsessional disorders are seen by psychoanalysts as the result of those unresolved conflicts.

So clinical psychologists adopting this approach tend to explore the person's childhood history, bringing unresolved pain or disturbance up to the surface, so that the person can learn to deal with it. Sometimes, this process is deeply traumatic, as in the case of child sexual abuse. But bringing it to the surface is the first step in being able to understand and work through the child's trauma at the time, and by doing so, allowing the adult to come to terms with the experience.

THE BEHAVIOURAL APPROACH

The behavioural approach in clinical psychology is quite different. Rather than looking at deeply buried, unconscious motives, it takes the view that some disorders are best treated in terms of the ways that they show up. The symptoms which show in the person's behaviour are seen as the entire problem – that is why the person requires therapy in the first place, and so that is the most appropriate focus for treatment.

This approach stems from a wider view of psychology which was very popular during the first half of the twentieth century. The behaviourist approach took the view that people were entirely a product of their learning experiences. From birth, we are exposed to a wide range of stimuli, and we learn to associate some of them together, and to link these with behaviours of our own. For example, a baby might learn to smile when it hears its mother's voice, because both the voice, and smiling in response, become linked with pleasant consequences – warm feelings, food, and so on. Basic stimulus–response learning like this, the behaviourists argued, could account for all human behaviour.

And it could even account for abnormal behaviour – irrational impulses, fears and phobias. These, they believed, arose from faulty learning: the linking of inappropriate responses to stimuli. But if a response has been learned, then it can be relearned, so they believed that therapy should be aimed towards helping the patient to learn a new, more appropriate set of responses to the stimuli which were producing the abnormal behaviour in the first place.

Nowadays, we no longer accept the behaviourist approach – or at least, not fully. But many clinical psychologists find it useful to approach a problem in a behavioural way, if not in a fully behaviourist one. That is, they will try looking at a problem as if it were a case of inappropriate learning, while still bearing in mind that human beings do also have thoughts, emotions, intentions, and those other aspects of mental life which the hard-core behaviourists denied.

Insight

The behaviourist assertion that most human behaviour is habitual and takes place without thinking may have a grain of truth, even though it is a bit overstated. It's worth taking notes during a typical day, and asking yourself just how fully aware you are of every single thing that you do.

In fact, the behavioural approach has been quite useful in clinical psychology, particularly when it is applied to very specific kinds of behavioural disorder. Obsessional reactions, for example, such as repeated hand-washing or avoidance of dirt, can often reach the point of becoming a real problem, and need treatment, and that type of problem can frequently be tackled very effectively using a behavioural approach.

Some behavioural methods are concerned with helping the client to relearn certain responses. For example, phobias are fear reactions that have become so extreme that they interfere with the person's day-to-day living. Many people are apprehensive about lightning if they are outside during a thunderstorm, for example. But some people become so apprehensive that they become unable to venture outside at all – even on a sunny day. In that case, what may have been quite a reasonable slight nervousness has become an unacceptable and irrational fear, which requires therapy.

Clinical psychologists often tackle these using techniques which replace the fears with other reactions. **Systematic desensitization** does this gradually, by training the person to relax in the presence of the feared stimulus, while **implosion therapy** does it by exposing the person to so much of the feared stimulus that eventually the fear just dies away (see also *Understand Psychology*).

Sometimes, the aim is for the client to learn a negative response. Some alcoholics, for example, have benefited from the use of the drug Antabuse, which causes the person to be sick if they take alcohol. The association of alcohol with sickness means that they learn an aversion to alcohol, which helps them to keep off it even when they are not taking the drug any more. This is a form of behaviour therapy known as **aversion therapy**.

At other times, a clinical psychologist might help someone to learn a new form of behaviour using a systematic programme of rewards. Or they may use modelling techniques, whereby the client is shown new ways of behaving and learns to copy, or imitate, the person who is showing them how to act. Different techniques are appropriate for different situations, and for different types of problem, which is why clinical psychologists are trained in so many different ones.

THE HUMANISTIC APPROACH

Another approach which clinical psychologists use when it seems appropriate is the humanistic one. In contrast to behaviourism, which sees people as being largely the product of a whole collection of different stimulus–response associations, humanistic psychology looks at the person as a whole. As a result, clinical psychologists adopting the humanistic approach tend to emphasize how people feel about themselves, and pay considerable attention to the person's self-concept.

One way of using this approach, for example, is to look at the differences between the person's ideal self-concept – that is, themselves as they would like to be – and their real self-concept (how they see themselves). Most people have some similarities between the two, but think that they could do with a bit of improvement. But researchers who have explored this idea found that people who came for therapy because of neurotic problems often had very little connection between their self-concept and their ideal self-concept. Their ideals were so unrealistically high and impossible to achieve that they lived with a constant sense of failure and inferiority, which produced their problems.

These researchers also found that humanistic therapy could help these clients a great deal. Teaching them how they could feel more at home with themselves and develop a more realistic, ideal self meant that they became more self-confident and their neurotic symptoms often disappeared. We will be looking at this approach in more detail in the next chapter.

An important part of applying the humanistic approach involves learning to listen to people, and to make sure that they are able to express their own ideas fully. Anxious people are often unwilling to express ideas which might be different from those of the person they are talking to. When that other person is a therapist – an expert – they can be even more reticent. So clinical psychologists and counselling psychologists (who also tend to use this approach) have a lot of training in ways of helping the person to relax and feel able to say exactly what they think.

....

Insight

Really listening to people is quite a rare skill. Humanistic therapists often use a reflecting technique, where they say

(Contd)

simply what they believe the client has just said, in slightly different words. This makes sure they have heard correctly.

In order to do this, it is important that they feel secure, in a positive atmosphere. Clinical psychologists have to learn how to adopt a **non-directive** approach which will help the person to express themselves. In the next chapter, we will be looking at the work of counselling psychologists, who also tend to use the humanistic approach, and we will see how this works in more detail there.

The humanistic approach also aims to promote **self-actualization** among clients. Self-actualization is the making real of different aspects of the self – discovering one's abilities, talents or skills and building on them, or exploring sides of oneself which were previously suppressed. In doing so, we become able to grow, psychologically, which also helps us to become mentally stronger and to deal with our problems more effectively. Again, we will be looking at this in more detail in the next chapter.

Insight

The humanistic approach emphasizes human agency – people making conscious choices in their lives – and psychological growth, or developing our own potential. So it is very different from psychoanalysis or behaviourism, which see the person as a passive victim of forces largely outside their control.

THE COGNITIVE APPROACH

The cognitive approach to therapy tends to focus on how people think about their problems. It takes the view that what matters is how we see what is happening to us. Some people, for example, are able to deal with all sorts of challenging problems in a positive and constructive way, while others become discouraged and depressed at the least setback. Cognitive therapy aims to teach people positive ways of thinking about their problems, which will help them to deal with those problems more effectively.

Different clinical psychologists have different ways of using this approach. In essence, though, cognitive therapy tends to focus on four different aspects of our thinking, and to show how someone can learn to use these differently. It takes practice, of course, so some of their work is concerned with helping the person to learn how to do this, but what results in the end is a much more positive style of thinking.

The first aspect of the person's thinking which cognitive therapists deal with is that of **expectations**. People always make predictions about what is likely in the future, and those predictions can have a tremendous influence on the decisions that they make, and what they do about things.

Some of our expectations are just about what is likely to happen. It is very easy for people who are neurotic or depressed to be very negative about these, when a more psychologically balanced individual might be more optimistic. Seligman (1991) discussed how useful it is for people to learn how to be optimistic. Although we might think it is better to prepare for the worst, in fact it isn't very good for us at all. It just adds to our current stress. Being optimistic, on the other hand, allows us to feel better and to make the most of things, and this gives us more psychological resilience to deal with problems if they do happen to come up.

Other expectations are to do with **self-efficacy** – how competent we see ourselves as being. Self-efficacy beliefs express how successfully we think that we would be able to undertake a particular task or role. They are important, because unless we believe that we are capable of doing something, we don't make any effort, and so we are more likely to fail. So it is important for people to recognize their own areas of competence and ability – and also to realize that even if they can't do something right now, they can learn how to do it. Cognitive therapists are often concerned with showing people just how much they can learn to change their ways of thinking. Enhancing their self-efficacy beliefs is often an important part of this.

Cognitive mechanisms such as self-efficacy can make all the difference to our reactions. The same situation can seem quite different if we feel helpless and out of control, than if we feel able to act to change it but choose not to.

A second focus for cognitive therapists is on the person's **appraisals**: that is, how someone evaluates what has happened in their lives. Sometimes, people make very self-defeating appraisals. For example, even very good students often manage to convince themselves that they have failed in an exam. The way they appraise the situation is unrealistic, and much more negative than it needs to be. It is psychologically damaging too. Beck (1976) showed how negative appraisals induce anxiety, which in turn can exaggerate other problems. So clinical psychologists using the cognitive approach teach their clients how to challenge negative appraisals – and most importantly, how to recognize that they are making them.

Another aspect of thinking which is often a focus for clinical psychologists using the cognitive approach is on the **attributions** which people make. An attribution is a reason which somebody gives for why things happen. We make unconscious attributions all the time, and the type of attribution that we make can have a direct effect on our behaviour. For example, if we see job promotion at our place of work as happening because of effort and commitment, we are much more likely to work hard than if we see job promotion as happening because of favouritism or seniority. The first is an internal attribution – the reason is something personal which we can do something about – while the second is to do with external factors that we can't do anything about directly.

Some types of attribution are much more psychologically healthy than others. In fact, there is a classic 'victim mentality', in which people's attributions tend to be external (unaffected by their own efforts), global (affecting everything rather than just that particular thing) and uncontrollable (so that nobody could do anything about it). Each of these styles of attribution has its opposite, and with help, people can learn to make internal, specific and controllable attributions instead; this gives them a much healthier attitude towards what is happening, and helps them to take action effectively when that would be useful.

Insight

The fundamental attribution error is to see our own actions as dictated by the situation, but other people's as dictated by their disposition or personality. It is really common in everyday life – try looking for examples in a typical day. You're bound to come across at least one or two.

A fourth focus for cognitive therapists is related to a person's **beliefs** about the world and about people in it. Sometimes, these take the form of personal constructs – the ways that people make sense of their worlds based on their own past experiences. There are specific forms of cognitive therapy based on personal constructs, although many just address beliefs in general rather than looking at these in particular. Clinical psychologists using the cognitive approach generally focus explicitly on the long-term beliefs that their patients hold, and on helping people to go about changing them into a more positive way of seeing the world.

There are several, more specific forms of cognitive therapy, and some experienced practitioners specialize in one or more of these. We will be looking at one of these – rational–emotive behaviour therapy – in the next chapter. But anyone who trains as a clinical psychologist learns how to deal with most of these approaches, and how to use them when they are appropriate. Everyone is different, and an approach which is suitable for one person may be entirely wrong for someone else. So if a clinical psychologist is to be able to deal with the wide-ranging set of problems which might arise during the course of their clinical work, they need to have expertise in a wide range of approaches, which will allow them to select the right approach for a person with a particular set of problems.

Family therapy

Sometimes, clinical psychologists find themselves dealing with a problem which can't be resolved just by individual treatment, because it has its origins in how a whole family interacts. It may be that one particular person has come for treatment: perhaps a child whose unruly behaviour has become a problem, or a young adult with extreme emotional problems. But what becomes clear as the therapy proceeds is that it isn't just about that single person. It is actually how the whole family works which needs to be changed.

So quite a few clinical psychologists work in **family therapy** clinics – specialist clinics which focus on the family's relationships, including alliances, feuds, and tendencies to make a single individual into a scapegoat for everyone else. Modern family therapists tend to look at the family in terms of working **systems**, with everyone being interlinked and affecting everyone else. Therapy aims to teach the members of the family to become aware of their impact on others, learning to respond sensitively to one another instead of just reacting to the other family members as a source of irritation or discomfort.

Often, the emphasis is not so much on looking at the dysfunctional aspects of family life – its problems and stresses – but on looking at its positive aspects, and seeing how these can be strengthened. Seeing the family as a working system emphasizes the need to provide **feedback** within the family. By letting the family as a whole recognize what is going on, it allows them to develop ways of adjusting to a more psychologically healthy style, so that all of the family members can interact with one another in a positive and constructive manner.

The methods which family therapists use vary considerably. Some therapists ask family members to act out crucial events which have taken place, so that they can re-examine how they and the other family members reacted at the time. Another approach involves drawing up charts or diagrams of the various alliances and splits in the family. Some therapists use a method known as **sculpting**, in which families arrange themselves without speaking to show how close or distant they are from one another. Like many of the others, this technique is a way for the family to receive feedback about itself, and the results can often come as quite a surprise. Some therapists even find it useful to see several families together. It's often easier to recognize disturbed functioning in someone else's family than it is to see it in your own, and looking at others can sometimes give valuable insights into your own situation.

We can see, then, that clinical psychologists apply psychology in a range of different ways. Training in clinical psychology is rigorous and lengthy. It takes at least eight years to become a qualified basic-grade psychologist, and much of that time is spent developing a range of expertise in the many different approaches and techniques used by clinical psychologists. In the course of their working lives, many clinical psychologists specialize in one particular area, but all have to have an initial training which will enable them to deal with a wide range of problems.

Insight

Many families have quite disturbed patterns of interaction, which family therapists can help to turn into something more positive. But until therapy is seen as an ordinary part of normal living, those who need it most will continue to avoid it.

In the next chapter, we will look at a branch of applied psychology which is very closely related to clinical psychology, but which usually (though not always) tends to deal with less acute problems, and often with people who would not be considered to have a clinical problem at all – the work of counselling psychologists.

10 THINGS TO REMEMBER

1 *Clinical psychologists help people to deal with psychological problems in living.*

2 *Clinical psychologists use clinical interviews, psychometric tests and direct observation to evaluate psychological problems.*

3 *The psychoanalytic approach sees the human mind as being like an iceberg, with most of it buried below the surface.*

4 *Behaviourists see psychological problems as arising from inappropriate learning.*

5 *Behaviour therapy uses conditioning techniques to help people to learn more appropriate behaviours and reactions.*

6 *Humanistic therapists provide a warm and safe emotional climate for people to overcome insecurities and low self-esteem.*

7 *Psychologists using the cognitive approach deal directly with people's expectations and beliefs.*

8 *Cognitive therapists help people to change their appraisals and attributions to a more positive pattern.*

9 *Some psychological problems arise from disturbed patterns within the family, and need intervention with the whole family to resolve them.*

10 *Family therapists provide feedback and guidance to help disturbed families learn new ways of interacting.*

7

Counselling psychology

In this chapter you will learn:
- *the meaning of the terms 'unconditional positive regard' and 'self-actualization'*
- *three techniques used by counselling psychologists to help people cope with stress*
- *how bereavement counselling can help people cope with the complexities of grief.*

Counselling psychology is a relatively recent area of applied psychology to emerge as a specialist branch of the profession. But psychologists have been doing counselling ever since the profession of psychology first began. It started with the work of Freud, which led to the development of psychoanalysis, and grew further as more and more clinical psychologists specialized in personal counselling. Sometimes, their work was (and is) based on psychoanalytic principles, but more often it adopts the humanistic approach which we looked at briefly in the last chapter and will explore in more detail here. Most often, counselling psychologists use a mixture of approaches. But since its beginning, counselling psychology has been applied in a number of fields, including helping people to deal with bereavements, family problems, and even the post-traumatic stress disorder which arises as a result of disasters or particularly disturbing experiences.

Approaches in counselling psychology

Counselling psychology, like all of the other branches of professional
psychology, involves a detailed knowledge of a wide range of
approaches and techniques. The training for becoming a counselling
psychologist is lengthy, involving a first degree in psychology,
specialized training in counselling skills and counselling psychology,
and a great deal of supervised practical experience. But by the time
someone has completed their training, they will have a good range of
expertise based on a wide and detailed knowledge. That will include
an awareness of the general approaches in clinical psychology
which we looked at in the last chapter, and of their application in
counselling situations, as well as more specialized techniques.

THE ROGERIAN APPROACH

The 'founder' of counselling psychology, if it can be said to have
one, is probably Carl Rogers, who was a clinical psychologist
and one of the pioneers of the humanistic approach to clinical
psychology. Rogers was particularly influential because his work
didn't just contain an explanation for mental illness, but also
included an approach to treatment – and one, moreover, which
emphasized the whole person rather than just their behaviour or
their unconscious impulses.

somewhat contemptuous attitude of medical and psychiatric
personnel in the 1950s.

Rogers specialized in the treatment of neuroses, and the more he
interacted with his clients, the more he became convinced that
many of their problems had their origins in the person's childhood.
He came to the view that what was important was whether parents
had given their children **conditional positive regard** – in other
words, positive regard (love or approval) which always depends on
good behaviour – instead of unconditional positive regard. Some
parents, for example, are able to communicate to their children
that they might dislike their behaviour, when they are being
naughty or disobedient, but they still love the child. Those parents
are communicating unconditional positive regard. But some
withdraw all love or affection, communicating dislike or hatred
to the child at such times.

Children who have that kind of upbringing grow up feeling
that they are only loved when they behave in ideal ways. As a
result, Rogers argued, they tend to develop unrealistically high
ideals. They feel that it isn't they themselves who are loved,
but some ideal person. So their view of themselves – their self-
concept – is that, if they are just being themselves, they are
unlovable.

But having positive regard from others isn't an option – it's an
essential need for all human beings. So people who grow up feeling
like that tend to suppress their real feelings, and go all out to
maintain an ideal 'front' when they are dealing with other people.
They spend most of their time seeking approval from others, in
order to gain the positive regard that they need.

The problem, though, is that trying so hard to win approval from
others means that they end up suppressing another vital need,
which Rogers called the need for **self-actualization**, or personal
growth. And that isn't psychologically healthy. It leads to neurosis
or other anxiety-based problems. So the goal of the therapist, in
Rogers's view, is to put the person back in touch with their own

self, and to create the conditions in which they can satisfy their own need for self-actualization.

In order to do this, it is important that the counsellor, or therapist, is able to create an atmosphere of **unconditional positive regard**. That means a relationship in which the person feels safe and approved of, no matter what they reveal about their inner selves. At the same time, Rogers believed, the therapist also needs to be as non-directive as possible. That means encouraging the client to say what they want or need, rather than suggesting anything. If the therapist suggests anything, the client's need for approval might mean that they end up agreeing even if it isn't exactly what they would have chosen themselves. So Rogers and others using this approach developed a range of techniques which counselling psychologists often use to help the client to express their own needs and ideas without being influenced too much.

Insight

It is human nature to keep learning – perfecting skills and acquiring new ones. Sport, video games and almost all other hobbies all involve this to some extent. This is self-actualization, and it is fundamental to our basic human nature. Unless it is interfered with – for example, by drugs – we carry on doing it right through to our very old age.

Counselling psychologists also need to develop very good listening skills. That might seem easy, but a great many people don't really listen to what other people are saying to them. We might think we are listening, but really we are thinking about what they probably mean, and putting our own interpretations on it – so much so, that we often think they have said one thing when actually what they said was quite different. Listening skills training helps a counsellor or therapist to become aware of this process, and to make sure that they are really paying attention to, and absorbing, what the person is actually saying.

Not many modern counselling psychologists use Rogers's methods in exactly the way that he developed them. It is generally acceptable nowadays for therapists to make suggestions, for instance, or to give the client their own interpretations of what is going on. But the work that Rogers did in developing what he referred to as **client-centred therapy** has become the foundation for many of the fundamental skills and approaches used in counselling psychology.

Insight

Client-centred therapy is particularly successful with YAVIS clients (young, articulate, verbal, intelligent and successful). But many people prefer a more directive approach than client-centred therapy offers: we often don't realize what our choices actually are until someone points them out to us.

RATIONAL–EMOTIVE BEHAVIOUR THERAPY

One of the more modern approaches to counselling psychology, rational–emotive behaviour therapy, or REBT for short, builds on basic Rogerian principles but goes about things in a very different way. This approach was described by Ellis, its founder, as a way of tackling problems at three levels: the rational level, in terms of how people think about or make sense of what is happening to them; the emotional level, in terms of how people feel about things; and the behavioural level, in terms of how people act. All three of these things, Ellis argued, were important in tackling people's emotional or personal problems.

Counselling psychologists using this approach often focus on dealing with the irrational ideas which neurotic people hold about themselves, other people, and the world in general. These tend to fall into three types. The first is the idea that it is absolutely essential to do well and win other people's approval all of the time. This isn't realistic, but many neurotic people believe it. So it is something which a counselling psychologist using this approach will challenge, helping the client to realize that it simply isn't a practical way of going about life.

The second irrational idea is that other people must act considerately and fairly towards that person at all times. Sometimes, people really do act unfairly, and we have to find ways of dealing with that. Recognizing that other people have their own stresses and emotions, and that these can sometimes mean that they don't act in absolutely ideal ways is an important part of coming to terms with the real world.

The third irrational idea is that the world, too, should be an absolutely fair and unfrustrating place. It would be nice if that were the case, but in reality the world is rather more tricky than that, and we all have to learn how to cope with it. Rational–emotive behaviour therapy aims to challenge these irrational beliefs, and to put the person in touch with a more realistic way of dealing with day-to-day experience. These ideas are illogical and self-defeating, but they are surprisingly common in people who have psychological problems.

Rational–emotive behaviour therapy deals with unreasonable ideas in three ways. The first is through reasoning and logic, showing the person just how irrational they are being. The second is by encouraging the person to learn new ways of feeling, which help them to respond emotionally in ways that are more in tune with a rational approach to the world. And the third involves developing a set of behavioural techniques to strengthen the new, psychologically healthy mindset which is developing through the therapy.

What is important in rational–emotive therapy, then, is partly the **cognitive restructuring** that is going on as the person learns to think in different ways, and partly the learning of new behaviours and psychologically healthy beliefs. It is very different from Rogers's non-directive therapy, because the therapist takes an active role in helping and sometimes directing the process of change, and sometimes confronts negative cognitive habits and destructive beliefs head-on. It can be quite hard work, psychologically speaking, for both the client and the therapist. But many people find it a valuable approach.

There are other approaches used in counselling psychology, of course, but the two that we have looked at are representative of the main ways in which most counselling psychologists operate.

Any professional needs to be able to draw on a wide range of techniques and approaches – that's part of what being a professional is. So counselling psychology training involves becoming familiar with these approaches, and with many others too. What we have looked at here is a very general overview, but counselling psychologists need to know about these approaches in great detail, so that they are able to use them, or parts of them, as and when they become relevant for particular problems.

Stress management techniques

As counselling psychology has become more widespread, it has come to be in demand in a wide variety of contexts and situations. Many counselling psychologists become involved in **stress counselling** of one sort or another, because stress has become a major factor in modern living, and is increasingly recognized as a costly and damaging force. As a result, many organizations are devoting time and resources to dealing with employee stress, and more and more people are turning to counselling psychologists for help in learning how to cope with the stresses of their day-to-day lives.

Insight

It is said that a healthy body makes a healthy mind, and certainly being physically fit and active does reduce our overall levels of stress. That's partly because we use the stress hormones constructively, and partly because of the extra oxygen carried in the bloodstream, which means our brains and bodies both work better.

COPING

At its most extreme, stress results in burnout and physical illness, and psychologists are often involved in helping people to learn how to manage these. But for most people, the stress they experience isn't as extreme as that. It's unpleasant, and makes their lives very difficult, but they manage to handle it, even over long periods of time.

It still has consequences, though. One of the problems is that when we are under stress, we don't have the mental reserves of tolerance and good-humour that we would have normally. So small things about other people become much more irritating than they would be normally. And when stress continues for a very long time, this can be extremely damaging to relationships.

Counselling psychologists who deal with relationship problems often find that couples who have come to them because they feel they can't make the relationship work any more often have a lot of external stresses. Chronic money problems are a common one, or continuing and unreasonable demands from a third person, which puts one or both members of the partnership under constant strain. The couple end up feeling that it is their relationship which is the problem, because they don't manage to communicate with one another effectively and end up arguing or not speaking. But often, it isn't actually the relationship that's the problem; it's the other stresses which they are trying to handle.

So counselling psychologists are often involved in teaching people **coping skills** – how to handle stress in a more positive kind of way. By teaching people how to cope, they can help them to manage their stress, so that it no longer interferes with their lives in the way that it has been doing. In some cases, it is possible to turn the whole thing around and make the stressful situation into a positive factor in their lives and not a negative one. That's hard to do with some things – lack of money to pay bills is a real anxiety which is difficult to think of positively. But sometimes, what people find stressful can be something which someone else would find challenging.

Not all stress is bad, you see. A lot of people thrive on challenges, and most of us prefer not to be bored. Sometimes, the difference between stress and challenge is only a matter of how we look at it. The situation may be real, but whether we see it as a threat or a challenge depends on a lot of different psychological factors. What we think we can do about it, how we have dealt with other situations in the past, how we feel at the time, whether we see its demands on us as unfair, and all sorts of other things influence how we respond to the various threats in our own lives. Counselling psychologists can help people to sort out this complex of reactions, in order to get a more realistic view of what is happening.

LOCUS OF CONTROL

One of the most important factors in stress management is a concept which psychologists call **locus of control** (see also *Understand Psychology*). This relates to how we think things happen – and most importantly, whether we believe that we can control them or not. If someone has an internal locus of control, this means that they (generally speaking) believe that they can control what happens to them. But someone who has an external locus of control sees any control over what happens as being exerted by something outside themselves – by other people, or by The System, or some other agency. As a result, they feel helpless and frustrated, and experience a lot more stress than someone with an internal locus of control.

Insight

Being helpless is one of the worst experiences for human beings. We all need to feel that we are in control of our own lives, but we often make our stresses worse by failing to look constructively at stressful situations and asking what we really can do about them. Instead, we avoid looking at them closely and just insist that there's nothing we can do.

In one study of mothers with pre-school children, for example, Stratton and Swaffer (1988) found that locus of control was really important. Some of the mothers they studied had an internal locus of control, feeling that they could influence their child's behaviour. So when the child was difficult or unreasonable, they would search for ways of dealing with it, such as looking for other activities that the child could do, or trying new approaches to discipline. Mothers with an external locus of control, though, didn't feel that anything they could do would make any difference, so they felt they just had to put up with it. As a result, they became very frustrated and experienced far more stress.

In fact, these mothers had come to the family therapy clinic because they were suspected of mistreating their children. So learning about their external locus of control helped the counselling psychologists at the clinic to develop an effective programme of action. They taught those mothers ways of controlling and influencing their child's behaviour, and gave them exercises they could try out at home. As the mothers learned that their children's behaviour was controllable after all, their stress levels came down and they were able to develop much more positive relationships with their children. The core of their stress had been the way that they felt helpless and unable to control what was going on.

Acquiring a sense of **agency** – a sense that we can actively influence what happens in our lives – appears to be one of the most effective ways of dealing with stress. We all tend to feel less stressed if we are involved in something, rather than if it is simply imposed on us by some outside agency. Later in this book, we will be looking at organizational psychology and the ways that it is involved in organizational change. One of the most important factors in how well organizational change takes place in an organization relates to 'ownership' – whether people feel that they have been involved and had their say in what is going on. And that, too, connects with whether we feel that we have some control over what is happening to us. Even if it isn't very much, it can make all the difference to the stress that we experience.

POSITIVE THINKING AND LEARNED OPTIMISM

That doesn't mean that all stresses can be handled in this way. Sometimes we experience things that we really can't control, and that we just have to put up with. But even then, there are positive coping strategies that we can learn which will help to minimize how much damage the stressful situations we are in do to us.

Psychological techniques for stress management also include teaching people how to think more positively about things. It is very easy always to look at everything from a gloomy point of view, but it also adds to our stress considerably. Seligman (1998) discussed how people who are optimistic as a general approach experience less stress and tackle day-to-day problems much more effectively than people who are pessimistic. And his research also showed how people can learn to be optimistic, even when they weren't particularly so in the first place. As they learned to use this style of thinking, their stress levels reduced dramatically. So **learned optimism** can be a valuable weapon in the fight against damaging stress.

Insight

Depressive attributional styles are stable, global and uncontrollable: 'It will always be like that, everything else is like that too, and there's nothing I can do about it.' Positive attributional styles recognize that things change with time, that a few bad situations doesn't mean everything else will be equally bad, and that control may be possible and is certainly worth trying.

Many counselling psychologists use methods which help the individual to begin to see the world a little more optimistically. This might include building up their self-efficacy beliefs – the beliefs they have about their own abilities to act effectively in particular situations. It also might include challenging their **attributional styles** – the reasons that they habitually give for why things happen. And it might include challenging unrealistic beliefs, as we saw in the section on rational–emotive behaviour therapy. Whichever methods they use – and most counselling psychologists will use more than one – they can do a great deal to help people to develop effective stress management techniques.

Insight

Compare these two explanations for failing a driving test: 'I didn't listen to my examiner properly, I let myself get too stressed and I should have practised more,' and 'I'm not good at tests; examiners are always so nasty and this car drove in front of me so I got too wound up.' Which is the more useful set of attributions?

Bereavement counselling

Counselling psychologists often find themselves helping people to deal with the kind of stressful life-events which all of us have to face at some point or other in our lives. One of the most common of these is bereavement. When someone who is close to us dies, the psychological effects are profound. To people who have not encountered this type of experience before, the depth of the emotional reaction can be quite bewildering, and a lot of people benefit from the help that counselling psychologists can provide.

In order to provide the best type of help for their clients, though, counselling psychologists need to have a good understanding of how bereavement usually affects people. Everyone finds their own ways of coming to terms with what has happened – indeed, that is what the whole counselling process is about. But an understanding that, say, anger is often a common part of grieving can help both the psychologist and the client to find constructive ways of coping.

Grief is a complicated emotion. It isn't just a single thing, but a mixture of all sorts of different feelings. Sometimes they happen at the same time, sometimes separately, and it can be very disconcerting for people who consider themselves balanced and rational to find their emotions shifting from minute to minute, and through such a range of different sensations. So a significant part of the job of the counselling psychologist in that situation can be in reassuring people that what is happening to them is (a) understandable, (b) to be expected and (c) not permanent.

Insight

Bereavement almost always involves strong feelings of anger, and one of the functions of all societies is to ensure that such feelings don't lead to savage reprisals or acts of revenge. The purpose of laws and judicial structures is to punish people who have committed crimes in a balanced and considered way. Social policies should not be dictated by strong emotions, even if they are understandable.

There are at least nine different components of grief, and for some people even more. I have listed them briefly in Table 7.1, but it is worth looking at them in more detail here. One of the components is a feeling of shock or numbness – a kind of sense that it can't really be true. Another is that the person often becomes disorganized, both physically and mentally, finding it hard to get even simple tasks done. People who are grieving often have times of simple denial, in which they refuse to acknowledge that the death has really happened. It may seem irrational, but even the most sensible people can slip into it from time to time.

Table 7.1 Components of grief

- *shock or numbness*
- *disorganization*
- *denial*
- *guilt*
- *anger*
- *depression*
- *despair*
- *anxiety or panic*
- *resolution and reintegration*

Almost all grieving includes some sense of guilt. People blame themselves for what has happened, or for failing to do something or other relating to the dead person, even when it is obvious to an outsider that their guilty feelings are completely unreasonable. And that guilt can often be mixed in with periods of intense hostility and anger. Sometimes, that anger is directed inwards, adding to the feelings of guilt and leading the person into self-punishment of one kind or another. Sometimes, though, it is directed outwards, at other people such as medical staff or relatives.

Grieving also includes feelings of depression and despair – periods in which someone simply pines for the person they have lost. These can be acutely painful, or mixed up with apathy to produce periods of mental and physical inactivity. But people also often have periods of anxiety or panic attacks mixed in with these periods of depression, which may happen because of the fear of being left alone and uncertainty as to how they will cope. The whole complex of feelings is so strong and so unlike how that person is normally, that they may wonder if they are going mad and panic as a result.

As the worst of the grieving dies down – which can take some time – the person begins to experience episodes of resolution, in which they begin to feel a little more capable and able to deal with things. At first, these periods tend to be short and temporary, as other feelings come up again, but they gradually become longer and more frequent. Similarly, as the grieving process proceeds, it includes a sense of reintegration as the person begins to reorganize their new life, and to come to terms with living without the person who has died. Many people find it quite hard to do this straight away, because it seems disloyal or callous, but the reintegration process is usually able to begin after a couple of weeks or so.

As we can see then, grieving is a complicated process, and one in which it can be very helpful to be able to talk things over with a qualified counselling psychologist who understands this complex of emotions and is able to offer constructive help where that seems appropriate. Grief is one of those intense experiences which often takes people by surprise, and which shows us just how deep our social bonds are.

Some of the most intense grieving often comes from people who had a very disturbed relationship with the person who has died. When that happens, it generally surprises everyone, including the person experiencing the grief – but it is partly because the person is grieving for the relationship which might have been, as well as for the relationship which actually was. Again, this is an area where counselling psychologists have a great deal to offer, and in which they are often involved.

But counselling psychologists don't just help people to come to terms with interrupted relationships. Many counselling psychologists also work to strengthen relationships, dealing with couples or families where the relationships between people have become strained or difficult. Organizations such as Relate employ a great many counsellors and counselling psychologists, and many others are employed in local medical practices, or in family guidance centres.

Counselling psychologists, then, deal with a wide range of different situations and experiences. Sometimes, they work with people who have experienced serious traumas, but equally they often work with people who just feel that they could do with some help in their day-to-day lives. This might be because they are coming to terms with a disturbed childhood, or because they have experienced something disturbing or traumatic recently, or perhaps just because they are finding everything a little more than they can handle.

Insight

Counselling itself may be one of humankind's earliest cultural practices. Counsellors and counselling psychologists can be seen in many ways as the modern equivalent of the wise person of the tribe – shaman, medicine woman or man, witch-doctor, or sometimes priest. All of these roles involve listening to people and reframing their problems in ways which help them to be resolved.

We can see, then, that the work that counselling psychologists do is very varied, and to do it they require very thorough training. Some counselling psychologists specialize, dealing with particular situations such as recovery from disasters and post-traumatic stress disorder. Some work in more general ways, as community psychologists dealing with all sorts of different aspects of social life. These might range from helping police to develop victim support, to working with voluntary organizations helping troubled children, to working with general practitioners and dealing with problems of loneliness or social isolation. Whatever they become involved in, counselling psychologists have a difficult and emotionally demanding job. Their specialized training helps them to deal with this aspect of their work too, as well as the immediate problems which people present to them.

10 THINGS TO REMEMBER

1 *Counselling psychologists provide psychological support for people experiencing difficulties or extreme life-challenges.*

2 *Rogerians believe that unconditional positive regard is needed for people to feel emotionally safe and able to develop.*

3 *Self-actualization is a basic need in people: we suffer psychological damage if it is suppressed.*

4 *The 'rational' part of REBT is about changing irrational beliefs which maintain disturbed behaviour.*

5 *The 'emotional' part of REBT is about helping people to feel more positive within themselves.*

6 *The 'behaviour' part of REBT is about learning new habits and behaviours.*

7 *Helping people to cope with stress is an important part of a counselling psychologist's work.*

8 *An internal locus of control, or sense of agency, is important for reducing stress and improving psychological health.*

9 *Positive thinking and learned optimism can dramatically improve physical as well as mental health.*

10 *Grief is one of the most powerful human emotions, and bereavement counselling is often helpful at such times.*

8

Health psychology

In this chapter you will learn:
- *the difference between the 'absence of illness' and 'positive health'*
- *the stages involved in changing a behaviour*
- *why a large part of health psychology is concerned with communication.*

Health psychology is one of the newer parts of applied psychology, but it has been growing rapidly since its recognition as a full branch of the profession in the 1980s. It developed in reaction to a growing number of challenges to the standard model of health which was common in the first half of the twentieth century. That model, which is known as the **biomedical model**, took the view that health was largely the absence of illness or disorder, and that illnesses and disorders were physical in origin. They might arise from outside the body, such as infections, or from within it, such as glandular problems, but they came about purely because of physical malfunction of one kind or another.

As our understanding of the body and its interactions grew, however, people increasingly began to recognize that things aren't that simple. Some diseases, for example, can be brought on (or at least made worse) by people's behaviour – smoking, failing to exercise, and so on. Some ailments seem to happen as a result of psychological stress, or worry, and are often closely linked with people in impoverished social circumstances. And ever since Freud, psychologists have recognized that some illnesses are closely linked to, and possibly caused by, buried emotional disorders. As the evidence for these, and other factors, became stronger the biomedical model came to be recognized as inadequate for a complete understanding of health and illness.

Insight

Models of health as the simple absence of illness are an example of how our society finds it hard to acknowledge the positive side of life. We have many ways to describe sickness or lack of health, but we don't even acknowledge wellness. Medical models include depression, apathy, listlessness and disturbed sleep, but they rarely include their opposites: enjoying new challenges, happiness, energy and sound sleep. Surely we should notice these just as much.

Health psychology brings together a wide range of psychological research and clinical knowledge, combining biological insights, psychological insights, and social insights into what has come to be known, rather clumsily, as the **biopsychosocial model** of health and illness. Some of the various factors which are brought together by this model can be seen in Figure 8.1, and an awareness of this combination of factors has contributed a great deal to our understanding of illness.

But there is more to health psychology than just a better understanding of what makes people fall ill. Healthiness is more than just an absence of illness, and a considerable amount of research and practice in health psychology has to do with promoting positive health. As a result, health psychologists also look at various types of communication concerning health and illness, and how they can be improved. They use research on healthy behaviours such as exercise to promote positively healthy lifestyles. And they also apply research into lifestyle factors such as diet and nutrition to help people to manage medical conditions.

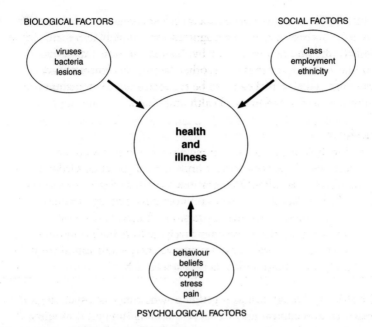

BIOLOGICAL FACTORS

viruses
bacteria
lesions

SOCIAL FACTORS

class
employment
ethnicity

health
and
illness

behaviour
beliefs
coping
stress
pain

PSYCHOLOGICAL FACTORS

Figure 8.1 The biopsychosocial model of health and illness.

Health communication

One of the areas where health psychologists have been
particularly active is health communication and, in particular, the
communication which takes place between health professionals
and their patients or clients. Health psychologists have explored
how different aspects of non-verbal communication – a doctor's
manner, the words and tones of voice they use, and even the way
that they dress – can help people to feel more comfortable with
their doctor, and to explain what is wrong with them clearly.
(If you are interested in non-verbal communication, you can
find out more about it in *Understand Psychology* and also in
Chapter 3).

Health psychologists have also carried out research into what patients actually comprehend of what their doctor tells them. One of the first rules of effective communication is that things should be put in ways that people understand. That might seem obvious, but a surprising amount of medical communication uses technical terms, and even when these are quite common, people often don't understand what they mean. A study of communications from health workers to women in a maternity ward illustrated this. The researchers tape-recorded the conversations between the health workers and the women concerned, and identified 13 technical but commonly used terms, such as 'breech' or 'antibiotic'. When they asked the women afterwards, they found that fewer than 40 per cent of them understood what these terms meant. Moreover, they found that the health workers only expected about that number to understand – they were using the words to the patients, but didn't really expect them to follow what they were talking about.

This, of course, raises the question of why they chose to communicate in that way in the first place, if they didn't expect to be understood, and why they didn't put things rather more simply. Sadly, the answer seems to lie more in some people's need to appear expert to other people, than in their belief in communication. This attitude is changing, slowly, as medical and health care professionals recognize the importance of understanding, and learn that people are unlikely to obey instructions properly if they don't understand the reasons for them. But it is largely the research from health psychologists and other psychologists working in this field which has alerted medical practitioners to the problem.

Insight

Unbalanced social status is at the core of problems in doctor–patient communication. Most people are intimidated by doctors in their professional roles, and find it almost impossible to express themselves freely. But doctors tend to be completely unaware of this.

If we are to use prescribed treatments properly, we need to understand what people are talking about, but we also need to remember what we have been told. Yet psychologists researching into doctor–patient communication have repeatedly found that people often leave the surgery with only a very vague, and sometimes entirely wrong, idea of what they are supposed to do. In one study (Ley, 1988), researchers asked patients what the doctor had told them just as they left the surgery. As a general rule, the patients only remembered about half of what they had been told. But when the researchers analysed what they did remember, they found some distinct patterns.

The patients Ley studied had a good memory for the very first thing they had been told. This is known as the **primacy effect**, and it applies in lots of other situations too. They also remembered information which had been clearly categorized much better than information which wasn't structured. And they remembered things more effectively if they already had a little bit of medical knowledge. These findings fit well with other psychological research into memory, and can be used to help medical practitioners communicate more effectively. Some findings were more surprising. They found, for example, that it didn't matter how often the doctor repeated the information – that didn't help the patient's memory at all. So the classic medical approach of using technical instructions and repeating them several times is one of the least effective communication strategies of all!

There are other aspects of health psychology which deal with how people communicate (for more detail on this subject see *Applying Psychology to Health* by Philip Banyard, or *Health Psychology* by Jane Ogden). Jane Ogden's book is quite detailed, so you may find Banyard a little more readable if you are new to this area.

Promoting positive health

One of the more important aspects of health psychology is concerned with promoting positive health by encouraging people to develop healthier lifestyles. In developed societies it is very easy for people to live a life which is mainly sedentary: that is, which doesn't involve much physical movement. People drive to work in their cars instead of walking, cycling, or using public transport (which generally involves a certain amount of exercise, even if it is only to and from the bus stop). Their work, or their studying, often involves sitting at desks and using computers for long periods of time. And in the evening, the main leisure activity for most people is watching TV, which can hardly be described as an energetic occupation.

In addition to this, modern lifestyles have produced changes in diet, so that as a general rule we eat much less fresh fruit and vegetables, and far more processed food – often containing high levels of synthetic additives. When you put all this together with the effects of environmental pollution and the high levels of stress in modern living, it isn't surprising that so many people experience illnesses of one sort or another. Nor is it surprising that people's general health can improve so much if they change their lifestyle to include a better diet and more exercise.

But telling people what they ought to be doing has never been a particularly effective way of getting them to do it. Health psychologists are able to draw on a large amount of psychological research into attitude change and behaviour modification which helps them to develop more effective strategies for promoting positive health. Sometimes, these strategies involve wide-scale communications, drawing on research into effective advertising and persuasive communication, such as the five-a-day campaign designed to encourage us to eat more fresh fruit and vegetables. Sometimes, though, they operate at an individual level, drawing on research which can help people to change established habits and damaging practices.

Insight

The 'five-a-day' campaign has been very successful in terms of increasing the amount of fruit and vegetables in people's diets. It is a good example of how well people can respond to being given definite, positive advice as opposed to scare stories or threats.

CHALLENGING NICOTINE ADDICTION

Persuading people to change damaging habits can be an important part of promoting positive health. Giving up smoking is the most obvious of these, and the health psychologist's knowledge of how habits are formed and how they can be broken is often very useful in developing a plan of action. No change of habits of this kind can be effective unless the person concerned actually wants to give up, of course, but for many people, wanting to give up and actually doing so are two entirely different things.

Insight

Psychologists have repeatedly found that appealing to fear does little to change negative habits. Yet anti-smoking campaigners continue to try to frighten smokers into giving up. Promoting the positive aspects of life without smoking is a much more effective strategy.

Health psychologists recognize that nicotine addiction acts at more than one level. There is, of course, the physiological addiction but that is only one factor. That can be tackled either straightforwardly, through abstinence, or gradually, though the use of nicotine supplements. Nicotine withdrawal has some psychological consequences, which have to do with the way that the drug works in the body, and health psychologists are often involved in helping people to understand exactly what is happening to them – why they have become more short-tempered, or more fidgety – so that they can develop effective ways of dealing with it.

The reason why this happens relates to the way that nicotine works in the body. It acts in the nervous system, where it interferes with the ways that our nerves pass messages to our muscles (see also *Understand Psychology*). So when we give up smoking, our muscles are receiving more information than they are used to. It's as if our nerves have had to 'shout' to our muscles in order to be heard. Now the muscles can hear clearly, but the nervous system continues shouting for a couple of weeks, before it adjusts to the new level.

That's why athletes don't smoke. They need as much control over their muscles as they can get, and nicotine interferes with that. They also need high levels of oxygen for their activities, and filling your lungs full of tar and poisonous gases like carbon monoxide isn't exactly the best way to achieve that either. But it isn't just athletes who benefit from avoiding smoking. As we know, smoking is associated with any number of long-term illnesses, ranging from heart disease and emphysema to lung and bladder cancers.

Moreover, freedom from nicotine is also associated with positive health. Doctors who work on post-operative surgical wards will tell you that it is easy to distinguish between patients who smoke and those who don't, because the non-smokers recover from their operations far more quickly – sometimes three or four times faster. The whole physical system operates more effectively – there is more oxygen coming into the system, the nerves communicate with the muscles more efficiently, the immune system acts more effectively, and so on. So abstinence from nicotine is a significant factor in promoting positive health, as well as in avoiding illness.

But for many people, it is the behavioural side of giving up smoking which is the hard part. There are particular times when people smoke, and situations which are closely linked with having a cigarette. Indeed, for many smokers the very first stage of getting control over their addiction is to begin to establish situations and places in their daily lives when (or where) they never smoke. It is a first step in learning new habits instead of the old ones.

Insight

Heavy smokers have quite fixed habits, and learning new ones can be the key. One strategy begins by extending the time between getting up and having the first cigarette to a longer but still manageable period. The smoker gets used to that over a couple of weeks, until it has become habitual, and then extends the time a little more, taking another couple of weeks to get used to that. So new non-smoking habits are built up slowly, and the body gets gently used to longer periods without nicotine. This gradual approach allows even the most hardened smoker enough time to develop new habits.

The habits and associations which are to do with smoking are difficult to abandon without putting something else in their place. They have become **conditioned responses** to situations and events. Health psychologists have a thorough knowledge of how these learned associations develop – of the processes of classical and operant conditioning which are involved, and how they can be changed. So they can design effective re-conditioning programmes to help nicotine addicts to change their habits.

Giving up smoking doesn't usually happen all at once, even when we understand what is going on. Prochaska *et al* (1992) identified five different stages in the process. These stages are shown in Figure 8.2. But getting rid of an addiction is a complicated process, and the evidence is that people often need several attempts before they are successful in giving up altogether. For this reason, Prochaska described it as a spiral model of behaviour change, because people sometimes spiral through the five stages several times. Not many people pass through each stage just once and complete the process of giving up the first time: most of us go back through it several times. But if you are one of these people, be encouraged: each pass through the spiral gives you more experience in how to do it, and makes you more likely to succeed in the end. So don't give up giving up!

Insight

As Figure 8.2 shows, there's a big difference between knowing and doing. We may be aware of an issue for some years before we actually adjust our lifestyles to do anything about it, and when we do we may lapse again. But without the initial knowledge we wouldn't even get started on the spiral of change.

EXERCISE AND STRESS MANAGEMENT

There are many other ways of promoting positive health. One of them is by encouraging people to take regular exercise. That doesn't just tone the body and help it to work more effectively. It also helps us to deal with stress, and with the consequences of stress such as high blood pressure or insomnia.

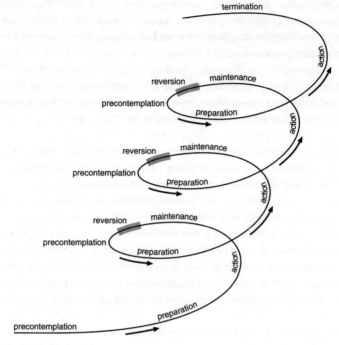

Figure 8.2 Stages in behavioural change.

Stress has profound physical effects on the body (see *Understand Psychology*, and also Chapter 4). One of these effects, which is closely linked with a lot of others, is that people who are under stress have a lot more adrenaline in their bloodstreams than people who aren't. This is because adrenaline is a hormone which prepares the body for action and makes us ready to respond quickly, at a physical level, to threats.

There are other times when we have high adrenaline levels in the bloodstream. One is when we are angry, and the other is when we are engaged in vigorous physical activity. The connection with anger is one of the reasons why we find it so easy to become angry and irritated when we are under stress. But the connection with exercise can work that way too. It makes the body more ready to engage in physical exercise. Getting the brain ready for it is another matter, though! We often think it would be too much trouble, or take up too much time. But once we begin exercising, the body responds straight away.

And in fact, doing strenuous exercise on a regular basis is one of the best stress management techniques that there is. The reason for this is that we have two separate physiological systems in the body: one for getting hyped up, and the other for calming down. They are known as the sympathetic and parasympathetic divisions of the autonomic nervous system. When we are under stress, we tend to hype ourselves up all the time, activating the sympathetic division, and it is this which keeps our adrenaline levels high. Unless we either use that adrenaline or learn to relax properly, it doesn't go away. When we exercise, we use up the adrenaline, and that gives the parasympathetic division a chance to become active. After the activity session, the body is much calmer than it would have been without it. As a result, even though our stressful situations are still there, we can think more clearly about them and deal with them better.

So finding ways that people can build regular exercise into their day-to-day lifestyles, and encouraging them to understand its importance and effectiveness, is another major contribution which many health psychologists make in maintaining positive health. Their understanding of how psychological, neurological and physiological systems interact means that they are able to help many ordinary people, as well as health professionals, to develop strategies for promoting positive health, and to gain a better understanding of what positively healthy lifestyles actually are.

Managing medical conditions

Another major area of health psychology is concerned with ways of managing existing medical conditions. There are a great many medical conditions which can't actually be cured, but which benefit considerably from certain types of behaviour or lifestyle factors from the person who has them. Diabetes is a classic example of this. Someone who is diabetic has a chronic condition – an imbalance of their physiology – which doesn't, at least at the moment, have any known cure. But it can be managed by the person who has it, so that it doesn't become acute or life-threatening, and most diabetics learn to live with their condition and accept it.

Lifestyle factors include diet and nutrition. Diabetes has to do with the way that the body uses and stores glucose – the energy source from food. The body keeps a certain amount of glucose available in the bloodstream for general activity and stores what is not immediately needed. The hormone insulin is actively involved in regulating available glucose levels, so that the body releases stored glucose when the blood-sugar level runs low, and stores it when it is too high. In diabetes, the regulatory system doesn't work properly, and some diabetics (though not all) need to take regular insulin injections to correct this. Others are able to manage the problem by being very careful about what, how and when they eat.

What they eat is important, because some foods produce higher glucose levels than others. Carbohydrates, for example, are converted into glucose in the body. Athletes need a high carbohydrate intake, because this gives them more energy, but diabetics need to watch their carbohydrate intake carefully. If they are exercising (which is also good for diabetes) then they need more, but if they are not, then taking in too much carbohydrate, or too little, can produce problems.

Insight

Many people don't realize how much moods and emotions can be affected by blood sugar imbalances. Diabetics or hypoglycaemics can be easily irritated or even fly into rages over matters which they would disregard when their blood sugar was at normal levels. And even people without these medical conditions tend to be more gloomy and less cheerful when they are hungry, than after they have eaten.

Managing the kind of diabetes which needs regular injections of insulin can also be a challenge. They have to administer regular injections to themselves, at the correct dosage; check their insulin levels by urine testing regularly; take regular meals and check their carbohydrate intake; take exercise; avoid alcohol; and attend clinics for regular check-ups.

All of these things can help to keep diabetics in good health, so it was moderately surprising when researchers found that something like three-quarters of diabetics didn't carry them out properly. Health psychologists have been able to identify many of the reasons for this, ranging from failure to understand the full reasons for the advice, to resistance to obeying orders (a much more important factor in human behaviour than we often realize – people really do need to have some say in what happens to them), to simple embarrassment. Understanding the factors involved made it more possible for health care professionals to work with the people concerned. They could develop maintenance programmes which patients felt they 'owned', and which they were able to fit into their day-to-day lives with fewer problems.

Insight

Having a properly 'owned' maintenance programme is vital for anyone trying to manage an illness. People need to feel in control of their lives, so they need to work out treatment systems which suit them. Being handed a ready-made programme by a health professional who has no awareness of their daily life is unlikely to be helpful.

CHRONIC PAIN

Another area in which health psychologists have been particularly active is in helping people to cope with chronic pain. Some people have medical conditions which give them constant pain. Sometimes, that pain can be treated with drugs but the kinds of drugs which can deal with high levels of pain are often dangerous opiates, which are extremely addictive and shouldn't be used over long periods of time. In addition, chronic pain doesn't respond well to painkillers. They work for acute pain, which is over relatively quickly, but not for long-term pain which can go on for years.

So psychologists in this area have been developing better ways of helping people to work with their pain and make it more bearable.

> **Insight**
> Chronic pain can be debilitating over time, leading to negative moods and depression. Part of the reason for this is the feeling of helplessness, so pain control strategies are helpful because they can give the person a sense of agency rather than of just being a victim.

Pain is much more than just a sensation carried by nerve fibres. Some pain doesn't seem to have anything to do with the nerve fibres at all. For example, some people experience **phantom limb** pain in a hand, arm, foot, or other part of the body which has been amputated. The pain is very real, but the part of the body it seems to be coming from just isn't there. What appears to be happening is that the brain is drawing on its memory of the part of the body to create what is called a phantom limb. If that memory also includes pain, then the pain is included in the phantom. Melzack (1992) gave an example of a logger in Canada who had got a painful splinter under his fingernail. On his way back from the forest, he had suffered an accident in which his arm was badly crushed and had to be amputated. When he recovered from the operation, he was still suffering the pain of the splinter in his phantom hand.

Even pain which has a physical origin can be stronger or weaker depending on our perceptions of it. Many pain management systems don't try to remove the pain physically, but try to give the patient ways of coping with it instead. One of the most important factors in this is learning self-control, and psychologists have identified a number of strategies for self-control training. Research into how effective these strategies have been have shown that they can make a great deal of difference to people's lives. They don't remove the pain, but they remove a great deal of the stress and frustration which it causes, and so they help people to bear it better.

There are other techniques explored by health psychologists in this area, such as **autohypnosis**, or self-hypnosis, and the constructive use of **placebos** – harmless substances like glucose which are presented as medicines. People can use autohypnosis to convince themselves that the pain is not as bad as they have been thinking, and some people find that they can use it very effectively. Similarly, placebos don't have any effect in themselves, but they work because the person concerned believes in them. Using these beliefs constructively can mean that someone with chronic pain can be helped to deal with it in a manner which works for them, psychologically, even if it doesn't have a physical source.

Insight

As we learn more about pain and the body, it becomes increasingly possible to change what were previously thought to be fixed or chronic conditions. So it is worth retaining hope, and re-examining the source of pain every so often. In addition, modern medicine is recognizing that some alternative treatments, such as acupuncture, can really make a difference in some cases, so it is always worth trying out a new approach if it isn't going to make things any worse.

In essence, then, most of the psychological approaches to dealing with chronic pain involve getting people to tap into hidden reserves of psychological strength, which didn't know they had. There are many ways of doing this, and each person will find a way that suits them. But once they have found one, they can often use it very effectively to minimize the discomfort they experience. Even when the pain has a physical source, the mental approach which we use in dealing with it can make it worse or better. Feeling sorry for oneself, and a helpless victim, inevitably makes it worse. Taking action to reduce the pain, even if that is only one's psychological experience of the pain, can make all the difference in making it feel better.

We have seen, then, that health psychologists work to promote positive health in a number of different ways. As usual, this chapter has only given a few examples of what is a detailed and complex area of the profession. But the work of health psychologists demonstrates just how effectively psychological knowledge can be applied to what used to be thought of as a purely physical affair.

10 THINGS TO REMEMBER

1 *Health psychology brings several different psychological approaches to the understanding of health issues.*

2 *Doctor–patient communication is very poor – people do not usually remember what doctors have told them.*

3 *Medical status-related behaviour interferes with effective doctor–patient communication.*

4 *Health psychologists often work to promote physical health through effective communication.*

5 *Challenging nicotine addiction is one example of a health campaign involving health psychologists.*

6 *Tackling any addiction is a spiral process, with reversals as well as times of success.*

7 *Exercise and diet are powerful tools in stress management.*

8 *Health psychologists help people to manage medical conditions which can be controlled by lifestyle changes.*

9 *Amputees often experience phantom limb pain, which is difficult to treat.*

10 *Chronic pain can be helped by psychological coping techniques such as autohypnosis.*

9

Forensic psychology

In this chapter you will learn:
- *two different approaches to 'offender profiling'*
- *how forensic psychology has improved the treatment of child witnesses*
- *why the 'cognitive interview' is more reliable than hypnosis in eyewitness testimony.*

Forensic psychology applies psychological principles to the understanding of crime and criminal behaviour. It is sometimes known as **criminological psychology**, and in recent years has been the subject of a great deal of interest on the part of the media and the general public. This has been partly as a result of psychologists' contributions in dealing with high-profile crime cases, partly an outcome of the huge success of the TV drama *Cracker*, partly the result of initiatives which have strengthened the professional standing of this area of applied psychology, and partly because people are just generally becoming interested in psychology.

Insight
Forensic psychology has become a popular goal for many psychology students – partly because of the influence of TV shows. But only those with serious ambitions in this area are likely to get through the rigorous training needed to become a qualified forensic psychologist.

Whatever the reason, forensic psychology has become a major area of professional applied psychology, and the training you would need to become a forensic psychologist is as rigorous as that needed to become a clinical or educational psychologist. Forensic psychologists tend to work in four main sections of society, as shown in Table 9.1. Becoming a forensic psychologist involves an approved first degree in psychology, a period of relevant work experience, a three-year approved training course and a probationary period of supervised practice, which can last for a further two years. By the end of that time, the forensic psychologist has acquired a great deal of specialized knowledge, which can be applied to many different aspects of crime.

Table 9.1 The work of forensic psychologists

1 In the legal system	e.g. contributing psychological understanding to the training and selection of police and magistrates, to interviewing processes, and to jury selection.
2 In criminal detection	e.g. helping police officers to identify offending patterns and to develop possible offender profiles.
3 In the prison system	e.g. developing treatment programmes for offenders and contributing to staff training and offender assessments.
4 In the political system	e.g. giving advice on the treatment of criminals, and also of their victims.

Insight

Many offenders can be helped by the right kind of treatment programme, and this can result in society being much better protected. So working in the prison sector can be rewarding and interesting as long as the prison authorities are prepared to back the programme and provide the resources to carry it through.

In this chapter, we will look at just three examples of forensic psychology: psychology's contributions to improving the quality of eyewitness testimony; the special requirements of child witnesses; and ending with a brief overview of offender profiling.

Eyewitness testimony

A great deal of the legal system depends on interviewing: interviewing witnesses to crimes, and also interviewing the offenders (or those charged with the offence) themselves. But the way that an interview is carried out can make a great deal of difference to what the person actually reports. Sometimes, if an interview is carried out in a certain way, it can distort the person's memory of what happened, so that they end up remembering something that didn't actually take place at all.

INFLUENCING MEMORIES

The reason for this is because memory is a much more personal process than people think. We all experience our memories as if they were objective records – tape-recordings of what happened. Yet in reality, our memories are a combination of the experiences we have actually had, and what those experiences actually meant to us. So the details of the experience tend to become adjusted in order to fit with our personal meanings and expectations. And sometimes, we bring in details which didn't actually happen.

Insight

Much of the judicial system depends on memory, yet memory is the most unreliable of all of our human experiences. We remember what things mean to us, and fit the details of what really happened around that. If fact and personal construction conflict, we cling to that version of the memory which most fits our personal understanding of the situation – regardless of what actually happened.

One of the classic studies which illustrated this was carried out by Loftus and Palmer. They showed a film of a car accident to a number of people, and then asked them to fill in a questionnaire. Half of the questionnaires asked 'About how fast were the cars going when they hit each other?', while the other half asked: 'About how fast were the cars going when they smashed into each other?'. A week after seeing the film, the participants in the study were asked to answer some more questions about it. In particular, they were asked whether they had seen any broken glass in the film. There hadn't been any, in fact, but nonetheless several of the participants said that they had seen it. Those who had received the second version of the questionnaire were twice as likely to say there was broken glass as those who had completed the first version.

If a simple adjustment to the wording of a question can make that much difference, then the fact that people interviewing witnesses often have their own strong ideas about what happened is very important. Psychologists involved in training police interviewers have to alert them to the need for very careful phrasing of questions, and ways of making sure that their questions don't accidentally influence what people remember.

Not only that, but people can pick up all sorts of non-verbal signals without really realizing what they are doing. We all check, unconsciously, to see whether the person we are talking to seems to agree with us, and we use slight signals such as their body language, or the tone of voice that they use, to give us the clues we need. Put that together with the human tendency to agree with other people – which is a very strong one and colours most of our social interactions – and that means it is extremely easy for witnesses to be influenced by the opinions of the person who is interviewing them.

Insight

People under stress are very sensitive to non-verbal cues, and can pick up impressions without the other person being aware that they have given anything away. Even keeping a deadpan expression carries its own messages.

So it is important that interviewers investigating witnesses
to criminal activity are very carefully trained, because those
witnesses may over-react to cues in an attempt to be helpful.

MEMORY AND HYPNOSIS

People can be influenced in other ways, too. In the 1970s and
early 1980s, there was a great deal of interest in the possibilities
of using hypnosis to 'recover' memories which appeared to have
been lost. Some police forces in the USA began to use it as a way of
obtaining evidence. But researchers into hypnosis showed that this
technique actually made the problem of distinguishing truth from
imagination far worse. The version of hypnosis we see in films
isn't anything like hypnosis in reality, and the idea that people's
memories can be unreeled like a tape-recording isn't valid either.

What hypnosis actually is, is a mental state in which we are
extremely open to suggestions from other people. All of the normal
social mechanisms which hold society together – our tendency
to conform to others, to do what we are told, to avoid open
disagreement, and to go along with things in order to avoid causing
a fuss – become active in hypnosis. Indeed, they are so strong at
this time that many psychologists doubt whether hypnosis is really
a special state at all, and it is clear that even people who believe
they are hypnotized won't perform actions which go strongly
against their conscience, even though they place so much trust in
the hypnotist that they often surprise themselves by doing things
they thought they were not capable of.

So the problem of using hypnosis for police interviews is that it
exaggerates the suggestibility of the witnesses. Because they are
even more socially compliant than usual, they are even more likely
to pick up subtle cues from the person asking the questions, and to
build these details into their evidence. In a series of studies on the
use of hypnosis in witness testimony, Gibson (1982) found that
it should really be considered as equivalent to tampering with
evidence, because it was so very likely to change people's memories
of what happened, and because once their memory had been

changed in that way, there was no way of telling the difference between that and a real memory.

Insight

People who are hypnotized are particularly suggestible, but in fact, most people in everyday life are pretty suggestible too. When Martin Orne was trying to find a way to distinguish between hypnotized and non-hypnotized people, he couldn't actually find any difference. For example, both groups would do equally pointless tasks for hours on end, if they thought it was what the investigator wanted them to do.

SENSITIVE INTERVIEWING

Criminological psychologists have contributed a great deal towards developing programmes for interview training which can help interviewers to avoid these problems. Interviewers also need to be trained not to give away their opinions or their knowledge of the details of the crime without realizing it, while at the same time being friendly and helpful so that people will feel free to talk to them openly. It's a challenging balance, and one where psychological training is very important.

In recent years, the question of interviewers influencing what people remember has come up again in the context of recovered memories of child sexual abuse. For many children, sexual abuse is such a traumatic affair, and so difficult to live with, that they end up repressing the memory of what happened to them, and sometimes only recall it again when they are adults. In some prosecutions for this type of abuse in the USA, the defendants argued that these memories were not true, but had been constructed because of suggestions from the therapists concerned.

However, a professional investigation into the area conducted by the British Psychological Society in 1995 looked at the evidence, and concluded that while that was obviously possible, most recovered memories of this kind are likely to be genuine. There are clinical signals which accompany abuse which would be difficult to fake, and a professionally trained clinical psychologist or therapist puts these together with the recovered memory evidence in evaluating the evidence, in much the same way as a forensic psychologist combines the interview information with other evidence.

Insight

Interviewing victims of rape is a difficult business, partly because of mental rehearsal, which means that details can become distorted. In one case, a woman was raped in her living room and later identified the face of her attacker as that of a famous interviewer who had been on her TV at the time. Her personal distress had caused the two memories to become fused together. Fortunately, the broadcast had been live, so the interviewer had a good alibi and the real perpetrator was eventually caught and identified.

THE COGNITIVE INTERVIEW

As we have seen, interviewing people without influencing them is a tricky business. But there are, nonetheless, ways of carrying out interviews which help people to recover more details than they would do in the normal run of things. That doesn't involve any 'magical' tricks like hypnosis. Rather, it involves applying a psychological understanding of the processes of cognition, and how these memories have been stored.

The **cognitive interview**, or CI, involves a standard interview procedure – that is, an interview approach which has been clearly set out beforehand. It begins with the person just recalling the event freely to begin with, and only afterwards answering detailed questions about it. The free recall period helps them to bring details to mind, and allows them to remember far more information than they would do if they were asked specific questions from the start. But there is more to it than just allowing the person to remember the scene. The cognitive interview also involves asking the person to relive the scene, mentally, recalling the sounds, smells and feelings that they experienced at the time. There is a great deal of psychological research which has shown how important context is to remembering, and this procedure allows us to make full use of it to bring back details we thought we had forgotten.

Another important part of the cognitive interview technique is asking the witness to report absolutely everything, even the most unimportant details. That too has been shown to help memories to come up more easily. The person is also asked to try remembering what happened using different time sequences – perhaps in reverse order, or in relation to a particular detail. And they may also be asked to imagine what the event must have looked like from a variety of different viewpoints – the point of view of different people who were there at the time.

These strategies, which are known as **retrieval mnemonics** (mnemonics are techniques which help us to remember, as we saw in Chapter 2), use psychological research findings to allow the person to bring out as much detail as they possibly can. Fisher and Geiselman (1992) showed that the CI procedure can bring out more than twice as much information about a particular event than an ordinary interview. Moreover, they found that this information is just as accurate as the information obtained from standard interviews. There are some variations in the technique which have been developed to help particular forms of remembering, such as recalling car licence plate numbers. These too have been found to be very effective.

Insight

The only way to deal with false memories is to make sure they don't develop in the first place. Once they have been implanted, it is impossible to tell the difference between them and the original memories. So any value that person may have had as a witness to what really happened is completely lost.

Interviewing witnesses, then, is an area where applied psychology has been able to contribute a great deal to professional practice. As a result, the training of police interviewers has become greatly improved during the past two decades, as better interviewing procedures have been developed and common misunderstandings about the nature of interviewing have been challenged.

Dealing with child witnesses

Most of the findings that we have just been looking at have concerned the interviewing of adult witnesses. But sometimes, notably in cases of child abuse, the only witnesses are the children who were the victims of the crime. Being interviewed is an intimidating situation for a child, and a child who has been a victim of that type of crime has almost always been threatened with dire consequences if they were to tell anyone. So interviewing children in that situation requires some very special skills.

The normal 'rules' of adult interviewing don't work in the same way when it comes to children, either. For example, a number of studies have demonstrated that if a child is asked the same question twice, it tends to change its answer, because it assumes that the first answer must have been wrong. In adult interviewing, the same question is often asked repeatedly, and changing the answer is seen as evidence that the first response was a lie. But in child interviewing, it is much more likely that the first answer was true, and that subsequent answers to the same question are the child looking for something to say which will satisfy the interviewer, since the first answer doesn't seem to have been good enough.

There are lots of other details like this which make applying the normal principles of interviewing inappropriate for children. And, perhaps as a result, there is also a persistent belief that child witnesses are less reliable than adults. This isn't particularly borne out by the evidence: Leippe *et al* (1992) showed that children's testimony for events is just as reliable and accurate as that of adults, even though many adults believe it is not.

Insight

Child abusers often frighten their victims with stories of awful things that will happen if they tell anyone. And the sad truth is that from the child's point of view, telling people about abuse from a family member often really is followed

(Contd)

by awful things – a complete breakdown of familiar routine, being taken from home and put into a strange place with strange people, being questioned by strangers and so on. It's one of the many reasons why child witnesses need to be handled really carefully by the courts.

This is made additionally complex by the way that society responds to allegations of child sexual abuse. Too often, people refuse to believe that sexual abuse has actually happened – even when the evidence is relatively clear – and, of course, those perpetrating the crime generally deny it. As a result, there have been a number of cases where children have been put through traumatic experiences in court, and even been returned to the care of abusers. For example, in 1987, over 100 children in Cleveland were taken into care as a result of a new method of diagnosing abuse. There was a huge public outcry, and the paediatricians concerned were hounded by the press. As a result, the children were returned to their parents without the allegations being investigated fully, and it is now thought that in 70–75 per cent of those cases, the children were returned to parents who really had been sexually abusing them.

Insight

The main problem with interviewing children is simply the imbalance of power. No matter how reassuring an adult tries to be, children are well aware that it is adults who can control their world and move them to places they don't want to go. And a child who has been abused is no longer a trusting, confident child. So interviewers have to be aware that a child's fear of consequences may make it difficult for them to be fully open about what happened.

Even when prosecutions are successful, the experience for the child is deeply traumatic. Not only do they have to relive the experience and talk about it over and over again, but they also often have to endure sustained cross-examination, and see (for a child) terrible consequences – the family being broken up, people being sent to prison and the like. The standard legal practice of expressing outright disbelief in the witness and accusing them of lying is also very difficult for children to handle, and many prosecutions for child abuse fail as a result.

In recent years, there have been a number of attempts to improve legal procedures when it comes to child witnesses. One of the most important of these concerns allowing children to record their evidence before the court case, on videotape. When it was first proposed, it was hoped that this would mean that the child would not need to attend court, but unfortunately the way it has been implemented means that this is still required, and the child still needs to undergo cross-examination. It is possible, though, for that cross-examination to take place via a live video link if the court considers that it would be too traumatic for the child to face the person they are accusing in court.

A number of professionals, including forensic and developmental psychologists, have been involved in drawing up codes of good practice to ensure that child witnesses are able to give their evidence as freely and as fully as possible. This includes establishing a good rapport between the child and the interviewer, so that the child feels safe to talk openly; allowing a period of free recall in the same way as is done in the cognitive interview; making sure that the questions that are asked are open-ended and not suggestive; and making sure that the interview ends in a way which is reassuring for the child. Similar guidelines are in place with regard to the obtaining of video evidence, where this is considered to be appropriate.

Despite these guidelines, it is clear that there is still a great deal to be done before children are able to report experiences of sexual abuse as freely as ought to be possible. Child molesters and those who are unwilling to believe in such things often assert that children make up these experiences in order to get the adult into trouble. However, in one study King and Yuille investigated 576 cases of alleged child abuse, and found that 92 per cent of them were true, and also that most of the untrue allegations had been made by other adults rather than by the children themselves. So examples of children making up such stories are actually quite rare. In any case, it is usually possible for a skilled child psychologist to be able to detect the specific details of a story which suggest that it has been fabricated.

Offender profiling

Another technique used by forensic psychologists, and one which has attracted a great deal of attention, is that of offender profiling. Essentially, what this involves is finding ways of narrowing down the search for a particular offender by identifying particular characteristics which they are likely to have. Traditionally, there have been two different approaches to offender profiling: the US approach, and the British one.

The US approach to offender profiling was developed by the US Federal Bureau of Investigation (FBI) in the 1970s as a result of interviews with a large number of serious offenders. It is essentially a probabilistic approach, which makes assessments as to criminals' likely lifestyles, personalities and places of residence based on statistical evidence. The profile which is obtained in this way is used to help the police to narrow down the list of suspects, and pick out people who seem to be particularly likely to have carried out the crime. Sometimes this approach can be quite successful, but there have been other cases which have been wildly inaccurate. Not all criminals conform to the general stereotypes, although many do.

The British approach is less general than the US one, and doesn't really go in for assessments of the likely personality structure of the person concerned. Instead, it focuses on patterns to their behaviour and very specific clues which have been left behind. It was developed by David Canter, who was asked by the police in 1985 whether it was likely that psychology could contribute to their criminal investigations. It became particularly widely known because of Canter's success in profiling a serial rapist and murderer, John Duffy, who was known as the 'Railway Rapist' and had carried out a series of crimes around North London.

Canter takes the view that people tend to act reasonably coherently, and that their behaviour often reveals patterns which can provide clues about other aspects of their lives (Canter, 1994). Those patterns may be linked with specific actions, with types of action, or with the types of social context in which the acts take place. The patterns are identified from very small hints in the crime itself and in the accounts of eyewitnesses. It has been described as a 'bottom-up' approach, working upwards from the data, whereas the US approach goes 'top down' from general information about typical offenders.

The US approach is mainly useful in identifying individuals who show disturbed or psychopathic behaviour, but the British one tends to be more appropriate for identifying people who are in other respects 'normal': that is, whose behaviour doesn't seem to be particularly out of the ordinary to their friends and neighbours. The technique itself is quite different from the way that it has been portrayed in the media, and of course in itself it is never the complete answer: it is always used in conjunction with any number of other investigative techniques. But it has sometimes been useful to police in helping them to narrow down lists of suspects, and focus on particular details or patterns in the information which might otherwise have been overlooked.

Insight

Critics of the US profiling system say that it relies too much on stereotypes and generalities. It may be quite accurate statistically, and have a number of successes, but it can also result in innocent people who fit the profile being wrongfully accused, while those who don't fit easily into preset categories walk free.

There is much more to forensic psychology than we have been able to deal with here. Forensic psychologists are involved in any number of other activities, not least of which is developing treatment programmes for offenders, and training programmes for probation officers and other professionals dealing with them. This chapter, as with all of the chapters in this book, can only give a general idea of some of the ways that psychology is applied in this context. But you can see from this, I hope, that the expertise that forensic psychologists are able to contribute to the legal process is considerable – so much so, that psychology has now become a recognized and valued part of a police officer's training.

10 THINGS TO REMEMBER

1 *Forensic psychology is a significant area of professional psychology.*

2 *Forensic psychologists work in the legal system, criminal detection, the prison system and the political system.*

3 *Eyewitness testimony is unreliable because people's memories change over time.*

4 *It is easy to influence people's memories by subtle use of words or suggestion.*

5 *Using hypnosis in police interviews is equivalent to tampering with the evidence.*

6 *The cognitive interview allows psychologists to find out information without using leading questions.*

7 *Retrieval mnemonics help to recreate contexts so memories can come back.*

8 *Child witnesses need special treatment, partly because of power issues and partly because of consequences.*

9 *US offender profiling involves describing a largely stereotypical offender, since this is the most likely fit.*

10 *UK offender profiling builds up an image of the person from specific clues and behaviour patterns.*

10

Educational psychology

In this chapter you will learn:
- *the main reasons for underachievement at school*
- *the duties and responsibilities of an educational psychologist*
- *how educational psychologists have helped to develop ways of tackling school bullying.*

Educational psychologists are applied psychologists who work with children with problems. They are often employed by the local education authority, and work closely with teachers, education authorities, courts and parents. Sometimes they work in specialist paediatric clinics, working as part of a team with social workers, psychiatrists and teachers to help tackle problems presented by seriously disturbed or maltreated children. And they work with other multidisciplinary teams in family therapy centres, assessment centres, community schools and children's hospitals.

The complexity of their work means that educational psychologists have to undergo a rigorous professional training. In common with other applied psychologists, they need to have taken an approved first degree in psychology, but they also need to be qualified teachers, and to have had a couple of years' teaching experience. On top of that, they then need to undergo the specialist training for educational psychology, which lasts for at least three years and includes periods of supervised practice as well as formal learning and examinations.

That training might sound demanding, but it is important because educational psychologists play an important role in the legal system. An education authority requires a psychologist's report if a child is to be sent to a special school, if a court case comes up regarding some particular aspects of a child's education, or if a child needs to be formally assessed for any other reason. So educational psychologists have to be able to undertake in-depth assessments of various kinds of learning problem or developmental disorder. They also need to be familiar with different types of intervention, because they often work with teachers, parents and educational welfare officers to solve behavioural problems which affect a child's schooling.

Evaluating special needs

One very specialized set of skills which an educational psychologist needs to acquire is that of evaluating any special educational needs which a child may have. There are any number of reasons why a child may have special educational requirements. One example is the one most people think of when they envisage special schools, which is that the children concerned are slower to learn than most others of their age group, and so they might be better off away from the pressure of their peer group, and in a school where they can obtain more appropriate help. In such a case, it may be that the child does have some general difficulty, but sometimes, for example, a child may appear to be slow to learn, but actually isn't. Instead, they may have another problem such as a specific hearing impairment, which is making it difficult for them to learn in the normal way.

Educational psychologists have to become familiar with a wide range of psychometric tests which can help them to identify these different kinds of problem. They use general intelligence tests sometimes, but they also use more specific tests designed to tease out exactly where any kind of specific deficit or problem lies. The tests they use are not available to the general public, because you need to be specially trained to use them and each one has its own specialized context and requirements. So one of the things which makes educational psychology training so demanding is the need to become familiar with so much detailed information.

Insight

Assessing special educational needs isn't only about identifying children who need additional support because they are finding learning difficult for some reason. It can also include finding enhanced or more demanding education for children who find it particularly easy to learn.

Most special educational needs, in fact, don't require a child to attend a special school, and there has been quite a lot of social controversy over the question of whether children with special needs should really be segregated from other, 'normal' children. In many education authorities, the ordinary schools have adopted a policy of integrating children with special needs into their classes as much as possible. Sometimes, this is a relatively straightforward practice. For example, accommodating children with physical disabilities means making sure that they are able to get around the school easily and use school facilities. That may mean making alterations to accommodate wheelchairs, or putting in handrails or lifts, but once these have been done, it doesn't make all that much difference to the actual teaching that goes on in the classroom.

Other types of physical disability may require a bit more adjustment on the part of teachers, and educational psychologists are often involved in helping them to adjust. For example, accommodating children with hearing impairments may involve the teacher learning sign language, or having people in the classroom who are skilled at signing and so can help the child to understand what the teacher is saying. But many schools are managing this type of integration too, and are finding a beneficial side-effect in the way that 'normal' – that is, non-hearing-impaired – children pick up sign language just as a result of their developing friendships. The initial adjustment may have presented some challenges, but the school as a whole often finds that it benefits in all sorts of ways once the adjustments have been made.

Insight

Educational assessment can be particularly useful when a child is underachieving as a result of stereotyping or other social pressures. When intelligence tests show that a child is 'brighter' than previously thought, this changes their teachers' expectations and, through that, the child's experience in the classroom.

DYSLEXIA

Some kinds of special educational need operate at the cognitive level rather than at the sensory one. That is, they are to do with the ways that the brain processes the information it receives, rather than with how we receive the information in the first place. One of the best-known of these is the problem known as **dyslexia**. Dyslexia is also sometimes known as 'word-blindness', and children who have this disorder have particular kinds of problems learning to read. The disorder takes various forms, but as an example, one type of dyslexia involves some very specific problems with processing visual information – such as being unable to distinguish between letters the right way round and the wrong way. That doesn't matter for most letters, but for some, like 'd' and 'b', it makes all the difference. A child with this problem is bound to have problems in reading, because they won't be identifying the correct letters in the words.

The challenge for the educational psychologist, though, is that not all children with reading problems have dyslexia. Learning to read is always difficult, and it takes a lot of practice. If a child doesn't have much experience with letters, simple mistakes can happen simply because the child doesn't realize how much it needs to pay attention to the details. Also, when we become fluent readers we recognize whole words on sight, simply by their shape, but that means we have to have learned what they look like. And that, too, takes lots of practice – particularly with some of the odd spellings we have in the English language. In families where parents don't read much either, many children don't see the point of trying to read, because they think they can get enough information from TV, and they don't see why they should put all that effort into something which doesn't seem to have many benefits. So a great many other factors can make a child slow to read.

An educational psychologist, therefore, needs to be able to distinguish between children who have reading problems because of environmental or social factors like those, and children who have reading problems because they really do have some kind of specific information-processing deficit. Again, this is where psychometric tests are particularly useful. They provide the educational psychologist with the detailed information they need to distinguish between other types of reading problems and dyslexia, and they also provide the information which allows the psychologist to identify just which form of dyslexia a child has. Some forms are more severe than others, and they all show up in different ways. The diagnosis of the particular type of dyslexia, and how severe it is, affects the recommendations an educational psychologist will make for how the school and parents should tackle the problem.

That part of the job isn't made any easier, of course, by the way that society has latched on to the label 'dyslexia'. As a result, people often label a child 'dyslexic' just because it doesn't seem to be learning to read as quickly as some other children. Once the child has been given the label, it is treated as if it were unable to learn, because of being supposedly dyslexic. That kind of labelling can easily become a **self-fulfilling prophecy**: if parents and teachers believe that a child is not capable of reading and writing properly, they don't put the effort into teaching the child and encouraging it, and the child too comes to believe that it isn't capable. Amateur diagnosis, in this situation, can be a very dangerous thing, and it is really only the specialized knowledge and tests of an educational psychologist which can provide a reliable judgement about whether a child really does have a disorder such as dyslexia.

Underachievement and poor school performance

The failure to identify specific learning needs can lead a child to underachieve in school. But there are other reasons, too, why children underachieve, and an educational psychologist will often be involved in identifying these, and developing intervention programmes which can help to tackle the problem. Fontana (1984) identified four types of reason for failures in academic achievement, which are summarized in Table 10.1.

Table 10.1 Reasons for failure in academic achievement	
Models of the human mind	e.g. beliefs about innate ability leading to labelling of children.
Individual problems	e.g. specific learning difficulties or sensory impairments.
The social and emotional environment	e.g. stress at home, inappropriate discipline.
The wider social environment	e.g. gender stereotyping.
	Source: Fontana, 1984

The first set of reasons concerns the models of human behaviour and cognition which are held by teachers and others dealing with the child's education. In the 1950s and 1960s, for example, education professionals tended to believe that success at school arose from the child's own inherited intelligence. A child was either capable, or it was not. As a result, children tended to be rigidly streamed, and those in the lower streams quickly got the message that they were not expected to achieve very much. Not surprisingly, they didn't put much effort into learning, and their teachers, as a rule, didn't put much effort into teaching them either. The whole thing had become a self-fulfilling prophecy, and the result was underachievement on a truly massive scale.

Nowadays, we recognize the importance of social expectations like those concerning a child's education, and we also recognize that underachievement can come from lots of other factors too, which are nothing to do with a child's intelligence. We can see the outcomes of these changes in the increasing proportion of children who succeed in school, and go on to university. But there are still a few teachers who hold to the old ideas about intelligence, and those kinds of belief can be very powerful in destroying a child's confidence, or its motivation to achieve. Once a child sees itself as stupid, or incapable of learning, then it is not likely to try to learn at school, and as a result will tend to underachieve dramatically.

Insight

Politicians emphasize 'parental choice' in education, but this disadvantages children whose parents don't push for them to be at a better school. Educational psychologists work to improve or enhance educational provision in all schools, not just the 'better' ones.

The second set of reasons identified by Fontana (1984) are those that we have already discussed. Some children underachieve because they have special educational needs which have not been identified. In many ways, these problems are easier to handle than the social ones, in that once they have been drawn to the attention of an educational psychologist they can be properly diagnosed and an appropriate schooling strategy developed. This might mean placing the child in a special school, or integrating it in an ordinary school, a combination of both, or some other type of educational intervention which will help to tackle the problem.

The third set of factors which can produce underachievement at school is the social and emotional environment in which the child is growing up. Rutter (1975) discussed how the emotional context in the family can be a major factor in underachievement and other social problems for children. Situations such as whether the atmosphere at home is very disturbed and stressful, whether a child's parents administer either excessively severe or very lax discipline, or whether there are long periods of parent–child separation or poor communication between family members, can all have a damaging effect on how a child performs at school. But children who are growing up in an environment which is encouraging, supportive and not too judgemental tend to develop positive and confident attitudes towards their work, and achieve much more as a result.

The fourth set of factors in underachievement, which an educational psychologist may encounter, comes from the wider societal or organizational environment. It may be that society in general, or the school in particular, has low expectations for its pupils and so does not provide them with the educational opportunities which they need in order to realize their full potential. If the staff in a particular school hold strong views about the domestic role of women and the lack of need for them to have high levels of education, then the girls who attend that school are unlikely to be encouraged to achieve as much as girls attending a more egalitarian one.

The problem can also apply to children attending schools in particular areas. In the UK, there have been several recent government initiatives which have aimed to challenge low expectations on the part of schools and head teachers, and make it clear exactly what children are expected to have achieved at particular points in their educational careers. Before these initiatives began, there was tremendous disparity, with many inner-city schools, and schools in the poorer parts of large towns, expecting far less of their students than comparable schools in other areas did. While the low expectations had some basis in terms of the greater social problems facing many of their children, it had nonetheless become so extreme that the children were becoming severely disadvantaged.

The introduction of the national curriculum, and of standards of attainment for particular year groups, has done a great deal to redress this balance and raise the expectations of teachers and parents. But educational psychologists still sometimes encounter this problem as a factor in the underachievement of a particular child, and this may lead to working with the head teacher, members of staff and education welfare officers to develop a form of intervention which can tackle the problem at a school level, rather than at an individual one.

Similarly, the reasons for a child's underachievement may arise from other children rather than from the official side of the school. This is still a school problem rather than an individual one, though. School bullying is a far more common problem than many schools like to admit, and in the past decade there have been a number of initiatives which have been developed to address the problem. It isn't a minor problem – a child who is being bullied at school can become severely emotionally damaged, and such an experience almost always results in educational underachievement. So many educational psychologists have been working closely with education welfare officers and others to address the problem.

Insight

School bullying can range from physical violence and intimidation to subtle but vicious verbal harassment. Children who are constantly ridiculed because of their appearance or personal difference are just as much victims of bullying as those who live in fear of being beaten up outside the school gates.

One of the clearest things to have emerged from research into the area, as well as from practical experience, is that bullying cannot be tackled at an individual level. It isn't a question of just singling out particular children who are bullies, and trying to stop them from acting as they do, because bullying is a cultural problem, to do with the informal culture which develops among schoolchildren, and not an individual one. Moreover, as any child who has been in that situation knows, it takes place at times when adults are unable to intervene, so the punishment of a single bully can all too easily rebound on the child who brought the problem to official attention.

Insight

Schools attempting to tackle problems with bullying have not been helped by the constant portrayal of bullying on 'realistic' children's TV shows. They define social scripts of bullying, and encourage children to believe that this is a normal or ordinary way of behaving.

Successful interventions on school bullying have always involved the school as a whole addressing the problem. Bullying needs to be officially recognized and tackled at a group and school level, with the aim of developing an anti-bullying culture among all of the children in the school. Once bullying is seen by other children as something to be despised rather than something to be feared and admired, the bully has lost most of their reasons for engaging in the activity. So addressing the problem at a school level is crucially important if the behaviour is really to be challenged.

At the same time, interventions with individual children are also needed. Those who have been bullied often need specific counselling, to help them to deal with the emotional consequences of the experience, and those who have been doing the bullying also need interventions. These are sometimes therapeutic, aiming to tackle the problem by identifying and challenging the emotional needs which have led the person to become a bully in the first place, but there have also been some very successful interventions which have tackled bullying as a group phenomenon. By bringing the whole set of bullies together, it is possible for a skilled psychologist or education welfare officer trained in group techniques to challenge how the various group members encourage one another, and so perpetuate the process.

Insight

Bullying is a cultural problem, and can only really be addressed by changing the culture of the school, so that bullying becomes despised rather than admired. Attempting to tackle it on an individual level simply makes children vulnerable to clever bullies who get their revenge in subtle or out-of-school ways.

Tackling educational underachievement, then, requires far more than just the ability to diagnose specific learning needs. What human beings do can be influenced by a wide range of factors operating at many different levels. An educational psychologist may need to operate at several of these levels in order to address a particular child's problems effectively.

Developing evaluation programmes

Another area where the expertise of educational psychologists is particularly valuable is in developing programmes to evaluate educational interventions. All psychologists, no matter what particular area of specialism they may adopt, undergo a rigorous training in research methods and analytical techniques. This gives them unique skills when it comes to collecting data from people and organizations. An educational psychologist, having the advantage of dual qualifications in education as well as in psychology, is also trained in research methods and evaluation issues in the educational context.

All of these skills come into play in educational evaluation. For example: it may be that a particular primary school has been trying out a new method for teaching children to read. Evaluating the effectiveness of the method isn't simple. It has to take into account any number of different factors: the method itself, the motivation of the children, the interest and involvement of teachers and parents, the resources of the school in material terms, such as books or staffing and available personnel, staff training, and a whole lot of other possible influences. Teasing out the various influences, and identifying just how far the reading method itself may be responsible for any changes, is a challenging task, and one where the extensive training of the educational psychologist is particularly valuable.

Evaluation doesn't just happen at a school level either. Sometimes, a whole education authority may decide to implement a new schooling policy: perhaps in terms of restructuring its sixth form provision, or as a result of a reorganization in the way that music education is arranged, or for some other reason. Changes like that may cut across several different schools, and affect large numbers of pupils, and again educational psychologists are likely to be called in to evaluate them.

Evaluation can take several forms. Sometimes, educational psychologists are asked to evaluate potential changes before they have taken place, to spot consequences and issues that will need specific attention. Sometimes, their evaluation consists of looking at how the changes have been implemented and what their effects have been. Most commonly, educational psychologists are involved in both types of evaluation, and their reports form an important contribution to education policy, at both local and national level.

Insight

Many educational psychologists have grave doubts about the usefulness of evaluating teaching through paperwork. Direct observations of classes and pupil–teacher interaction may need more organizing than looking at forms, but they are much more useful both to the school concerned and to the organization doing the assessment.

We can see, then, that the work of an educational psychologist is both varied and complex. The rigorous training that educational psychologists experience gives them skills which they can use in dealing with problems at all sorts of levels – ranging from the level of individual cognitive deficits, to the organization of whole areas of schooling. Dealing with problems at a multiplicity of levels is one of the distinctive skills of applied psychologists, because of the way that psychological training requires us to be able to deal with human beings, and human beings are never simple.

Insight

It takes longer to train as a fully qualified educational psychologist than it does to become a medical doctor. And even then, as trained professionals, educational psychologists must continually renew and refresh their professional skills and knowledge, throughout their working lives.

There are other applied psychologists who work within the educational system. In some countries, notably the USA, they too are called educational psychologists, but in the UK and other countries which follow the UK model, the profession of 'educational psychologist' has been explicitly defined by law, and so these other psychologists don't use that name. Sometimes, they are called school psychologists, but that isn't really accurate because they also work in further and higher education too. What they are really concerned with is the applied psychology of teaching and learning – applying psychological insights to our understanding of what exactly is going on in the learning process, and how it can be improved. We will be looking at some aspects of their work in the next chapter.

10 THINGS TO REMEMBER

1 *Educational psychologists assess children for courts and for educational purposes.*

2 *They can use a wide range of psychometric tests, including specialized diagnostic tests.*

3 *Educational psychologists are able to diagnose dyslexia accurately.*

4 *There may be over-diagnosis of dyslexia by some teachers, to cover common difficulties with spelling.*

5 *Some children may underachieve due to low social expectations in their area or school.*

6 *Stress at home can also produce educational underachievement.*

7 *Being bullied at school can produce lasting emotional damage as well as underachievement.*

8 *Schools need to tackle bullying as a cultural and social problem. Individual solutions don't usually work.*

9 *Educational psychologists are often involved in evaluating educational programmes and policies.*

10 *The term 'educational psychologist' has a different meaning in the USA than it does in the UK.*

11

Applied psychology of teaching and learning

In this chapter you will learn:
- *two aspects of learning that differ between adults and children*
- *how psychological knowledge can improve the experience of exams*
- *how an understanding of the psychology of learning can improve teaching.*

Educational psychologists, as we saw in the last chapter, are primarily concerned with children. But adults, too, are involved in education; in fact, most people engage in some kind of study at some time in their adult lives. Some people undertake full-time courses at college or university, while some take part-time ones and continue working at the same time. Some people do evening classes as a hobby or recreation, while others do them because they can be a passport to a better job. Some people are sent on training courses by their employers, or take in-service training courses within their own company or organization.

Applied psychologists working in the field of teaching and learning may work in any of these areas. Their main concern is with helping to improve the teaching and learning process – helping the students to be able to manage their learning better, and helping those who are providing the education or training to do so in a way that is effective and motivating. Sometimes an applied psychologist specializing in teaching and learning will be employed by a particular college or university, as a specialist in staff development or in teaching quality. More commonly, though, they act as independent consultants or advisors.

> ## Insight
>
> Many adults returning to study have little self-confidence, especially if they left school without qualifications: they fear they may be too stupid to learn. The first stage in their education, therefore, tends to focus on building up self-efficacy beliefs and showing them that they really are capable of learning.

Like other applied psychologists, those specializing in this field have to go through a systematic process of professional training and education. In the UK, the main way that they do this is through the particular qualification in this area offered by the British Psychological Society. First, they need to have taken a recognized first degree in psychology, and to have had some years' experience as teachers or lecturers. Usually, this experience is in teaching psychology itself, either at degree level, at A level, or to other professional groups, but sometimes people teaching other subjects decide to develop their professional qualifications by undertaking training in this area. The qualification itself is obtained through a mixture of exams, coursework and a lengthy period of supervised professional practice involving a number of case studies and a research project.

The work of an applied psychologist specializing in the teaching and learning process can take many forms. They may work at the college level, for example, developing an integrated curriculum policy for the college or university as a whole, or implementing teaching quality assurance systems. They may run workshops or in-service training courses for lecturers or teachers, helping them to improve some aspects of their teaching, or course delivery. They may be involved at the individual level, helping students to make appropriate educational choices or to improve aspects of their learning. And, of course, they conduct research into the many different psychological aspects of the teaching and learning process.

Social and motivational aspects of learning

One of the ways in which the work of applied psychologists in this field is different from that of educational psychologists is that they are usually dealing with adults rather than children. Adults and older teenagers have different kinds of social relationships than children do, and their motivation for studying is also different. As a result, they have to be more self-directed in their learning, and the work of their teacher or lecturer often has more to do with helping them to manage their own learning, than with teaching them directly.

The consequence is that the social and motivational aspects of learning become extremely important. Applied psychologists working in this area need to have a thorough knowledge of the types of influence that social factors can exert on learning, and of how these can be managed so that their influence is positive rather than negative. They also need to be aware of how the learning process can be managed in such a way as to enhance the students' own motivation, and so help them to put in the time and effort needed for successful studying.

Insight

People who have taught both schoolchildren and adults returning to study often remark on the differences between them. Schoolchildren tend to be more self-confident, but adults are more highly motivated in their learning – they know exactly why they are doing it, and it matters to them.

SOCIAL INFLUENCES

Social influences on learning can take a great many forms, ranging from the body language used by the lecturer or teacher, to the social representations or shared beliefs held by everyone concerned, and take in attitudes, social scripts and expectations along the way (see also *Understand Psychology*).

As we have seen in other chapters in this book, people convey information to each other in all sorts of ways – not all of which are conscious. The way that we dress, stand, and organize the space around ourselves can be just as informative to other people as the actual words we say; our facial expressions, gestures and tones of voice supplement that information. This **non-verbal communication** occurs whenever people are in contact, and the process of teaching and learning inevitably involves people coming into contact with one another.

In the 'traditional' teaching situation, the implicit messages which are conveyed by non-verbal signals are all about power and authority. The teachers dress differently – more formally – than the students, which conveys an impression of being socially distant. They have more space to move around in, and a much larger desk, which conveys messages about having control of the space and how people are organized. They manage the talking, and do most of it, with the learners expected to be passive recipients, which conveys messages about the control of information, and about authority and power. And so on.

That traditional approach to teaching, however, isn't always the best way of going about it. Students learn better if they are active in their learning, and able to make some choices about what they are doing. When it comes to adults, those choices become particularly important, because everyone is studying for their own personal reasons and needs to be self-directed. So the emphasis needs to shift away from an authoritarian model of information transmission, towards a more collaborative model, in which the lecturer is working with the student to help them to learn. And that means that the non-verbal signals need to be changed, too.

Insight

Authority has become almost a dirty word in some educational contexts, but it is important to recognize that teachers are the authorities on their subjects, and do have both the duty and the right – not to mention the knowledge – to direct the learning process. There's a big difference between collaborating with students and designing learning experiences so they can draw on their personal knowledge, and handing over complete control of the learning experience.

The teacher or lecturer does know more about the subject than the student does, so they need to have some authority. This means that some of the non-verbal signals are still useful. It may be useful for a lecturer to dress a little more formally than the students, for example, and if their interactions are conducted in a friendly and approachable manner the slight amount of role distance which it signifies will be helpful rather than repressive. The challenge is to distinguish between those signals which are actually helpful in the learning process and those which interfere with it.

For example: conversations work much better when the people who are talking can make eye-contact with one another. So if the course includes discussion, and students are expected to work together in groups, or to talk over issues with one another, it is quite important that they are able to see one another as well, and that often means rearranging the furniture to allow them face-to-face contact. Having all the students seated in such a way that they are looking towards the front of the room is going to make any discussion stilted and awkward. On the other hand, if the lecturer or teacher is actually conveying large chunks of information, then that is likely to be the best type of seating arrangement for that situation. It just depends on what is going on at the time.

Insight

There is still a place for traditional methods of teaching in some contexts. Large lectures, for example, offer little scope for student involvement but can be useful in establishing an overall context within which more detailed study topics make sense. So psychologists might seek to enhance a lecturer's presentational and performance skills as part of developing their teaching and learning.

MOTIVATIONAL FACTORS

There are many other ways that a good knowledge of social psychological processes can aid students' learning. Motivational processes are also important, and are often closely linked with social factors. In terms of adult learning (and children's learning too, for that matter) one of the most important motivational processes is that of developing positive self-efficacy beliefs.

Self-efficacy beliefs (see also *Understand Psychology*) are the beliefs that we have about what we are capable of doing. Positive self-efficacy beliefs are beliefs that we can act effectively in a particular area. In the context of teaching and learning, positive self-efficacy beliefs relate to having a sense of being able to learn, and to deal effectively with assessments. They aren't quite the same as self-confidence, because they are much more specific. Someone might have positive self-efficacy beliefs when it comes to learning history or social studies, but low self-efficacy beliefs when it comes to statistics or science.

So an important part of managing the learning experience consists of creating opportunities for students to enhance their self-efficacy beliefs, because if people believe that they are capable of learning, they are much more likely to put in the extra study time and effort which is required to succeed. If they believe that they are too stupid to learn, or that the work is too hard for them, then they are less likely to put in the necessary effort. This means that teachers and lecturers need to provide students with opportunities to realize that they are capable of succeeding.

Applied psychologists in teaching and learning become familiar with a wide range of ways in which this can be achieved. It might take a number of forms. One way, for example, is by developing appropriate assessments or practical work which will provide students with constructive feedback as they progress through their course. It might involve discussions in tutorials, creating small tasks which students can perform to use the knowledge they have been acquiring. Or it might involve the development of individual study programmes which have been broken down into a series of manageable goals.

A psychologist providing assistance in this area will use their knowledge of the context and the various factors involved to identify the strategy which is most likely to be effective in that particular course and for those particular students. That knowledge also helps them to develop an implementation programme which will address a particular problem or situation, identifying any training requirements or resources needed to put it into practice.

There are, of course, many other factors which influence people's motivation to study. And there are other ways in which students' learning can be enhanced by the application of psychological knowledge. One of them is in how we handle and retain the information itself – the cognitive side of learning.

Cognitive aspects of learning

An applied psychologist specializing in teaching and learning will often be involved in **skills training** with both students and lecturers. Thinking skills, study skills and presentation skills are all important aspects of the learning process, and most students can enhance their performance by consciously developing some of these. Knowledge of how your own cognitive processes work is known as **metacognition**, and many psychologists working in this area develop programmes for training students in metacognitive skills.

Teachers and lecturers, too, often benefit from this training. A teacher who has undergone training in thinking skills, for example, is often able to revise their course in such a way as to make it more challenging and educationally effective for the students who are taking it. A knowledge of how these skills can be taught can be useful in developing better ways for structuring and presenting information. It is also useful in developing more appropriate assessments for that particular area of knowledge, so both teacher and students benefit as a result.

Similarly, a detailed knowledge of memory processes and how memory works is useful in helping students to come to terms with large amounts of information. A knowledge of cognitive structuring and the organization of knowledge helps a lecturer to present information in a manner which means that it will be more readily understood. And a knowledge of the different ways in which students can acquire information, and the benefits and disadvantages of each, allows the whole teaching and learning process to be managed in a way which best suits that particular course.

Insight

Metacognition – the recognition and understanding of one's own cognitive processes – is at the heart of successful learning. We need to be aware of what we find easy to remember, and how we can improve our own memories. We also need to recognize what we find easy and when we need to put in more effort. Metacognition grows with experience and self-knowledge, so it's not really surprising that adults tend to be better at it than children.

Sometimes, this involves the complete restructuring of a course. It might involve, for example, shifting from a knowledge-based approach, to a problem-based one, in which students are expected to use the knowledge to tackle specific problems, rather than just learning it as dry, academic knowledge. In one Canadian university, for example, the entire medical curriculum was revised in this way. Instead of learning vast amounts of information about the body and its systems by heart, students were presented with a series of real-life medical problems. Understanding what was going on in each of these cases meant that they had to come to terms with the same information that they would have had to learn in the traditional way, but this time they were using it in a practical context. The result was that those students obtained a much deeper understanding of physiological systems and the way that they work together in the body, which helped their eventual development as doctors a great deal.

It helped them by sustaining their motivation too. They had, after all, come to medical school to learn to become doctors, and seeing how the information they were handling was relevant in the context of actual medical problems helped them to remain interested, and to put effort into acquiring that knowledge. Effective learning and motivation are very closely tied together: if students know that they are progressing, and acquiring useful knowledge, that in itself can be a motivating factor which helps them to continue to put time and effort into studying.

So an applied psychologist working in this area will have detailed knowledge of the effects of different methods of teaching on the acquisition of knowledge. That includes things like memory from lectures. Sometimes, lectures really are the most effective way of imparting information, but sometimes they are the only method that lecturers or teachers can use because of the sheer number of students they are dealing with. It also includes a knowledge of learning styles, and metacognition – that is, understanding one's own cognitive processes and using that understanding to work effectively.

Exams and assessment

It is in preparing for examinations, of course, that a knowledge of how our cognitive processes work really comes into its own. Examinations involve learning and remembering very large amounts of information, but psychologists have been studying memory for over 100 years, so we know a great deal about how it works. As a result, applied psychologists working in this area often find themselves giving advice on revision techniques or strategies which will help students to learn information.

Insight

Thinking positively, practising realistically, eating and sleeping well, and believing in success have all been shown to be significant factors affecting success in sport. They apply just as strongly to exams – but how many people follow those principles?

THE PSYCHOLOGY OF REVISION

There are any number of ways of improving student learning when it comes to revision. What they all have in common is that they rest on the fundamental principles of memory which have been identified through psychological research. One of the most useful of these is known as the 'levels of processing' approach, because it relates to a psychological theory of how memory works which originally had that name. (The theory has been modified by researchers since it was first developed, but its basic principles still hold true.)

Effectively, what this theory is saying is that the reason we forget things is because we haven't processed the information deeply enough. By 'processing', we mean cognitive processing: that is, thinking about the information, exploring its implications and meanings, and generally making sense of it. When we are dealing with information, we can either receive it superficially, and not really think about what it means, or we can process it deeply – and we very rarely forget information that we have really processed thoroughly. The trouble is that many students aren't really very interested in the kind of information they are trying to learn for exams, or they don't have the habit of trying to think about what it really means. They don't forget information about their friends and family, though, because they do process that.

Fortunately, though, the psychological research which revealed how important levels of processing can be, also showed that just about any kind of cognitive processing will improve memorizing – even if it is only changing the form of the information into some other words, or into sounds or pictures. A great many revision techniques are based on this principle. They involve changing the form of the information in some way – such as converting a couple of pages of notes into a diagram or a summary chart. The process of doing this forces us to think about the information, and so helps us to remember it. But we do have to do it ourselves. Just copying someone else's summary isn't going to help – it only gives you more to remember. It is the act of actually processing the information which helps to place it in the memory, not the end result.

There are some other principles of how memory works which applied psychologists use when they are developing strategies to help people with their revision. One of them relates to the connections between memories: our strongest memories are those which link up with other ones – like the memories that come back in response to particular songs. So revision techniques aimed at connecting up different bits of information and identifying the connections between them – such as developing flow-charts and tree diagrams – are also very effective.

Another important principle is that the brain has only a limited capacity for remembering meaningless chunks of information, but nobody has yet found a limit to how much meaningful information we can remember. So revision techniques which force the person to understand the information concerned are particularly useful. Summarizing, converting it into diagram form, or even telling someone else about it are examples of methods which draw on this principle as the basis of revision strategies.

Another principle of human memory is that visual images are usually easier to recall than words. So some revision techniques involve creating memorable images – either on paper or as mental imagery – to help the person to learn the information they will need to remember in the exam. This isn't the whole answer, and it can sometimes be a fairly superficial kind of processing, but sometimes there is information which simply has to be learned by heart, and at such times mental or physical imagery can be very useful.

EXAM STRESS

Another area in which applied psychologists of teaching and learning are particularly active is that of exam stress management. Stress is a significant part of our day-to-day experience, and it can make all the difference to successful exam performance (see also *Understand Psychology*). A certain amount of stress is good, because it encourages people to make an effort and do well, but beyond a certain point it can work the other way, and cause the person to do less well than they might otherwise have done.

So psychologists working in this area often conduct exam stress management workshops for groups of students and lecturers, as well as individual stress counselling sessions. Generally, these workshops emphasize how stress has a physiological dimension as well as a mental one, and show how effective coping strategies will address both of these dimensions rather than just one. There are techniques to reduce mental stress, such as positive thinking exercises and mental relaxation techniques, which are all useful at exam time. A lot of these techniques are similar to the ones used by sport psychologists to enhance performance in competitions, so we will be looking at them in more detail in Chapter 16. When you think about it, taking an exam and competing in a sporting competition have a lot in common: we have lots of opportunity for practice and preparation, but just the one opportunity to do our very best. So the methods which help sports people can also help people doing exams.

One of the areas which teaching and learning psychologists often address is that of attributional styles. I mentioned these when we were looking at clinical and counselling psychology (Chapters 6 and 7), and they will come up again when we look at sport psychology, in Chapter 16. Effectively, attributions are the reasons that we give for why things happen, and the particular attributional styles that we adopt can make a great deal of difference to how much stress we feel. If the reasons that we give for exam failure, for example, are stable (unlikely to change), global (applying to just about everything to do with exams) and uncontrollable – for example, seeing ourselves as too 'thick' to succeed in any exams – we will feel very stressed at exam time. But if we see exam failure as coming from unstable, specific and controllable causes, such as not doing enough revision for that particular exam, we have used attributions which allow us to see how we can do something about it, and so we don't feel as much stress.

Everyone feels some stress when they do exams – without it we wouldn't be likely to do very well at all! But there are ways of ensuring that the body can deal effectively with its stress levels, and that helps our minds to think more clearly. We saw in Chapter 8 what a difference exercise can make to stress levels, and this applies as much during exam times as it does at any other. Similarly, a healthy diet and avoiding anxiety-inducing drugs like caffeine can do a great deal to bring the emotions which people are experiencing down to manageable levels. And that can be surprisingly effective in helping us to be more successful in exams – even if it is only giving us the mental energy that we need to create a sensible answer from the little bits that we remember!

There are two types of revision – learning and practice. Learning involves getting the stuff into the brain, and practice involves getting it out again in a form which means the examiner will give it marks. So practice is best done with sample questions and past papers, under timed conditions, but learning needs to involve as many different ways of reframing and reviewing the material as possible, so that it becomes interesting and memorable.

EVALUATION AND RESEARCH

Helping people on a personal level isn't the only way that applied psychologists are active in the area of exams and assessments. They are also involved in evaluating different forms of assessment, and developing assessment programmes which will connect most appropriately with the skills and knowledge that the students are supposed to acquire.

They also carry out research. Psychologists specializing in teaching and learning have conducted research into all sorts of aspects of the learning process. These range from investigations of cheating in examinations, to the question of gender inequality and other forms of bias in the marking of assessments and examinations, to explorations of the personal development which students undergo as they go through particular courses. When acting as consultants within the educational system or in organizational training, they are able to draw on and apply this knowledge as it becomes appropriate.

As a result, this area of applied psychology is becoming increasingly well known, and the applied psychology of teaching and learning is becoming an increasingly well-recognized branch of the psychological profession.

10 THINGS TO REMEMBER

1 *The applied psychology of teaching and learning uses psychology exactly as its name suggests.*

2 *Motivation is the key to successful learning with both adults and children.*

3 *There are both helpful and unhelpful forms of non-verbal communication in this area.*

4 *Good lecturers/teachers create opportunities for students to enhance their self-efficacy beliefs.*

5 *Understanding cognitive processes helps to improve both memory and learning strategies.*

6 *Successful revision always involves cognitive processing of the information.*

7 *Organizing information into meaningful chunks can help people to remember.*

8 *Visual images are easier to remember than words.*

9 *Exam stress responds well to psychological stress management techniques.*

10 *Evaluation and research are an important part of the applied psychology of teaching and learning.*

12

Occupational psychology

In this chapter you will learn:
- **three different uses for psychometric tests**
- **three types of occupational test**
- **what the terms 'time and motion', 'job enrichment' and 'occupational stress' mean.**

Occupational psychology, as its name suggests, is all about applying psychology to occupations – to work, in other words. It is concerned with how we choose people for different jobs – with occupational selection; with how people are appraised and rewarded in terms of their job performance; and with analysing the characteristics of different types of work and their particular impact on the individual person.

Psychologists have been involved in this area almost since the beginning of the psychology itself, and occupational psychology has been a recognized part of professional applied psychology for over 70 years. In earlier times, occupational psychologists were trained on the job by senior psychologists working in the same organization. Nowadays, like other areas of professional psychology, training to become an occupational psychologist requires a recognized first degree in psychology, a substantial period of relevant work experience, and an approved higher degree in occupational psychology. The training is detailed and complex, because occupational psychologists can find themselves working in so many different areas.

Occupational testing

Occupational psychologists are particularly highly trained in the use of **psychometric tests**. These are tests which are designed to measure some aspect of the person's psychological functioning – from general assessments of personality or intelligence to the identification of characteristic learning styles. Other psychologists use psychometric tests too – as we saw in Chapter 10, for example, educational psychologists use psychometric tests to diagnose specific learning problems in children. However, they use psychometric testing for different purposes, so the tests are different. The tests used by occupational psychologists are all work-related in some way.

USING PSYCHOMETRIC TESTS

Psychometric tests are not perfect, and nobody would use a psychometric test as the only basis for making an important decision. But they do provide good background information to help us to make decisions. Occupational psychologists use psychometric tests quite frequently, and in a variety of contexts. They are used for any number of different purposes, but perhaps the three most commonly used ones are for recruitment, promotion and vocational guidance.

Every organization needs to have staff who will help to make it work. Recruitment – that is, selecting people for jobs – is a regular requirement in modern society, and organizations often go to considerable trouble to make sure that they are appointing the right person. Many occupational psychologists specialize in recruitment, and all occupational psychologists are trained in the skills and knowledge required to give effective advice to prospective employers, and to undertake appropriate psychometric testing.

> ### Insight
> Psychometric tests generally contain specialist lie-scales, which can detect if the person is lying. They do this by asking particular questions which are likely to attract lies if the person is not being truthful, but only the test designers and the psychologists are aware of which questions these are.

No psychometric test can really predict exactly what someone is like, or how well they will do in a particular job, because people change according to the situation. Different organizations bring out different skills and characteristics of a person (we will be looking at organizational psychology in the next chapter). Psychometric testing can add useful information to the decision-making process, but one of the reasons it should only be used by trained professionals is that it is very easy for the results of a test to be misinterpreted, or taken as more definite information than they really are. An occupational psychologist uses test results as a diagnostic device to be used alongside other sources of knowledge, rather than as an absolute statement of fact.

For example, a small computer firm might streamline its recruitment process by asking would-be employees to take an **aptitude test** – a kind of psychometric test which explores whether you can undertake the kind of reasoning or thinking which would be suitable for that particular type of job. Aptitude tests are not concerned with whether people already have skills and knowledge – they will learn these at work – but with whether they have the right kinds of abilities which will allow them to do that learning effectively. Someone who found logical thinking difficult, for example, wouldn't be likely to take to computer programming very easily.

Another common use of psychometric tests is in selecting people for promotion. Potential candidates for high-level management positions, for example, are often sent by their organizations to what are known as 'assessment centres' – although these have nothing to do with the assessment centres used for troubled children! At these centres, they are put through a battery of psychometric tests, and also have to undertake a series of practical exercises designed to reveal leadership and communication skills, and the like.

The psychologists running the assessment programme observe the candidates carefully, and also conduct a series of interviews and discussions with them. They use the information they gain from all this to produce a full report on each candidate's abilities, aptitudes and skills. The report is passed on to management and also, usually, given to the candidate. The organization's management can then take that information into account when they are making their promotion decisions.

Insight

People applying for high-powered jobs are often asked to take a whole battery of psychometric tests. These will identify job aptitude, personality and leadership profiles, and may also cover motivational and spiritual qualities. Not all of them will be paper-and-pencil tests – some will involve practical exercises too. But all of these will only be used as supplementary information – the job interview is still, usually, the deciding factor.

A third area in which psychometric testing comes into play is in **vocational guidance**. This involves helping people to choose the particular careers or occupations which are most likely to suit them, and occupational psychologists are often used for this purpose. They are also sometimes involved in training careers officers to use the appropriate psychometric tests for this purpose. The idea behind these tests is to identify the person's interests, preferences and aptitudes.

That information is then used to suggest particular jobs or lines of work which the person may find most suitable. Someone who likes paying attention to small details and prefers indoor activities, for example, might be well suited to a job dealing with paperwork in an insurance office, while someone who feels that they need a high level of physical activity would probably be entirely unsuitable for that type of work. That's a simple example, of course, and the real tests are much more subtle, but it should give a general idea of what this type of occupational testing is all about.

> ### Insight
> Vocational guidance testing can help people realize that they may be suited for jobs that they hadn't even considered. If someone is considering a change of career, vocational guidance tests can sometimes be really helpful.

TYPES OF OCCUPATIONAL TEST

Most of the psychometric tests used by occupational psychologists can be fitted into one of four categories. The first category is that of **general mental ability tests** – the tests that people often refer to as intelligence tests. These are not often used on their own, but as part of a group of tests, and they are used as an overall indicator as to whether someone has a basic level of mental competence. There has been a lot of controversy surrounding the use of intelligence tests for job selection, mainly based around the way that the questions and scoring of such tests often show an unconscious bias against people from particular cultures or ethnic backgrounds. So they are rarely used on their own as the basis for any kind of recruitment.

Occupational psychologists are much more inclined to draw on the information from **personality tests**. Typically, these tests involve asking a series of questions designed to provide a picture of someone's personality in terms of a number of different personality factors. One of the most commonly used occupational tests, the OPQ, is based on a model of personality developed by Cattell, back in 1946. Cattell's model gives a profile which shows how someone has scored on 16 different personality factors. The factors are all bipolar: that is, they have two ends, such as 'reserved–outgoing', and the person's score shows how close they are to one end or the other. Figure 12.1 shows what a personality profile based on Cattell's 16 personality factors might look like.

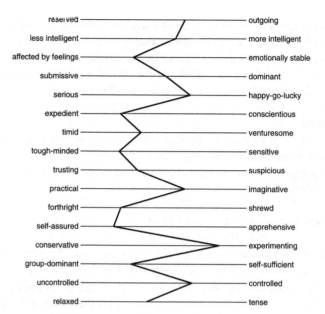

Figure 12.1 A personality profile.

These tests (or more modern versions of them) are used in occupational selection to give useful information as to whether someone appears to have the characteristics needed to 'fit in' to the job or not. For example, there would be little point in choosing someone whose profile indicated that they were 'submissive' rather than 'dominant' to a leadership role which required strong management of large numbers of people. But again, the test results wouldn't be used on their own: the person's previous track record and their performance in interviews and on other types of test would need to provide supporting data as well.

Insight

The main problem with personality tests is that they can't take account of how we change in different situations. Someone can be bright and confident in one setting, but diffident and shy in another. But this wouldn't come out in most personality tests.

Aptitude tests are another type of test commonly used by occupational psychologists. As we have seen, these are tests which have been designed with a particular type of job or work in mind. Their function is to show whether the person who is tested has the right kinds of skill for that particular job. For example, a PR firm which wanted to recruit and train sales representatives would try to make sure that they were taking on people with the interpersonal skills and communicative abilities which sales promotions require. So an occupational psychologist helping them with recruitment would be likely to include an appropriate aptitude test as part of the information that they were gathering.

Some aptitude tests are paper-and-pencil ones, but others take the form of scaled-down versions of real tasks which the person would encounter in the job. One popular exercise in management recruitment, for example, is known as the 'in-basket exercise', in which people have a limited amount of time to deal with a set of letters, memos and other tasks such as might appear in a typical manager's in-tray. The way that the person deals with the information, how they prioritize different things, and what they actually decide, all provide information which can be very useful for managerial job selection.

Some other aptitude tests may be much more specific and, in some cases, they merge with the fourth type of test which an occupational psychologist may use: **diagnostic tests**. There are many situations in the working context where an occupational psychologist might need to use a particular diagnostic test, to identify the source of a particular problem or difficulty at work. For example, they might test for closed head injury which has happened as a result of an accident at work, and use tests based on the research which we looked at in Chapter 4. Or they might use a test as an aptitude test – for example, telephone engineers have to have good colour vision, because they deal with so many different colour-codes in their wiring systems. So selecting someone to work as a telephone engineer almost always involves a diagnostic colour-vision test, to identify any slight forms of colour blindness the person may have without realizing it.

Diagnostic tests relate to specific disorders, and there are a great many of them. So not all occupational psychologists are equally trained in the use of every single diagnostic test. But all tests of this kind which come on the market require the people who intend to use them to have had general professional training in test use, and also to have undergone the specific training required for a particular test. So occupational psychologists requiring this type of knowledge often find that they are continually developing their professional skills, by undertaking additional training in the different types of test they use in their work.

Diagnostic tests, as we saw in Chapter 10, are not for the amateur. They require very specific expertise, and are available only to trained psychologists. But some types of occupational test are more available. All psychometric tests require training, though, so the British Psychological Society issues Certificates in Occupational Testing which state whether the person is properly qualified to administer these tests. Occupational psychologists all have these certificates, but it is also possible for non-psychologists to take special courses run by occupational psychologists, which will qualify them as well. So people working in personnel or recruitment who want to use psychometric tests to help their decision making can obtain the appropriate training.

Having the right training matters, because proper psychometric tests need to be administered and interpreted very carefully. Psychometric tests are more than just questionnaires – they are very carefully constructed, based on large research samples, and each test item is individually evaluated before it is incorporated into the test. As a result their outcomes are quite different – and much more accurate – than those from an ordinary questionnaire. There are lots of amateur 'tests' on the market, but it is easy to tell the difference, because no reputable test publisher will sell their tests to people who have not been properly trained in their use. So if you can just buy a test without showing evidence of your competence, you know that the test you are buying is not a proper psychometric test, and may not be all that useful.

Occupational tests, then, can be quite diverse, but they all need to have gone through rigorous processes of reliability, validity and standardization, and they need to be administered by people who are trained in them and understand how to use them. They can be useful in providing information to help guide job recruitment; in helping managers to make decisions about promotions; and in helping people to decide what types of job might suit them best. So administering, evaluating, and sometimes even developing occupational tests is an important part of the occupational psychologist's work.

Job analysis

Job analysis is another aspect of working life that occupational psychologists have been involved in for a very long time. It is always thought to have begun with the work of F.W. Taylor, in 1911, who (the story goes) was watching labourers load pig-iron onto railway trucks one day, and was struck by the inefficient way that they went about the job. Typically, each man loaded about twelve and a half tons of pig-iron a day, but Taylor was sure they could manage much more than that. He secured the agreement of one particular labourer, asking him to do exactly as Taylor told him to do – lift when he was told, rest when he was told – for the whole day. By the end of the day, the labourer had loaded forty-seven and a half tons.

TIME AND MOTION

Taylor's work was influential in the development of **ergonomics** – the study of efficiency, which we will be looking at in Chapter 14 – and it also formed the basis of a type of job analysis known as **time and motion,** which became widely applied. This approach was very popular with management, and in the first half of the twentieth century a great many occupational psychologists were employed to carry out job analyses of this type. But it was not popular with the people doing the work, because of the way that they were expected to act like robots, and had no personal say in what they were doing. As occupational psychology became more sophisticated in the second half of the twentieth century, managers began to realize that there was value in having motivated, interested staff, and that this was cheaper in the long run because they stayed longer and had fewer days off sick.

Modern types of job analysis, therefore, are quite different from the time and motion approach founded by Taylor. They also tend to deal with far more complex occupations, since people as a general rule undertake more complex activities in their day-to-day lives than they did during the old factory-based era. Far more people nowadays work in service industries or office jobs than on production lines, and even on those, jobs have become more complex as managers have learned to value the competence of their workforce more.

Insight

Many people nowadays are deeply suspicious of job analysis practices – partly because of an engrained cultural memory of the rigid and inhuman demands of the original 'time and motion' studies, and partly because they are often precursors to redundancies. Occupational psychologists need to overcome these anxieties to undertake job analyses properly.

So carrying out job analysis requires far more than just observation. It involves gathering a wide range of information about the job itself, about the amount of variety and change there is from day to day, about levels of responsibility and scope for decision making, and a number of other such attributes. Once it has been carried out, a job analysis might contribute to overall management policy, such as providing baseline knowledge for a management restructuring; it might be used for an individual's appraisal to determine their pay level for the coming year, or their suitability for promotion; or it might be used to inform a recruitment advertisement.

JOB ENRICHMENT

Another way that a job analysis (or a set of job analyses) performed by an occupational psychologist might be used is as the basis for a deliberate programme of **job enrichment** which the management of the organization has decided to adopt. Job enrichment involves aiming to enhance people's motivation and personal commitment to their work by ensuring that some of it, at least, is intrinsically satisfying and gives them a sense of achievement or competence. That can mean allowing them to make more of the relevant decisions in their work, or reorganizing what they do so that they can take responsibility for a particular case or person and follow what happens to them throughout their dealings with the company.

A job analysis might also involve identifying some of the special skills which a particular task requires. Sometimes these can be entirely unexpected, at least on the part of management, and it is only the job analysis which shows what is actually required. Very often, the use of job analysis by occupational psychologists shows up massive inefficiencies in the ways that people use their time, which have been brought about by the ways that decision making or paperwork are structured in that particular organization. As they collect information from interviews, observations, and other sources of data, the occupational psychologist is often in a position to see how this can be improved and to make recommendations which will make the job concerned a great deal easier to carry out.

Occupational stress

Another area where occupational psychologists are particularly active is in identifying and dealing with occupational stress. Stress, as we have seen several times in this book, is one of the areas where the broad-ranging knowledge that applied psychologists have is particularly relevant. Organizational stress is stress which arises as a consequence of work, and many occupational psychologists run workshops or staff training sessions which help employees to deal with it.

Stress, as we have already seen, has both a physiological dimension and a psychological one. The physiological dimension is based on the old 'fight or flight' response, which we have in common with all mammals, and which prepares the body either to run away or to fight in response to threat. It's a set of physiological reactions designed to give the body extra energy, but these are particularly inappropriate in a modern world, and so can become a serious problem, not to mention a threat to health and well-being.

Insight

Anything which is even slightly unpleasant or arousing can be called 'stressful' by some, but that is not what the term 'stress' really means. Damaging stress is long-term and severe, not short-term and unpleasant.

On the psychological side, someone who is experiencing stress is much more ready to perceive threats than they would be otherwise, and will often end up reacting to situations as if they were threatening when this isn't really appropriate. They are also more likely to make errors, as all of us are when we are anxious, which can also be a problem in working life. In the short term, stress results in an inability to concentrate, irritability and emotionality, and the loss of the person's sense of humour. Over the long term, it leads to poor decision making, tiredness, absenteeism and apathy, and also to stress-related illness. So having employees who are under stress can be a serious problem for an organization.

SOURCES OF STRESS

There are a number of different ways that organizational stress can happen in organizations. Cartwright and Cooper (1997) identified six different sets of factors which are involved in producing occupational stress, which are listed in Table 12.1.

Table 12.1 Factors in organizational stress

Job factors	e.g. noise, pollution
Career development	e.g. being unable to achieve promotion or diversify at work
Role in the organization	e.g. having little say in relevant matters
Non-work factors	e.g. family stress
Organizational structure and climate	e.g. lack of co-operation between departments
Relationships at work	e.g. working with hostile or difficult colleagues

---

Psychologists often make a distinction between job factors and role factors. Job factors which can produce stress include the general working conditions which people are facing, whether they are doing shift work or long hours, whether their job involves travel and simple work overload. Role factors, on the other hand, are more concerned with exactly how people are expected to carry out their work. They include role ambiguity, when it is not clear what they are supposed to be doing or where their responsibilities lie, and role conflicts, where someone has to address two conflicting sets of demands as part of their job. Job analyses performed by occupational psychologists can be useful in identifying, and sometimes dealing with, both of these sources of stress.

In addition to this, occupational psychologists often use job design strategies to minimize workplace stress. These are likely to include establishing effective workloads, which are enough to keep people busy but not so busy that they are never able to get the work done. They may also include job enrichment programmes, to ameliorate repetitive or mechanistic work, and sensible shift systems which don't end up straining people's health. Reducing stress through job design might also include role clarification – helping to remove ambiguities or conflicts by making it clear exactly what role the person is supposed to be playing, and also some level of job control or empowerment, which makes it easier for people to do the work they are expected to do.

Stress workshops held by occupational psychologists can also be useful in identifying stress produced by relationships at work – a particularly bullying manager, for example, or conflicts between two individuals which are affecting others that they work with. Sometimes, too, sources of stress become apparent as a result of appraisal interviews, or other types of investigation which highlight people's concerns about job security, job performance, or the way that their personal career portfolio is building up. In these cases, the expertise of occupational psychologists can be useful in counselling the individuals concerned.

Insight

Organizational bullying has become increasingly recognized as a work problem. But the concept is more problematic than it seems, because some people habitually express themselves in a forceful and direct manner which others find intimidating, even when there is no intimidating intention at all.

Sometimes, organizational stress comes from the overall organizational structure, or climate. It is generally stressful for people if they are unable to participate in any decision making about their work, or unable to voice their opinions. Sometimes, too, organizational decisions are made at a level which is so remote from the actual work that they are completely impractical. Cases like these, which involve the functioning of the organization as a whole, are generally outside the scope of an occupational psychologist, as are the kinds of non-work stressors which come from families, divorces and bereavements. But even though they may not be able to address the source of stress, occupational psychologists are often able to set up behavioural interventions which can help the people concerned to develop coping skills, and so reduce their levels of stress.

We can see, then, that the work of the occupational psychologist can be quite varied and complex. There is much more to it than we have been able to deal with here, of course. The ways that people interact with their work are many and varied – even the different types of work that occupational psychologists deal with are complex, and when you add to that social factors, ambitions, motivation and all of the other complications of being human beings, you can see that there is plenty to do. Occupational psychologists tend to deal with the individual at work, but there are other applied psychologists who work at the organizational level, dealing with the social aspects of management and working life. We will be looking at their work in the next chapter.

10 THINGS TO REMEMBER

1 *Occupational psychologists are mainly concerned with individuals at work.*

2 *Psychometric testing can be an important part of an occupational psychologist's job.*

3 *Candidates for important jobs often have to take many different psychological tests.*

4 *Mental ability tests include IQ tests and other tests of reasoning and mental skill.*

5 *Personality tests look at aspects of personality such as timidity, confidence and conscientiousness.*

6 *Aptitude tests assess how suited someone is for a particular job or occupation.*

7 *Diagnostic tests are used to uncover specific problems.*

8 *The old-fashioned approach to job analysis treated people like machines. Modern approaches are very different.*

9 *Stress at work can come from many sources, and is very costly to an organization.*

10 *Occupational psychologists develop programmes to reduce stress.*

13

Organizational psychology

In this chapter you will learn:
- *the difference between a 'group' and a 'team'*
- *what is meant by 'organizational innovation'*
- *why understanding an organization's culture can enable better management.*

Occupational psychologists, as we saw in the last chapter, are primarily concerned with individuals and the jobs that they do – in other words, they are mainly focused on people's occupations. Organizational psychologists, on the other hand, work at the level of the organization itself, dealing with questions of groups, management, and the various social factors which can influence organizational life.

Some very large organizations employ their own organizational psychologists, who specialize in areas such as management training, teamworking and organizational change, but as a general rule, organizational psychologists work from outside the organization. They come in as consultants, either independently or from big consultancy firms. Some organizational psychologists also have academic posts with universities, which gives them a good base to conduct research. It also benefits their students, and many universities actively encourage staff conducting research in this area to do independent consultancy for that reason (and because it helps to bring in research income).

Organizational psychologists used to begin their careers with a similar kind of training to occupational psychologists, but specializing in organizational theory and research during their higher degree, rather than on psychometrics and selection issues. In recent years, though, the training for organizational psychologists has become more distinct and separate from that of occupational psychologists, as the needs of constantly changing organizations has highlighted the need for understanding the social psychological aspects of organizational life. It still follows the usual pattern for a professional psychologist, though – a recognized first degree in psychology, followed by relevant work experience, an approved higher degree, and a period of supervised practice.

As a result, an organizational psychologist will be familiar with a wide range of issues concerning organizational life. This will range from an understanding of the complexities surrounding management structure and leadership, to an understanding of the processes of organizational change and the resolution of organizational conflicts, to detailed knowledge of group processes and decision making, and many more areas. Like other psychologists, their knowledge spans several different levels, ranging from the level of individual cognitive processes and how issues affecting organizations are understood by the people working in them, to the level of organizational culture, and the distinctive history, practices and customs which make each organization unique. In this chapter, we will look very briefly at just three areas of organizational psychology: teamworking, organizational development and organizational cultures.

Groups and teams

People in groups often act differently from when they are on their own, and this applies just as much in organizational life as it does in any other area of day-to-day living. In recent years, organizations have come to recognize that this can be a positive force – that people like to work co-operatively, and that providing opportunities for them to do so often helps them to remain motivated and interested in their work. And if a team is really working well, the members can inspire one another to work better. Organizational psychologists are involved in teamworking at many levels, ranging from research into what makes teams effective, to the development and implementation of teamworking strategies in the organization as a whole.

One of the important distinctions to make is between a group and a team. A group is a collection of individuals who have come together, perhaps for a reason and perhaps not. Just being with other people in a group is enough to trigger a number of psychological processes – pressures for conformity, for example, and for compliance and co-operation. A knowledge of these processes is important for understanding just why groups of people act as they do (see also *Understand Psychology*).

Insight

Teamworking is useful to modern organizations, because an effective team can be far more productive than the same people working as individuals. The whole is more than just the sum of the parts.

There are other processes which come into play in groups, as well. One of the most damaging, at the organizational level, is that of **groupthink**. Groupthink was first identified when researchers began to explore just why some organizations ended up making totally disastrous decisions, whose failure could easily have been predicted. It was first discussed by Janis, in 1972, who showed that these decisions tend to be based on an entirely unrealistic perception of the situation. That unrealistic perception is generated by the group, which dismisses outside information and operates entirely on the basis of its own assumptions.

Insight

In modern society it is much too easy for members of a particular subculture or group never to meet people from outside that group. This means that they are rarely faced

> with dissenting ideas or serious challenges to their values. It is
> why politicians, bankers and bureaucrats are always so out of
> touch with ordinary people, and it leads directly to groupthink.

All groups of people have a natural tendency to assume that
their way of looking at the world is the only possible one, and
groupthink is an example of what happens when that is carried to
extremes. Moorhead, Ference and Neck (1991) showed how the
disastrous decision to launch the space shuttle Challenger in 1986,
despite warnings by the technical staff, was a classic example of
groupthink. The committee had all of the symptoms of groupthink,
and thought only of the managerial and publicity advantages of a
successful launch. They never even considered the possibility of an
unsuccessful one and, as a result, almost lost the entire US manned
space programme.

A more recent example can be seen in the global banking crisis of
2008/9, where the major investment banks were so carried away
with their risky investment behaviour that they brought the world's
entire financial system into crisis. The bankers concerned were
entirely taken up with their own beliefs, so much so that they failed
to make any real-world checks on what was actually going on. The
symptoms listed in Table 13.1 were just as clear in their decision-
making processes as they were in the case of the Challenger launch.

Table 13.1 Symptoms of groupthink

▶ an illusion of **invulnerability** – that all decisions will work out
successfully
▶ a tendency to **rationalize** away unpopular solutions
▶ **stereotyping** and deriding opponents rather than arguing a case
logically
▶ pressurizing doubters to **conform**, rather than investigating the
source of their doubts
▶ **self-censorship** – people with doubts about the wisdom of a decision
keep quiet rather than speak up
▶ an unrealistic impression of **unanimity** among the group members

(Contd)

▶ members acting as **mindguards**, *by censoring undesirable information and opinions – directly, or by gentle hints*

▶ an **illusion of morality** *– the belief that the group's actions or decisions are intrinsically right, and moral.*

Source: Janis, 1972

There are a number of safeguards which an organization can put in place to ensure that groupthink doesn't happen, and this is one area where the organizational psychologist's understanding of group processes and other aspects of group decision making often comes in useful. Organizations are full of groups – committees, working groups, informal 'canteen cultures' and many others – people are intrinsically social (see also *Understand Psychology*). So knowing how social influences act on people can contribute a great deal to helping an organization to run effectively.

Insight

Facing up to and accepting dissent is one of the hardest things for a powerful group to do. But it is the only way to be sure of combating the totally disastrous decision making which can result from groupthink.

TEAMWORKING

A team, on the other hand, is a bit more than just a group. A team is a group of people with complementary knowledge and skills who have been brought together for a specific purpose. There are several different types of team, but the main way that a team is different from a group is that it is much more task-focused. That has other consequences too – for example, teams tend to be quite explicit about what they consider to be appropriate conduct for the team itself, and much less concerned with non-team activities than groups are.

Insight

Effective working teams can help an organization in many unexpected ways. They foster pride in the organization, enhance employee beliefs in its value and energize people at work.

West (1995) argued that what makes a team distinctive is that its members share common values. West and his colleagues carried out an extensive programme of research into multidisciplinary team building in the health services, and came to the conclusion that developing a shared vision was the one factor which was absolutely essential if a team was to function effectively over a sustained period of time. Table 13.2 lists the main dimensions of team vision identified by West.

Table 13.2 Dimensions of team vision	
Clarity	The team need to be clear about what their values, purpose and goals are.
Motivating value	The team need to have a shared sense of the importance or value of their work.
Attainability	The team need to perceive the team goals as reachable, and something which they will be able to attain in the time, and given their abilities and effort.
Sharedness	All members of the team, and those managing it as well, need to share the team's vision. In order to achieve this, all team members need to have been involved in its development: it cannot be prescribed from above.
Ability to develop future potential	The team vision needs to be able to develop with time, and in response to changing circumstances, skills of the team members and changing values.

Source: West, 1994

Other approaches to team building emphasize the social process of social identification, or 'them-and-us', which is so powerful in human thinking. In some of my own research (Hayes, 2002) I discussed how effective teamworking is really about harnessing these mechanisms – the psychological processes of social identification – and ensuring that they act positively, to strengthen the team members' sense of commitment to one another and their awareness of the positive contribution they can make to the organization. Social identity mechanisms include the importance of classification, social comparison, and also pride in the group, and are useful motivators for people. They also work together with the shared values identified by West, and together form a powerful set of mechanisms which can make the team a very positive force within an organization.

An organizational psychologist who is concerned with implementing teamworking in an organization will tend to draw on these approaches, and also bring in other aspects of team-building, such as the development of effective team skills and the establishment of appropriate training for teamworking. That doesn't just mean developing the specific technical knowledge the team requires. It also means training the team members in interpersonal and liaison skills. Most people's experience is in working as individuals, and they sometimes need explicit training in the kinds of skill which are required to work effectively as a team.

Organizational development

Another area in which organizational psychologists are particularly active is in organizational development – the planned and controlled change of organizations. The modern economic climate means that organizations have to be constantly changing, to adjust to shifts in the market and in working practices. So organizational practices which have worked well for a couple of decades sometimes have to be changed completely.

RESISTANCE TO CHANGE

Implementing change, though, is not easy, and people are often highly resistant to it. Employees who are resisting change can be a major problem, since almost all organizational functioning depends on the goodwill and co-operation of the people working in that organization. Not all resistance is bad, of course. Sometimes, it is justified, in the sense that some changes really do result in a lowering of quality, and the resistance shown by employees serves to alert management to the damaging consequences of what it is that they are doing. But often, resistance to change happens because of other factors. Organizational psychologists are often employed to identify those reasons, and suggest solutions for them.

Insight

Those who oppose organizational change are not always wrong. Sometimes, they can see the consequences more clearly than the management can.

One common reason for resistance to change, for example, is simply lack of communication. If people don't know what is going on, then rumour and misinformation spread around the organization, and quickly acquire the status of fact. People are not passive: they don't simply accept what happens to them without trying to understand what is going on. Nor do they wait until things happen before they begin to think about them – employees in an organization are quick to detect the unusual, and if nobody tells them what is going on, will speculate about it. So establishing effective communication is an important part of implementing organizational change successfully.

Another source of resistance to change is helplessness and passivity. It has already been noted how important it is that people should have a sense of control over their lives (see also *Understand Psychology*). Being helpless is deeply stressful, and when people are under stress they exaggerate all of the negative aspects in their thinking. So they are likely to resist the changes because they expect the worst. On the other hand, if they are involved in the change process in some way, such as by being consulted and given an opportunity to make suggestions, then they have some sense of 'ownership' of the change, and that can make all the difference to whether they resist it, or whether they try to make it work.

Mistrust of the change agents – the people who are causing the change to happen – can also be a factor in resistance to change. Organizational psychologists who adopt this role know how important it is that they should give employees an opportunity to know who they are and what they are doing – and also, how their expertise can be a positive factor in the change process. A group of people who come in from outside, don't bother getting to know the organization and its culture, and implement change in an arbitrary and dictatorial fashion, are unlikely to be successful.

THE PSYCHOLOGICAL CONTRACT

Another issue which comes up in organizational change, and can be an important factor in resistance to it, is when it gives employees a sense of betrayal. There is what has become known as a **psychological contract** between employees and their organization – an implicit, unspoken agreement that each will fulfil their obligations and duties towards the other. Sometimes, that psychological contract can involve assumptions that the organization is no longer able to fulfil, and when that becomes apparent, the consequences can be profound.

For example: a few decades ago, it was acceptable for people to regard a large organization as providing them with a job for life. If they worked hard for the organization, then the organization would respond by providing them with job security. More recently, the competitive environment of many organizations means that they are no longer able to sustain that type of assumption. When IBM – a classic example – suddenly initiated a policy of redundancies in the early 1990s – the psychological shockwave was enormous!

In that particular case, there were other positive managerial practices, such as openness of conflict and debate, which meant that the organization was able to weather the storm. But many other organizations making similar decisions have suffered serious consequences in terms of reduced motivation and commitment on the part of their workforce. As psychological research into the process has continued, organizational psychologists have developed a clearer understanding of how these problems can be addressed, and of ways that organizations can overcome them.

Insight

Just because a psychological contract isn't written down doesn't mean it isn't there. Employers have duties to their employees, in the same ways as employees have duties to the employers. It may be implicit, but it becomes very obvious once such a contract is broken.

The psychological contract at work does not need to be based on the idea of jobs for life, and increasingly organizations are recognizing this. A great deal of research and consultancy on the part of organizational psychologists has been focused around ways of building organizational commitment, even in a relatively short-term workforce. By highlighting other aspects of the organization's commitment to its employees – for example, the idea that the organization will take seriously its employees' 'career portfolios', and help people to develop skills which will also be useful to them when they leave – it is possible for an organization to develop a positive psychological contract with its people which is still based on openness and trust, but doesn't contain uneconomic or unmanageable assumptions.

Insight

The psychological contract also applies between a government and its armed forces. For example, sending troops to war without adequate equipment is generally seen as a clear breach of the psychological contract between the government and the armed forces.

Managing organizational change, therefore, does involve a certain amount of re-evaluating assumptions. Lewin (1951) described it as being a three-stage model. The first stage consists of 'unfreezing' – challenging people's established ideas, recognizing that the organization has different needs which have to be addressed, and combating resistance to change through argument and explanation. The second stage is the change process itself, which involves adjusting the tasks, structures and technology in the organization, and also changing the people who are doing the work, by giving them different responsibilities and appropriate retraining. And the third stage which Lewin described is that of 'refreezing' – that is, consolidating the changes which have taken place by allowing them to work for a period, making any necessary modifications, and evaluating how effective they have been.

INNOVATION

One of the alternatives to the kind of massive organizational change we have just been looking at is the idea of continuous innovation. The idea originally came into Western organizations from Japan, where the practice known as **kaizen** – continuous development through small refinements and improvements – is common. By involving all of the workforce in finding ways that working practices could be improved, the organization as a whole would be constantly changing, and wouldn't need the major upheavals which are involved in the Western-style approach of keeping things the same for years on end, and then changing everything all at once.

Many organizations in the Western world have also taken on the principle of kaizen, although their cultural and status differences often mean that they seem to have problems involving the workforce in quite the same ways. Certainly the idea that continuous organizational innovation is preferable to massive restructuring appears to have taken hold in many organizations, although not all.

Insight

Organizations have to change to keep up with the economic climate. But it is open to question whether all of the organization should be in constant flux, or whether some elements need to be stable. Too much change can be as damaging as too little.

West (1990) produced a model of the innovation process which is illustrated in Figure 13.1. As you can see it forms a cycle, from recognition of the problems which need to be solved, to the initiation of a change process in terms of identifying what needs to be done and putting into place the necessary resources to do it, to the implementation of that process, to a period of stabilization and evaluation. That period of evaluation will in turn identify problems which need to be addressed by more innovation, and so the whole cycle continues.

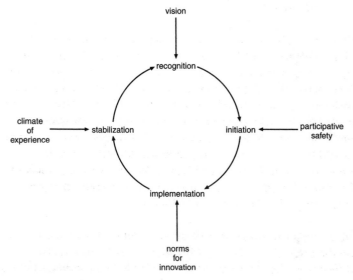

Figure 13.1 West's model of the innovation process.

Each stage in the cycle is improved or enhanced by certain qualities of management. Having a clear vision, for example, will improve the process of recognizing and identifying changes which need to be made. Having an organization in which people feel that they can make contributions or challenge ideas safely will help in initiating actual changes and making sure that they are set up properly. Having group and team norms in which innovation is recognized as a positive thing rather than a negative one will help when the changes are actually implemented in the organization. And having an organizational climate in which employees value excellence and high-quality performance will help in the stabilization and evaluation stage of the cycle.

Understanding organizational change, then, and helping management to develop effective programmes for implementing it is an important part of an organizational psychologist's work. In order to do this, organizational psychologists also need to have a reasonably good understanding of some of the special aspects of organizational cultures.

Organizational cultures

Organizational cultures are what makes each organization distinctive, and different from others. Each large organization has its own distinctive culture, and the habits and working practices which take place in one organization may be completely different in another. There have been various ways of analysing organizational cultures, ranging from typologies, which try to sort them out into different types, or groups, to systems approaches which look at the kinds of system which operate within the organization.

One of the best-known approaches to organizational culture, however, was put forward by the psychologist Edgar Schein. Schein defined culture as being the pattern of underlying assumptions within a given organization. Many researchers into organizational culture had looked at the kinds of rite, ritual and artefacts which organizations use, but Schein argued that organizational culture actually goes deeper than that. In fact, it is about deeply held beliefs, shared by everyone in the organization, and it is these shared beliefs which hold the culture together.

In Schein's model there are three levels of an organization's culture. The first is a kind of surface layer, containing the visible signs of culture – flags, emblems, logos, mottos, anecdotes and so on. The second is a layer of values, which informs the kinds of ways that the organization makes decisions, and what things are considered to be important. But the basic, fundamental layer underneath both of these is a layer of shared beliefs and basic assumptions about the nature of reality, human nature and relationships.

Organizational cultures are characterized by distinctive symbols and legends. But these have become significant gradually, through the history of the organization, and express implicit understandings. It is a mistake to think we can change the culture simply by changing the symbols.

SOCIAL PSYCHOLOGY OF ORGANIZATIONAL CULTURE

Building on this idea, Hayes (1998) proposed that organizational cultures could be usefully seen as social representations, and that seeing them in this way could provide some useful indicators as to how organizational cultures might be changed. Essentially, social representations (see also *Understand Psychology*) are the shared social beliefs which people use to structure social discussions and practices, and they are often anchored in shared metaphors or images – like the way that genetically modified foods have come to be referred to as 'Frankenstein foods'. The surface layer of organizational culture, and the deeper social assumptions which they symbolize, all fit closely with social representation theory.

There are other psychological processes which are involved in organizational cultures, too. We looked earlier at how an understanding of social identification processes is helpful to organizational psychologists dealing with teamworking; and it is also helpful when we come to understand what holds cultures together. Organizations aren't just single entities – they consist of lots of smaller groupings, or subcultures, each of which has their own ideas and beliefs, and also their own sense of 'them-and-us'. It is the overlapping of the different social identities and social representations in these smaller groups which makes an organizational culture strong.

Hayes and Lemon (1991) showed how the basic aspects of social identity processes – categorization, social comparison and self-esteem – could be used in management consultancy. By converting these into practical organizational terms, they allowed managers to strengthen the sense of unity and commitment in their departments, and also strengthened the overall sense of belonging to the organization as a whole. In fact, the researchers found, these recommendations often formed an underlying thread in other management consultancy recommendations, even though they were often not recognized as such.

THE LEARNING ORGANIZATION

Other researchers have explored different issues relating to organizational cultures. Starkey (1996), for example, explored the question of the learning organization – organizations which have established a culture of learning and responding to their environments. Because it has become such a deeply rooted part of the organization, necessary changes just happen – they don't have to be forced or implemented deliberately.

The learning organization has certain characteristics which researchers have identified, and which many organizational psychologists aim to establish in the organizations with which they are concerned. One of them is that they tend to be person-centred, valuing their staff as assets and valuing expertise. They also tend to have fluid relationships, in that the people working in them can be flexible in the roles that they adopt and the work that they do; and they are often very results-oriented.

At the same time, such organizations are often experimental and creative, ready to explore new ways of doing things and to see whether they will work or not. They don't feel the need to get everything right the first time, because they know that they can readjust and change something that isn't working. And that leaves them freer to try out new things and experiment with new systems.

Insight

The most effective organizations are those which listen to all of their employees, because people at lower levels often see much more clearly where things are going wrong. But in most organizations, middle-level bureaucracy prevents information getting from the bottom levels to the top.

There is, of course, far more to the work of the organizational psychologist than we have been able to look at here. But we can see from this how organizational psychologists are able to bring some rich insights into the ways that organizations work. By applying their knowledge of human psychology, and in particular their knowledge of social psychological processes, they can help organizational researchers and managers to gain a better understanding of what is going on in their organizations and, in the end, help them to manage them better.

10 THINGS TO REMEMBER

1 *Organizational psychologists deal with working life in the organization as a whole.*

2 *Groups at work can have negative effects on decision making, producing groupthink.*

3 *Teams are focused groups with explicit tasks, aims and values.*

4 *Organizational psychologists use social identity processes to help build teams.*

5 *People tend to resist change in organizations. This is sometimes damaging, but sometimes justified.*

6 *Resistance to change may be stronger because of poor communication and mistrust of management.*

7 *The psychological contract may not be visible, but is very important to employer–employee relationships.*

8 *Many firms feel they need constant innovation to deal with the ever-changing economic situation.*

9 *Organizational cultures have three layers – symbols on the surface, values deeper down and shared assumptions about the world at the base.*

10 *Organizational cultures can be seen as social representations, with social identification as the 'glue' holding organizational members together.*

14

Engineering and design psychology

In this chapter you will learn:
- *two examples of ergonomic design*
- *the components of human–machine 'systems'*
- *why 'surprise' could be a crucial component of an exhibit in a museum.*

In the past two chapters we have looked at two ways that applied psychologists are involved in the world of work: as occupational psychologists, and as organizational psychologists. This chapter will explore a third area of psychology at work, which is concerned with how people interact with machines and other artefacts. Engineering and design psychology looks at how human factors need to be taken into account when designing complex systems; it looks at the implications that human information processing has for the design of everyday objects, and how psychological knowledge can be used to enhance design processes.

Engineering and design psychologists work in a number of contexts, but many of them are based in or with engineering firms, working alongside designers and production engineers to develop and refine various types of machine – cars, kitchen equipment, videos and hi-fi systems, or even aircraft. Others are based in universities, carrying out research into human factors and ergonomics, and acting as independent consultants for various industrial projects.

> ## Insight
> Engineering and ergonomic psychologists tend to be highly
> valued by the engineers and technologists they work with.
> It's only those who haven't worked with psychologists who
> think that they are not necessary.

An engineering or human-factors psychologist may be involved
at any stage in the design process, but as a general rule the more
successful projects involve psychologists from the very beginning.
There have been several instances where complex designs have
had to be modified at the last moment because the testers suddenly
discovered flaws in the designs which made them difficult for people
to use, or which made it much too easy for people to make simple
and costly mistakes. Last-minute modifications are costly, and often
don't work particularly well. Building knowledge about the end-user
into the design from the very beginning makes the whole process
much more economical, as well as being more energy-efficient.

The professional training for engineering psychologists usually takes
much the same form as that of other professional psychologists, but
with their higher degree specializing in human factors, ergonomics or
industrial psychology. Some psychologists, however, begin to focus
in human factors or applied cognitive psychology during their first
degree, and come into the area as a result of undertaking a specialized
doctorate in some aspect of design or engineering psychology. Some
high-powered psychology graduates with an interest in the area are
recruited directly as graduate trainees by engineering firms or similar
organizations, and develop their expertise through a combination of
on-the-job training and part-time further study. Some psychologists
focus on other areas, such as cognitive psychology, and become
interested in engineering psychology as they develop specialized
knowledge and experience through research projects and consultancy.

Human–machine systems

One of the central concepts in engineering psychology is the idea
of the **system**. It concerns how human beings and artefacts work

together, not independently, and it is the way that they function as a system which is important. A system is always viewed as a cyclical process, illustrated in Figure 14.1. As you can see from the illustration, there are several different elements in the system, and only one of them is the machine itself. In the diagram, the machine is a computer, but it could just as well be a car, food mixer, hair-dryer, or any other kind of machine.

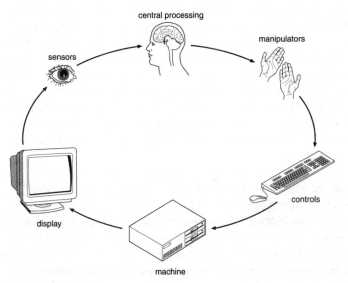

Figure 14.1 A human–machine system.

The machine on its own isn't enough, though. There also needs to be some way that the human being operating the machine knows what it is doing – some kind of **display**. That might be as simple as the position of an on-off switch, or it might be as complex as the multiplicity of dials and displays in an aircraft cockpit, but the purpose of the display is always the same: to inform the human operator of the machine's functioning. So a display presents the information in a form which can be picked up by a human being's senses. If it consists of warning sounds, for example, those sounds need to be pitched in a range which can be detected by human hearing and overcome background noise. If it makes visual signals, they need to be clear enough to be seen.

That may sound obvious, but there have been many examples of machines which have displayed information in a form which was either too faint, too inaccessible or too confusing for human beings to interpret. In early aeroplanes, for example, some accidents happened because the cockpit dials were set out in such a way that those which gave vital information were too easily overlooked. Redesigning how the dials were arranged cut down on those accidents dramatically. Studying how people pick up information from displays has been a major area of research in human-factors engineering for several decades.

After the information has been picked up by the human sensory system, it is then passed to the brain of the person operating it. At this point, a number of different aspects of psychological knowledge come into play. In Chapter 2, we looked at applied cognitive psychology, and at the kinds of factor which can influence our attention, both in terms of sustained attention over long periods of time and in terms of selective attention, or noticing particular things when there is a lot else going on. Many applied cognitive psychologists work closely with engineering psychologists in human factors and systems design.

Once the information has been taken in and processed, the person needs to take action of some sort. So the human–machine system includes the kinds of **controller** which the person will be using. That might be just using a finger to press a button; it might involve speaking, in the case of voice-activated systems; or it might involve complex co-ordination of different parts of the body. Driving a car, for example, means co-ordinating arm and leg movements, which takes some learning at first but which most people can learn fairly effectively.

The actual controls of the machine also need to be designed with the human being in mind. Foot pedals need to be of an optimal size, and engineered in such a way that they provide the right amount of resistance to give the operator proprioceptive feedback for their actions ('proprioception' is the sense we have which tells us about the positions of our muscles and joints). Similarly, a button must not be so stiff that it is difficult to press, but nor should it be so light that it responds to the slightest touch. The shape, size and action of controls can all make a considerable difference to how effectively the human–machine system is likely to operate.

I have talked about the human–machine system here, but engineering psychologists use the concept of system in the design of other artefacts, too. When new coins were introduced in the UK, for example, applied cognitive psychologists were closely involved in their design. In order to explore the optimal size, weight and shape of these new coins, the psychologists found it useful to consider coin usage as a system. So they looked at it in terms of the physical and social acts involved in using coins, everyday human behaviour, and cognitive factors such as human perceptual processes. In fact, systems analysis is applied to a wide range of human activities, because looking at things as working systems helps us to express and to analyse quite a lot of the complicated ways that people interact with their environments.

Ergonomics and efficiency

Modern ergonomics is all about adapting work to the human being who is performing it – fitting the job to the worker, as opposed to fitting the worker to the job. It first developed as a side-branch of the engineering industry, using insights from psychophysics and other aspects of experimental psychology, so most of the early practitioners tended to be engineers rather than psychologists. After World War II and its recognition of the importance of human factors, however, psychologists became more and more involved. Modern ergonomics is a multidisciplinary study, bringing together specialists from engineering, psychology and cognitive science to solve questions of human factors in design.

> **Insight**
>
> Ergonomics has to do with efficiency – the most effective way of getting work done. But as we saw in Chapter 12, being efficient in terms of work done can mean expecting people to act like robots. And at that point it becomes inefficient: people don't work well that way and days become lost through boredom, sickness and even unconscious sabotage.

We have already looked at several examples of ergonomics, and the one which has recurred time and time again is that of aircraft cockpit design. This is partly because it was that early research – and particularly the redesign of the cockpit of the Spitfire – which gave ergonomics the boost it needed to develop as a special part of the industrial design process. Since then, of course, ergonomics has become relevant in far more than just military contexts, and the advent of consumer society has meant that it has reached into just about every aspect of our lives.

One specialist branch of ergonomics, for example, deals with seating. In the modern world, we spend a great deal of our lives sitting down, and during the past five decades chair design has become a very large area of ergonomics. Research projects evaluate weight distribution, stressors, the consequences of different types of posture with particular designs of seat, and all sorts of other factors. The result is a huge diversity of different designs of chair, ranging from the simple classic dining-room chair, to specially designed office chairs, to trendy and sometimes avant-garde living-room chairs.

The reason for the huge interest in the ergonomics of chair design is twofold. One factor was the advent of widespread lifestyle consumerism in the 1960s. As people explored different lifestyles, new and imaginative furniture designs emerged. But many of these were designed with appearance in mind, and when people actually came to use them, they were uncomfortable or awkward. As the novelty wore off, consumers began to expect comfort and ease of use to become a part of the design, as well.

The other major factor was the development of health and safety at work legislation. Despite the fact that manual labour is becoming less and less common, back problems are on the increase; this is partly caused by the length of time that people spend sitting down at work. So researchers in this area began to explore the various ways that gravity and other forces act on the body, and what types of chair would be best to deal with them.

PSYCHOLOGICAL ASPECTS OF ERGONOMICS

One of the main problems of ergonomics, though, is that straightforward ergonomic solutions to problems are often not adopted. One of the most efficient of all office chairs, for example, is a kind of kneeling stool, which keeps the body in a kind of supported crouch, with the back straight. This design has been shown to be remarkably comfortable for sustained use, and to produce very little strain on the back or legs. Yet it has never really become popular. It takes a little getting used to, and many people are not prepared to give it an extended trial. They find its approach to sitting just too different from the chairs that they are accustomed to, and despite the evidence which shows that the body doesn't actually find it fatiguing, they feel that constantly keeping the back straight and not slouching will become a strain. So although the design is efficient, it is working against cultural assumptions, habits and expectations, and as a result has never become particularly popular.

Insight

Ergonomic designs are all very well, but people have to be persuaded to use them. Most changes in human behaviour are built on existing patterns, and we can accommodate a certain amount of novelty. But if a change is too different and takes people out of their 'comfort zone' of familiarity, then they won't take it up. The Sinclair C5 and many other innovations have failed on this principle.

A similar situation exists with the QWERTY keyboard which is in such widespread use for typewriters and computer keyboards. This particular arrangement of letters was actually developed in order to slow down typists, because they were operating early typing machines too quickly and there was a danger of the machines being shaken apart in the process. Sanders (1998) showed how ergonomic research reveals that there are many more efficient designs for keyboards, including designs in which the keys are used in combination, as chords, rather than just singly as they are at present. But these other designs have to fight against the massive cultural adoption of the QWERTY keyboard, and the typing habits which people have so painstakingly acquired. Efficiency, it seems, is not always the deciding factor.

Ergonomic specialists have had rather more luck with their research into the optimal ways of displaying verbal information. Although there are still many examples of badly constructed notices around, the systematic research which has been put into this area has produced some straightforward and practical recommendations, which those designing public notices often use to good effect. For example, it is often easier for people to read text in lower-case letters, because these give more information and can be read more quickly. Similarly, information should be presented using simple grammar and phrasing, and not very much at a time. There is also a great deal of research into the choice of colours and width of lettering which is most effective for different forms and levels of illumination. Designers of road signs and public safety notices frequently use these findings in their work.

Insight

Despite the extensive research into the readability of signs, it is amazing how many public notices are so badly designed that their messages are almost unreadable. Roadside signs with too many words, or with the key information in print that is too small, are classic examples.

There are, of course, many other areas of working life with which ergonomics is concerned. The control cabins of forklift trucks, cranes and other types of industrial machinery, for example, have incorporated the results of a great deal of ergonomic research over the years. The operators of these machines need controls which are straightforward and easy to use, but which will also give them manoeuvrability and rapid response times – they are so powerful that they could do a lot of damage if they did not respond rapidly to their controllers. They also need to offer good visibility and ease of access in all sorts of terrain, since they might be working in confined spaces or other difficult situations. So almost every aspect of these machines has been researched in detail, and the consequence is that they are very much easier to operate than their equivalents of 40 years ago.

Insight

Feedback is another essential factor for ergonomic design. People need to find necessary actions easy, but they also need to know and feel that they have made them. There is a precise science to adjusting the resistance in a fork-lift truck's controls, or the keys of a computer keyboard, so that they give the right feedback to the operator.

Design and interactivity

Ergonomics, as we have seen, is very closely associated with design. But there are many other aspects of design in which psychologists have been involved, and where the insights which can be gained from applying psychological concepts have been useful. There has been, for example, a great deal of research into colour preferences, and how people respond to different colours in different contexts. Colours are not just experiences: they can also be symbolic. It is not just coincidence that toothpaste packets always contain lots of blue or green and white. Those particular colours are closely associated in our minds with freshness, and that is exactly the association the toothpaste manufacturers want us to come up with when we look at the packet. Both advertisers and designers are very sensitive to how we use colour, and the messages we transmit with it.

Psychology is involved in other types of design, too. For example, in the 1990s, I was working with a number of designers and evaluators on the psychological aspects of interactive exhibits. Interactive exhibits are common in science centres, museums, zoos and many other places. They are exhibits for visitors which allow them to do things, in order to make things work – to pull levers, push buttons, turn wheels, balance objects and so on. People clearly enjoy interactive exhibits, and that is because they involve a number of different psychological mechanisms. The work I was doing with Science Centre personnel involved identifying and exploring those mechanisms, and showing how they lead to different types of outcome.

Figure 14.2 shows the overall model. On the surface, it looks as if the design of the exhibit produces the outcomes, but what is really happening is that it is triggering off a number of different psychological processes, which are what actually produce the outcomes. Looking at interactive processes in this way has been useful to a number of designers working in this area, as well as being useful for people who are evaluating interactive exhibits.

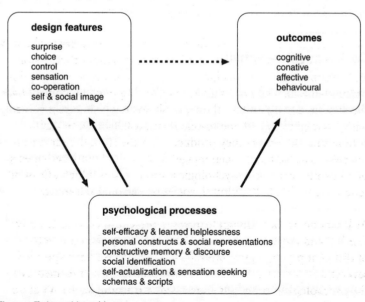

Figure 14.2 The interactivity model.

Insight

The psychological design features used in this model can be applied in many other contexts. Some teachers, for example, have used them as the basis for constructing interesting and enjoyable learning experiences in the classroom.

DESIGN FEATURES

The model identifies six sets of design features, but no single interactive exhibit is likely to encompass all six of them, and some of the design features can also be found in non-interactive exhibits. The first design feature is surprise and unexpectedness, which is largely self-explanatory. Some exhibits are explicitly designed to surprise people, or to present the visitor with counter-intuitive experience or information. The second feature concerns choice and multiple outcomes. This is the way that some exhibits allow people to make decisions, and to choose the actions that they will make when engaging with the exhibit, so as to produce different effects. The third design feature is co-operation and social interaction, and is about whether the exhibit involves people working together, undertaking joint actions or making joint decisions.

The fourth design feature is labelled 'sensation'. It refers to the way that some exhibits require people to use senses other than vision and hearing – they may include touch, smell, taste, proprioception or kinaesthesia. The fifth is all about exerting physical control over the exhibit. Some exhibits allow people to engage in direct control, with a straightforward one-to-one relationship between their actions and the results they produce. And the sixth design feature is referred to as 'self and social image', and is all about how aspects of an exhibit can elicit psychological mechanisms which affirm or reflect the individual's cultural, social or personal self-image.

At least one of these design features is present in every interactive exhibit, and most contain more than one. They elicit a number of different psychological mechanisms, of which I have specified several different sets. But they are also, sometimes, informed by the psychological processes concerned. For example, it isn't at all uncommon for an interactive exhibit to be designed in such a way that it is particularly relevant for a certain group of people, such as teenagers. It works by attracting their interest because of their belief that, as teenagers, they are different from other people and have special interests. And the design of the exhibit is adjusted to suit the interests of that particular group. So it is a two-way relationship, not just in one direction.

PSYCHOLOGICAL MECHANISMS

The psychological processes which are discussed in this model are also grouped into six sets, which is really just a coincidence – they don't match the six design features at all. The first group of mechanisms have to do with self-efficacy, and its counterpart of learned helplessness. Self-efficacy beliefs are all about how effective, or competent, we feel ourselves to be (see *Understand Psychology* or Chapter 11 of this book). A typical interactive learning task is designed to allow the individual to participate as an active agent in the learning experience, rather than as a passive recipient of information. In so doing, it challenges learned helplessness, and increases the person's sense of self-efficacy.

Insight

It is always good for us to feel competent and capable. This is why activities which heighten our sense of agency or raise our self-efficacy beliefs are so popular.

Another set of psychological processes relates to how we understand our worlds. People do not just approach knowledge passively. We act as scientists in our day-to-day lives, collecting experiences and formulating our own theories, or personal constructs, so that we can understand those experiences. We also draw on widespread shared social representations, about all aspects of human behaviour as well as about scientific topics. Both personal constructs and social representations are involved in how we make sense of interactive exhibits and the experiences that they give us. Indeed, science exhibits which are able to reflect or challenge commonly-held social representations can have a powerful, and memorable, impact on our understanding.

Other processes are concerned with constructive memory and discourse. The schemas and social scripts that we use as plans for action are active in our experiences – we have expectations about what is likely to happen and how we ought to behave, and exhibit designers often deliberately use established social scripts to make an exhibit memorable. We saw in Chapter 9 how memory is far from being a factual process, and the conversations that we have with people both during and after the event do a great deal to shape our experiences of it.

Insight

We all carry around a series of 'scripts' for how people ought to behave in particular circumstances, and they are important criteria which we use for judging social actions. Someone who doesn't conform to the scripts can be seen as anything from 'different' or 'odd' to 'abnormal' or even 'creepy'.

Some psychological mechanisms are to do with the mechanisms of social identification and positive regard. Social identity is all to do with group membership and, as we have already seen and will be seeing again in Chapter 19, it is deeply fundamental to the human psyche. An exhibit which can draw on social identity processes – a football-related exhibit, for example – will find a receptive audience. Similarly, people need to have positive regard from others. Embarrassing yourself in front of your peers can be a major turn-off, depending on the context, but appearing daring or achieving can be very attractive.

Another set of psychological mechanisms operate at a more physical level. One of these is sensation seeking. We actively seek experiences which break monotony and present us with challenges. There are individual differences in this, though. Some people actively seek out experiences which are physically challenging, while others prefer to have such experiences vicariously, through IMAX films, Wii or simulators. At a more mundane level, too, there is enjoyment to be gained from exploring and utilizing senses which we don't normally employ consciously, and many interactive exhibits draw on the way that we enjoy exploring sensory information.

The psychological processes that I have mentioned here are very well-established ones, which is why I have not gone into much detail about them. Different exhibits bring out different psychological mechanisms, but a great deal of the appeal of interactive exhibits has to do with how the human mind works, and the psychological processes going on in the background.

EVALUATING OUTCOMES

Exhibitors have often found it difficult to establish whether people have learned anything from their exhibits. Just asking people doesn't really tell us much, but this model identifies four different types of outcome, each of which has its own implications for evaluation: the cognitive domain, the conative domain, the affective domain and the behavioural domain. These domains have a long history, going back to the ancient Greeks, who identified three of them in the human psyche: cognitive, conative and affective. The cognitive domain consists of learning, thinking and remembering. The conative domain consists of planning, will-power and intentionality. And the affective domain consists of feelings: sensations, emotions and impressions.

These domains, the Greeks believed, were what activated the human mind. It works like a chariot being pulled by two horses: the cognitive domain is the charioteer, controlling and directing the horses, while the conative and affective domains generate the energy, or motivation, for movement.

In the early twentieth century, though, psychology came under the influence of modernist thinking and, in particular, behaviourism. Behaviourists argued that human beings did not really have will or intentionality at all. Instead, human behaviour was entirely a product of conditioning and environmental influences. As a result, they replaced the conative domain with the behavioural domain, concerned with actions, activities and habits. Nowadays, we see value in both the conative and the behavioural domains, so we end up with four outcome domains rather than three.

Interactive exhibits can have outcomes in the cognitive domain, in that people learn about a particular topic from them. Interactive exhibits also have outcomes in the conative domain, in that they may foster intentions or readiness to engage with 'science' – or at least with new learning experiences – in the future. Interactive exhibits have outcomes in the affective domain – they generate new sensations, they present challenges, and (most importantly) people enjoy them. And interactive exhibits have outcomes in the behavioural domain, in terms of what people do with them, how much time they spend with them, and also in terms of how people act towards them on future occasions.

Insight

When we are evaluating human activities, it's very important to separate intentions from behaviour. We can intend to do things and never get around to it, but even failed intentions may still influence later acts or beliefs.

This model has been used by designers, in developing interactive exhibits; by planners, in terms of articulating what the motivational aspects of a proposed interactive exhibit are, and what its outcomes are likely to be; and also by researchers evaluating interactive exhibits. It is just one way that applied psychology can be involved in design.

We can see, then, that engineering and design psychology is another very rich area, in which applied psychologists of one sort or another have been active in many different ways. What we have looked at here are just a couple of examples but, as with every branch of applied psychology, there are, of course, many more.

10 THINGS TO REMEMBER

1 *Engineering and human factors psychologists work with engineers and designers in refining various types of machine and system.*

2 *Human–machine systems always involve a display, a machine, and controls for the human to operate.*

3 *Including the human being as part of the system helps professionals to get better designs.*

4 *Ergonomics is about finding the most energy-efficient ways of doing things.*

5 *Health and safety at work has helped ergonomic design in some ways, but hindered it where it has become unreasonable.*

6 *Some of the best ergonomic designs are not accepted because they are too different from current use.*

7 *Colours can be important in how people react to products.*

8 *Interactive designs have specific psychological features which aid people's responses to them.*

9 *Design features draw on several well-established psychological mechanisms.*

10 *Outcomes for interactive designs can be in the cognitive, conative, affective or behavioural domains.*

15

Space psychology

In this chapter you will learn:
- *how psychology is involved in astronaut selection*
- *why psychological research can help individuals to function better in space*
- *about the work of the 'psychological support crew' who monitor Russian cosmonauts.*

We have seen how applied psychology covers almost all aspects of our daily lives. In a book of this size, it has only been possible to give an overview of some of the major areas, but applied psychology continues to grow, and to expand into new fields. This is happening partly because psychological knowledge is continually becoming better developed and more useful, but also because people are becoming more aware of just how valuable psychological knowledge can be.

The areas of applied psychology which we have looked at so far have relevance for very large numbers of people. But applied psychology also deals with some very special and distinctive areas of human experience, and the broad-ranging expertise which psychologists are able to bring to human problems has particular relevance when it comes to looking at how people adapt to, and deal with, unique sets of problems.

Space psychology is an example of this. It isn't – at least at present – a particularly widespread area of psychology, and it doesn't have all that many practitioners. But space flight is becoming a well-established commercial arena, and many nations are involved in space programmes of one sort or another. Even the UK, which is notorious for its lack of interest in space exploration, has its satellite research programmes, and a high economic dependence on satellite technology.

Space is developing as an industry. The regular service flights carried out by space shuttles and other spacecraft provide maintenance and adjustment services for many satellite networks, while the establishment of long-term bases in space such as Mir, Skylab, and the current Space Station, has opened up commercial opportunities which are being actively taken up by pharmaceutical firms and other manufacturers. These activities all involve human beings, often for long periods of time. Space psychology is concerned with maintaining those people's optimal functioning while they carry out a job which is stressful and demanding.

Insight

The space industry has already developed as a significant and essential part of human activity. Modern life is almost entirely dependent on satellites, for instance. But new applications are developing all the time.

Space tourism is one of the newer areas of economic activity in space. It might have developed decades earlier, but it was set back by the Challenger disaster of the 1980s, in which the first American civilian to go into space – a young school teacher – was killed along with the rest of the crew, because of bad decision making on the part of the launch committee. Modern moves towards space tourism began after John Glenn proved that it was not necessary to be young and in the peak of physical fitness to undertake space flight, and continued with short space flights being offered to tourists who could afford it by Russian and other space agencies. More recently, Richard Branson's Virgin organization has moved into the provision of leisure space travel, and plans to offer trips for 'space tourists'. The short bursts of weightlessness offered by high-speed aircraft looping through the upper levels of the atmosphere have also become popular leisure activities for those who can afford it and want to get a taste of the 'space experience'.

Being such a specialized area, space psychology doesn't yet have an established career structure. Many of the advances in this area originated with the Soviet space programme, although they have continued to develop since the collapse of the Soviet system. There has been some applied psychology involved in the US space programme, although many critics have argued that this has been far less than it should have been. Indeed, in 1986 Harrison argued that NASA had shown active resistance to the involvement of psychologists, either with the astronauts or in the conduct of space missions. That position is changing now, but it contrasts dramatically with the Russian experience, where an active psychological support team was directly involved both with the astronauts and with planning and ground control teams.

That psychological involvement was highly valued by the cosmonauts themselves. When a Mir cosmonaut returned to Earth after two years in space, a journalist asked him what advice he would have for anyone spending such a long period of time in such a confined environment. His reply was unequivocal: 'Listen to the psychologists.' The advice they had given him, and the ways they had responded to his changing needs, had provided the vital support he needed to see the experience through. Many other astronauts participating in the Russian space programme have found the same, and the first man in space, Yuri Gagarin, even co-authored a book on space psychology with one of the Soviet psychologists.

That doesn't mean, though, that space psychologists are only found in the Russian space programme. Psychologists have been active in researching various aspects of the space experience, and in developing better forms of evaluation and assessment for astronaut selection. Perhaps not surprisingly, much of the US-based research tended to emphasize the individual and their responses to space flight, while the Russian approach tended to integrate these with the social and environmental factors which are also involved. But international collaboration means that the two are coming together a bit more than they did before.

Astronaut selection

One of the first qualifications for astronaut selection, of course, is physical fitness. Potential candidates are put through a battery of physical tests designed to see how they will deal with weightlessness, spinning, and other kinds of disturbances of balance, as well as investigations of their general all-round health and strength. They are also tested for stamina and endurance, as well as short-term strength.

The assumption has always been that physical fitness would be needed because space flight is arduous and demanding. However, better design of spacecraft may be reducing some of the physical demands of the experience, and the recent experiment of sending up John Glenn, one of the first American astronauts, at an advanced age allowed researchers to evaluate just how essential being at the absolute peak of physical fitness actually is.

On the psychological level, selection for astronaut training with NASA tends to emphasize two areas. The first of these is making sure that candidates have a high level of skills and aptitudes for the complex tasks that they will be carrying out as part of their work. This includes the manipulative skills involved in fine precision work; perceptual skills, since accuracy in perception and judgement can be essential; and co-ordination skills, since they will be faced with learning entirely new ways of co-ordinating their physical movements while they are weightless.

The second area has been screening for psychological disturbance of any kind. The extreme crowding, physical discomfort and lack of privacy involved in space flight are highly demanding, psychologically speaking, and people need to have a high level of tolerance and mental adaptability to be able to cope with them. Someone who is subject to bouts of depression, anxiety or slight paranoia would be likely to find these exacerbated by the stresses of space flight, and that could produce problems for other colleagues, as well as for the mission as a whole.

On the Russian side, the selection of cosmonauts involves considerable attention being given to the psychological aspects of their training. They have to be fit and able to respond well to stressful situations, of course, and like their American counterparts they have careful psychiatric evaluation. But they are also given many different psychological tests, and their social interaction skills are carefully monitored. They are taught biofeedback techniques for regulating autonomic functioning and other physical systems, and they are also monitored during challenges which explore how they cope with uncertainty and other sources of stress. The emphasis on their social and interpersonal skills was developed as a result of considerable experience in seeing people through prolonged periods of time in space. We will be looking specifically at this area of space psychology later in this chapter.

The individual in space

Ever since Yuri Gagarin's first flight, researchers have been investigating the effect of space on individual functioning.

Much of this research has been physiological, investigating the effects of zero gravity (or microgravity) on digestion and other human body functions. But there has also been a considerable amount of psychological research into biorhythms, sleep patterns, the sensory illusions produced by being in such a very different context, and other aspects of individual psychology.

FUNCTIONING IN MICROGRAVITY

The experience of weightlessness is very different from our everyday experience, and we really don't experience it in any other context. There are some slight similarities with deep-sea diving, but gravity is always present in diving, even though movement may be freer, so it isn't really the same. How the body copes with microgravity has been a major focus of interest ever since space flight first started. When Gagarin first went into space, there was a lot of anxiety as to whether his body would be able to survive weightlessness at all, and great relief when the researchers discovered that it seemed to be a relatively harmless experience, at least for short periods of time.

But adjusting to weightlessness does present a bit of a challenge. We are so used to gravity acting on us all the time that we are often unaware of just how important it is. One of the studies carried out on the very first space shuttle flight was a psychological experiment, looking at how our subjective experience of weight changes in different gravitational fields. It consisted of a precisely calibrated set of balls, all of identical size but different weights, and the tests were designed to see how accurately the astronauts could distinguish between them. Other studies investigated the orientation illusions which astronauts often experience as they adapt to weightlessness. They feel that their bodies are in one position, where really they are in another. Kornilova (1997) observed that these illusions disappear as the astronauts adapt to weightlessness, but found they often reappear spontaneously, although briefly, after 50 or so days in space.

Other psychological research has included tests of cognitive skills, to see whether long-term space flights make any difference to individual functioning. Manzey and Lorenz (1998) reviewed a number of studies, and found that the only skills which seem to become disturbed as the result of a prolonged period in space are visual-motor tracking and multi-tasking: that is, carrying out two or more tasks at once. There were no impairments to memory or other complex cognitive functions, and the researchers believed that the effects which they did find were more likely to be a side-effect of adaptation to lower gravity conditions than an actual mental impairment.

SLEEP PATTERNS

Astronauts face considerable disruption of their normal circadian rhythms. These rhythms can be very powerful, and are strongly influenced by daylight and other such factors. All of the normal routines maintaining these rhythms are disturbed during space flight, and as a result many astronauts suffer from sleep disturbance or other problems. Stewart et al., (1995) developed a way of addressing this by administering simulated daylight at specific times of day, before, during and after two shuttle missions. The astronauts who had received the light treatment reported that they had slept better and felt that they had been in better moods and able to work more effectively as a result. Their ratings were compared with other astronauts on the same flights, and the researchers came to the conclusion that this would be a useful form of treatment for astronauts generally.

Insight

The fact that even astronauts are affected by circadian rhythms and respond to artificial daylight tells us just how powerful these factors are. We need much more sensitivity to these factors when we are engaging in activities which need far higher levels of alertness and precision than usual.

There are, though, a lot of individual differences in circadian rhythms, and it appears to be possible to minimize the disruption in other ways too. In another space shuttle study (Monk et al., 1998), the schedule was specially arranged so that it would fit as closely as possible to the astronauts' own established rhythms. The researchers collected a wide range of data, from assessments of mood and alertness to measures of brain activity during sleep. For the most part, they found that the circadian rhythms of the four astronauts on board were largely unaffected by the shuttle flight under the new system, although they did sleep less, and the sleep that they had was lighter. Under the old system, they had suffered much more disturbance.

Long-term space missions

Keeping people in space for prolonged periods of time has been going on for over 30 years. It first became possible with the launch of Salyut 6, in 1977, which was the first space station. This was followed by Salyut 7, and later by the Mir space station, and each of them became better equipped to support cosmonauts for long periods of time. The personnel who staffed these stations came from a variety of ethnic and educational backgrounds, and had to be prepared to experience close confinement, lack of privacy and a number of other stresses.

The purpose of these long missions was always as preparation for a future flight to Mars. This project is now also being discussed by NASA, and there is a distinct chance of such an expedition being launched at some time in the future. But being in space for two years or more is very different from spending a few months on a space station, and the Russian experience shows how important space psychologists are in those situations.

Space psychologists have drawn on other experiences of long-term isolation of small groups, such as submarine crews and Antarctic expeditions, to provide data for crew selection. Cheston (2004) outlined a number of aspects of psychological fitness for a long-term mission. Mixed-sex crews have been shown to get on better, perhaps because there is less competition and fewer internal arguments than in all-male crews. There also need to be enough people to provide a balance of personalities, and some studies suggest that between 6 and 8 people would be optimal.

Part of helping a crew to work effectively together is giving them the right kind of training. Having the right information matters – for example, research shows that if crew members know from the outset that conflicts and problems are going to arise when people are cooped up together in a small space for so long, they can handle those conflicts better when they do arise, and they feel less stressed as a result. Some psychologists have recommended that the crew should already have experienced a prolonged period together before beginning the mission, in order to identify and sort out personality problems which could become serious. But others argue that a much shorter period should be enough to show up any really serious problems, and others can be dealt with along the way. As the Russian experience showed, psychological training in group sensitivity and communication can do a great deal to maintain tolerance, and make sure that crew members can work together effectively.

In one study, researchers asked astronauts to identify the qualities needed for long-duration space missions. They found that traits such as agreeableness, extroversion and expressivity – that is, being able to express their emotions and ideas easily – were regarded by the astronauts as very important, while other traits that related to individual competences or skills were not. That doesn't mean that competence is completely unimportant, because as we have already seen, astronauts tend to be screened for those kinds of quality before they are even chosen to be part of the programme. So they probably just took that for granted. What the research does suggest, though, is that astronaut selection and training could usefully emphasize teamworking and social skills, as well as individual aptitudes and abilities.

Insight

It is uncertain whether personality tests would really be helpful in astronaut selection, apart from identifying obvious problems like over-anxiety or excess aggression. There is a danger in looking too hard for the 'right type', because a successful mission would need a mixture of personalities rather than just one sort.

CHANGING EXPERIENCES

A cosmonaut's experience during a prolonged mission is not all the same. The first two to six weeks tend to be periods of adaptation, in which the crew members are learning to deal with everything, and the psychologists' main role at that time is to help them deal with sensory overload. Later, though, things slow down and can become monotonous. At this time, the psychologists focus on providing novelty and variety – they might broadcast lively, stimulating music, or vary activity schedules and contact times. Sometimes, too, after several months the cosmonauts can begin to find loud sounds or unexpected stimuli disturbing, and at such times the psychological support group will brief the ground control team to make sure that their communications will take account of this, and not become too stressful. Towards the end of a mission, they focus on preparing the cosmonauts for their return to Earth, and the psychological demands which they will face at this time.

The psychological support which a cosmonaut experiences doesn't end as soon as they return to Earth. Space psychologists also help the person concerned deal with the consequences of their return. Some of this is physical – on their return to Earth after a prolonged stay, the demands of Earth gravity hit hard. Although they use special suits on board to help them prepare for it, they still have to re-adapt to standing and carrying weights again. The sudden transition from being physically strong and active to being as weak as a kitten is a tricky one to handle, and here again the psychologists can provide the mental assistance that cosmonauts need to deal with it.

Insight

Going from the peak of physical fitness to effective invalidism in one day can be quite extreme, yet that is what happens when a long-term cosmonaut returns to Earth. Psychological support is vital in such cases.

Psychologists also help cosmonauts to deal with the sudden fame which results when they return to Earth. This can be a big shock, particularly after such a long period of only being in contact with two or three other people. Adjusting to family life takes time too – both for the cosmonaut and for the other members of the family – and the psychologists sometimes have a role to play in helping them to deal with this as well.

THE PSYCHOLOGICAL SUPPORT GROUP

As you might have gathered from the previous section, the Russian space programme has always had a very active psychological support group, which monitors the crew of the space station throughout the mission. Their monitoring includes direct contact with the cosmonauts, and services such as counselling and advice if they feel they need it. But they also monitor several other sources of information which can indicate potential problems. Table 15.1 lists some of the measures which are constantly checked by the psychological support group in case they give an indication of a build-up of stress or some other problem.

Table 15.1 Stress indicators used by space psychologists

▶ *Spectral analysis of speech patterns in ground–space transmissions.*
▶ *Linguistic analysis of speech timing and intonation.*
▶ *Observations of body language from television images.*
▶ *Observations of interpersonal behaviour from television images.*
▶ *Direct personal communication with crew members.*
▶ *Evaluation of physiological indicators (e.g. heart rate, breathing, galvanic skin response).*

The psychological support group employs a number of trained operators who listen to the audio transmissions made by the cosmonauts all the time. They are trained to recognize five psychological states: the normal at-rest state; tension from work overload; tension from emotions; tension from fatigue; and tension from exhaustion. The human voice is subtly different in each of these conditions, and once one of the stressful states has been identified by a listener, that section of tape is subjected to formal analysis. The analysis includes looking at talking speed and how long silences last, as well as intonations and other kinds of signal.

It can be very useful in alerting the support group when someone is under more strain than usual.

Insight

Being able to detect stress at an early stage is essential for successful long-term missions. Voice stress analysis isn't perfect, but it does give useful hints, and alerts the psychologists to the need for intervention.

One of the areas where the psychological support group has been particularly active has been in the improvement of interiors, so as to provide the cosmonauts with an environment which they will find more comfortable. The lessons learned from the Salyut stations resulted in Mir having not only better-designed instrument panels, but also more colour and more pleasant illumination in the interior, and also having private areas where cosmonauts can have time to themselves. These improvements were highly rated by the cosmonauts, and their suggestions were taken into account by the psychological support group, who had been involved in the design of the Mir station from the very beginning. Many of these were also integrated into the design of the present Space Station.

The psychological support group also gives a lot of attention to the cosmonauts' free-time activities. Cosmonauts are well equipped with music and video systems, and a good range of different types of entertainment. Supply missions and visiting astronauts almost always bring new material with them, and they also bring favourite foods, letters and other minor luxuries. The crew have colour monitors so that they can have realistic two-way conversations with family, friends and the various celebrities who want to be seen talking to cosmonauts, and the psychological support group also uses these on occasions to broadcast music, news, and sometimes Earth sounds such as rainfall or birdsong. They also make sure that the cosmonauts have opportunities for personal, private communications with their family and friends. In such a confined environment, a small amount of personal privacy is really essential.

Space psychology, as you can see, is a very highly developed area of applied psychology, even though it has not been widely recognized in the West. Space psychologists are active in Japan, India, and many other countries with active space programmes, as well as in the ex-Soviet countries. As the Russian expertise in this area is being shared with NASA and the other partners in the Space Station programme, many of the people working in the field expect this area of applied psychology to become more widely known, and certainly more widely used. The lessons which have been learned from the Russian experience have already proved useful on many occasions, and will become even more so if the nations concerned ever do succeed in their avowed goal of human beings travelling to Mars.

The lessons learned from space psychology are not just of use for those who are off this planet. They have been put to use in other contexts too, such as in Antarctic exploration, with submarine crews, and in other situations where people are forced to remain in closed, cramped environments for long periods of time. Applying psychological insights in these areas can make a huge difference to how people survive the experience – and sometimes, even, to whether they manage to survive them at all.

There are many other types of specialist applied psychology – there is even a specialist area of survival psychology, in which applied psychologists conduct research into the best ways to survive in various types of disaster, and also help people to deal with the aftermath of being involved in them. There isn't, though, the space to deal with all of them in this book, so in the next chapter we will return to one of the more 'mainstream' areas of applied psychology, and look at how applied psychologists use their knowledge to help sportspeople to enhance their performances.

10 THINGS TO REMEMBER

1 *Psychologists have been involved ever since the very beginning of the space race.*

2 *Space psychology is becoming more established as space develops as an industry.*

3 *Russian cosmonauts have found the advice of space psychologists invaluable.*

4 *American astronaut selection emphasizes individual skills and physical fitness.*

5 *Microgravity can distort judgements of weight and other perceptions, but does not seem to affect other cognitive skills.*

6 *Applying psychology can help to minimize the disturbance to circadian rhythms felt by astronauts.*

7 *Long-duration space missions are seen as preparation for a future voyage to Mars.*

8 *Crews for long missions need to be carefully selected to ensure they can get on together for the whole time.*

9 *Cosmonauts have different psychological needs at different times during long missions.*

10 *Russian psychological support groups have extensive experience of supporting cosmonauts for long periods in space.*

16

Sport psychology

In this chapter you will learn:
- *four different types of skill required in sport*
- *how skills become automatized*
- *how mental activity can enable a sportsperson to achieve physical success*.

Sport psychology has become an increasingly important area of applied psychology. As society in general has become more conscious of the value of sport and the health benefits it brings, there is more and more interest in the many different factors that can influence sporting performance. Psychological factors of various kinds are involved in sport, ranging from an improved understanding of motivation, to the development of better practising routines and schedules, to the use of mental training to aid athletes or other sportspeople to achieve peak performance.

Insight
Sport has always been such an important part of everyday living that it isn't really surprising to learn how long-established sport psychology is.

Like professional psychologists in other areas, sport psychologists are required to have a recognized first degree in psychology, some relevant working experience, and further professional training in the form of a higher degree and supervised practice. They work in a variety of contexts. Some are employed full-time by sports teams or coaching centres; some work as independent consultants with several different clients; and some are based in universities, where they carry out research into sport psychology and also engage in consultancy with teams and sportspeople.

Interest in the psychology of sport has existed for a very long time, and research in this area goes back to the 1920s, and sometimes even earlier. As a result, there has been a wide body of knowledge built up, concerning all sorts of different aspects of sport. These include studies of the personality characteristics of sportspeople – which have often seemed to be a little inconclusive, since people of so many types undertake sport at all sorts of levels. They also include learning studies, in which psychologists investigate the best way of arranging practice sessions to optimize skill learning, and all sorts of other questions. There isn't space in this chapter to cover them all, so we will look at just three areas here: at the question of motivation in sport; at skill learning; and at psychological approaches to achieving peak performance.

Insight

The drive to perfect and master skills seems to be inbuilt in the human being. It may be one of the distinguishing features of the human animal, it may be something which all mammals share and only human beings are aware of, or it may be an example of the human being's 'extended childhood'. Whatever its origins, though, it's a powerful motivator.

Motivation

What motivates people to do sport? It's very apparent that some people are keener on it than others, but what is it that makes the difference? Why do people take to some sports rather than others? Why do some practise seriously while others are content with just one session a week, or even less? And what is it that makes people keep on learning or performing a sport, even when that leads to actual physical discomfort, or even pain?

People do seem to be highly motivated to become competent at things. Even when we are small babies, we take delight in mastering physical skills, and this is a distinctive characteristic in children too. In part, this comes back to Carl Rogers's idea of the importance of self-actualization to human psychology. Self-actualization (see also *Understand Psychology*), is a very fundamental need in people, and it involves making real, or actualizing, our potential. Learning physical control, and how to express just what one's body is capable of is an example of this. So the Rogerian explanation for sporting motivation would be that physical development and achieving maximum performance is deeply satisfying for so many people because it satisfies their basic need for self-actualization.

PERSONALITY AND BEHAVIOURAL TRAITS

Other psychologists see the key to sporting motivation as coming from certain personality characteristics, or typical behaviours. One of these is the need to achieve success. Achievement can take many forms – it might simply mean reaching a personal best, or managing to perform a complex activity in a skilled manner, rather than winning a trophy. But in the 1960s and thereabouts, **achievement motivation** was seen as being a relatively stable trait, which people could have more or less of.

Achievement motivation has been described as having two distinct sides. One side is the motive to achieve success, while the other is the motivation to avoid failure. These sides have different characteristics, and different people tend to have one or the other type of achievement motivation. They can be distinguished because those people also have very different ways of behaving and thinking about their sport.

People who are mainly motivated to achieve success tend to look actively for challenges, and to be concerned with developing excellence in their performance. They also try harder and longer to master a difficult skill, and value feedback from other people. Typically, too, they are not afraid of failure, and attribute their performance to their own efforts. If they fail, for example, they see it as having been due to poor concentration or not enough effort; while if they succeed they attribute their success to the hard work and effort they have put in. Perhaps because of all this, such people enjoy performing in situations where others are evaluating their performance.

Some people, though, seem to be mainly motivated to avoid failure. They tend to avoid taking on difficult challenges, but instead choose easier matches or situations. They also tend to worry a lot about the idea of failing, and they dislike situations in which other people might evaluate them, and in which they might fail, because they regard failure as shameful. Perhaps as a result, such people tend to perform worse in competitive situations or if their performance is being judged by others. They also – which is quite a key finding for trainers and coaches – tend to attribute their performance to external factors, such as luck or being prevented by circumstances from practising at some crucial time.

Insight

There are certain differences in personality which can lead us to be more or less prepared to put in the effort needed to be successful. Attributional styles have a lot to do with it, as does self-efficacy, but it seems likely there really is a personality trait which can be summed up as 'achievement motivation'.

Atkinson's model has some drawbacks, but it raised some interesting issues. For example, the question of attributing success or failure to internal or external factors is a very important one in sports training (see also *Understand Psychology*). People who make internal attributions about their success or failure take personal responsibility for them. As a result, they work harder to overcome them, and are much more likely to be successful. People who attribute their success to external factors, on the other hand, rarely manage to achieve peak performance. Because they attribute failure to bad luck, to the situation, or to problems with their equipment, they don't work as hard to improve their performance. And as a result, they don't manage to achieve their full potential.

INTRINSIC AND EXTRINSIC MOTIVATION

Another approach to understanding motivation is to look at the difference between intrinsic and extrinsic motivation. Intrinsic motivation is motivation that comes from the person themselves – working to achieve a personal goal of some kind. Extrinsic motivation is motivation which comes from outside sources – working for rewards such as medals, or praise from other people.

As with internal and external attributions, intrinsic motivation is an extremely powerful force. Many older people who take up sporting activities do so purely on the basis of intrinsic motivation. They want the satisfaction of developing a personal skill, or of feeling fitter, and they recognize that they are unlikely to achieve much in the way of awards or certificates, because of having begun so late in their careers. Indeed, some sports – notably golf – are almost entirely dependent on the huge numbers of people who join the sport when they are older, even though the high achievers in the field are those who began playing it at a very young age.

Sport provides many opportunities for extrinsic motivation: there are certificates of achievement, medals, competition trophies, and any number of other types of reward. These are important for the structure of the sport, and for providing the participants with a sense of achievement. But coaches and sport psychologists recognize that working purely for extrinsic rewards is not a good thing in the long run – that some level of intrinsic motivation is also needed if the individual is to put in the massive amounts of time and effort required to achieve their personal best. On their own, extrinsic rewards are not usually enough for people to keep up sustained effort.

That doesn't mean, though, that extrinsic rewards are bad. Their value in sport is that they act as evidence of achievement – as definite statements that the person concerned has reached a particular standard, or a particular target. When they act as 'signposts' in that way, they can be extremely useful in helping the person to strengthen their internal sense of achievement, and in providing them with manageable goals that they can reach.

There is a story of an old man who wanted to stop kids hanging around his garden and making a noise. Instead of telling them off, he offered to pay them, saying he enjoyed hearing them around. He kept this up for a couple of times, but then offered much less money on the grounds that he couldn't afford any more. Disgusted, they said it wasn't worth it and went away to play somewhere else.

Many of the reward systems for beginners run by sporting organizations work on the principle that providing novices with certificates of achievement will encourage them to progress through the difficult early stages, until their competence reaches a level where they can obtain personal satisfaction from their performance. They each represent a set of small, manageable goals which the person can work to achieve. The amateur 'Fun Skate' certificates, swimming certificates, and similar reward systems operated by other professional sporting associations have been established deliberately with this in mind.

Sport psychologists working at higher levels in the sport also use **manageable goals** – sometimes with extrinsic rewards but more often without – to structure an individual's training and skill acquisition sessions. People work harder when they believe it is possible to achieve the goal they are working for, but if they think that what is expected is too difficult or too remote, it is hard for them to retain motivation. So part of the job of a sport psychologist in that situation will be to work with coaches and others to establish manageable goals which will motivate athletes or players, and help them to put in the training and effort that is needed.

Skill learning and practice

Sport psychologists are also involved in carrying out research into skill learning, and in developing the optimal type of skill learning programme for the particular sport with which they are concerned. The types of skill required by different sports are very variable. Weightlifting is an example of what is known as a **gross motor skill** – that is, a skill which involves lots of muscular effort, but not too much precision. Ice-skating, on the other hand, is a sport which involves a high level of precision and accuracy. Since the performer is – quite literally – balanced on a knife-edge, and sometimes even jumping on and off it, every muscle has to be accurately positioned and carefully controlled. That is known as a **fine motor skill** – not 'fine' as in 'good', but 'fine' as in 'precise'.

Most sports, of course, fall somewhere between these two extremes, but the amount of precision or the amount of sheer strength involved will affect the type of training programme that the person performing the sport needs. A footballer, for example, needs to have general fitness, strength and endurance, in order to maintain a high level of performance throughout a 90-minute match. But footballers also need to practise precision skills when it comes to dealing with the ball itself, so that they are able to capitalize on any opportunities which may arise.

Another useful distinction which sport psychologists make is between open and closed skills. This is all to do with how predictable the environment is, in which the skill is being performed. Archery, gymnastics and figure-skating are examples of **closed skills**, in that they tend to take place in very predictable situations, and most attention is focused on the performance of the skill itself by the individual. Football, wrestling and ice-hockey, on the other hand, are **open skills**, because there is no way of predicting exactly which action is going to be relevant at any given time. That depends on the opponent or the other team members, as well as on the situation the person is in and where the ball is.

Open and closed skills require different approaches to training. The type of practice which is needed for closed skills tends to focus on muscular precision and being able to repeat activities accurately. The type of practice which is needed for open skills tends to focus on reading cues in the environment, and responding rapidly to changing situations. But as with gross and fine motor skills, sport psychologists have found that almost all sports respond well to a combination of both types of training. Being able to adapt to unexpected situations may not be a common skill in figure-skating, but someone who is able to do so generally has a better overall command of their skill than someone who cannot, so some training in different situations is often very useful. Similarly, closed skill training can be useful to refine the technique and improve focus in people who normally perform open skills. A champion tennis player will spend as much time refining precision and muscular technique as they spend on their response time and reactions, because both of these are valuable in the game itself.

AUTOMATIZATION

Understanding skill acquisition also involves understanding the process of **automatization**. In simple terms, a skill isn't a skill until it has become so well learned that we don't even have to think about it. The process becomes automatic, so that all we have to think about is what we want to achieve, and that is enough for us to carry out the skill properly.

All physical learning involves automatization. Perhaps the best way for most people to think about it is to think about what happens as we learn to drive a car. At first, we have to think, consciously, about all of the controls and what they do. Changing gear involves recognizing when it is appropriate from the situation or the sound of the engine, depressing the clutch pedal, moving the gear lever, bringing the clutch pedal back up, and so on. As we get more practice, these actions begin to combine themselves until they happen automatically.

Insight

Automatization is at the heart of skill learning, but the only way it can happen is through practice – doing the same thing over and over again. Without practice, even people with talent will not be able to develop really high levels of skill and expertise.

Automatization actually involves a shift in the part of the brain controlling the activity (see also *Understand Psychology*). Conscious movement is mediated by a part of the brain known as the **motor cortex**, more or less at the top of the head. This is the part of the brain that we use when we make a deliberate muscle action, such as deciding to raise a hand, or wave a finger. But when we make unconscious actions, the control comes from another part of the brain, known as the **cerebellum**. That is at the back of the head, and it co-ordinates all the different small muscle actions so that what we do is smooth and even.

Shifting control of a series of actions from the motor cortex to the cerebellum is all about practice. The more practised we are at doing something, the more that particular sequence of actions becomes stored as a routine, and the more the cerebellum gets involved. And that is what is involved in skill automatization. There are other parts of the brain involved in performing skills too, of course – we need, for example, to have the sensory systems involved, so that we can use visual or auditory information to tell us when to act. But cerebellar control is the key to performing actions smoothly and without having to think about them.

Annett (1989) explained how complex skills are often built up by the combination of lots of different smaller skills. This is a model which is frequently used by sport psychologists in developing training and practice programmes. Some of the training programme is based on **part-learning**: that is, practising a small part of a complex skill until that part, at least, becomes automatic. But another section of the training programme is based on **whole-learning**: that is, practising the complete skill. The combination of whole- and part-learning helps the sportsperson to gain the fine control they need, while not losing sight of the way that the skill needs to be applied in context.

Practising complex skills can be quite a demoralizing process for people who are unaware of the psychology of skill acquisition. Typically, when we learn a new skill we show a gradual improvement for a while; this is known as a **learning curve**.

Either the time taken to do something, or the accuracy of how we do it, gradually improves as we practise it more.

Insight

Most of us have had the experience improving at something and then going through a period where that improvement stops. But if we persevere, we eventually start to improve again. Sometimes, the brain just needs to consolidate what it has already learned.

But that only lasts for so long. Once someone has learned a basic level of skill, they quite often go through a period in which they don't seem to be improving at all. These periods are known as **plateaus**, and they happen often in the course of learning. In fact, what is happening is that the skill is becoming consolidated at a deeper level in the brain and as 'muscle memory'. So although it seems as though the person isn't improving, what they are actually doing is establishing a better baseline for future performance. If they keep practising and don't give up, they eventually begin to improve again – and when they do, it is on a much firmer basis.

Another important concept in skill acquisition – and therefore in sport training – is the idea of **feedback**. Nobody can improve on a skill if they don't have any idea of how they are doing. But sometimes we need more specialized feedback as well. Professional athletes often gauge their training quite closely on the basis of exact timing or other performance indicators. They are constantly trying to improve on their personal best. People who are just engaging in sport for hobbies tend to have different feedback needs: they do need a general idea of how they are getting on, but often they are content with the feedback from their own performance and how they felt on that particular occasion, rather than needing to compare themselves to other standards.

Insight

We can't learn skills without feedback, because we need to be aware of what we've already done to be able to improve it. You couldn't learn to play darts blindfold, could you?

Achieving peak performance

Another important area of sport psychology is in helping athletes or other sportspeople to achieve peak performance. We have already looked at some ways that this might happen, particularly through dealing with the internal and external **attributions** which people make for success or failure. A sport psychologist may often work quite hard with an individual athlete helping them to change their typical pattern of attributions, and the way that they think about the source of excellence in their own performance.

Insight

Exams and sporting competitions have a lot in common. There is just one occasion when you have to do your best, but you have plenty of time to prepare. The advantage of applying psychology is that it helps you to know the best ways to do that preparation.

But there are other ways that sport psychologists can help people to develop more positive mental styles. One of them is in the use of **mental imagery**. We tend to assume that the images we conjure up in our minds have very little to do with how our muscles behave. But actually, this isn't the case. There is a very close relationship between mental imagery and the physical reactions of our bodies.

MENTAL PRACTICE

We saw something of this in Chapter 9, when we looked at how lie-detector tests work by detecting the slight physical changes which happen when someone has an anxious thought. There also seem to be changes in muscle tone when people imagine themselves moving particular muscles, and many modern sport psychologists train their clients into what has become known as **mental practice**. It can be surprisingly effective.

In one study, for example, a group of researchers asked people to imagine performing a finger exercise 20 times a day, over a four-week period (Smith *et al.*, 1998). They had another group of participants who were actually performing the exercise rather than just imagining it, and those people improved their muscle strength in that finger by 33 per cent. But surprisingly, the group who had only imagined the exercise also improved their muscle strength, by 16 per cent. Mental practice is no substitute for physical practice, obviously, but it does seem to be able to contribute something to the process of learning.

Insight

Whenever we imagine physical movements, we send tiny nerve messages down to our muscles. They aren't big enough to move the muscles properly, but they still help performance, probably by strengthening the nerve pathways.

Coaches and sport psychologists also find that mental practice is useful in refining exactly how people perform complex skills. They ask their clients to imagine performing the exercise correctly, often and at regular intervals. Those sportspeople practise physically too, of course, but what the trainers find is that backing up the physical practice with mental visualization can help the skill to become properly learned in a much shorter time. It's important, though, that the person visualizes doing the skill exactly right, so they do have to have had at least one physical experience of having managed it to make sure that the mental imagery is realistic.

VISUALIZING SUCCESS

High-performing athletes have yet another use for mental imagery, and that is in visualizing success. There has been a great deal of research on the value of positive mental imagery when people are preparing for competitions and high-level tests. David Hemery, the Olympic gold medallist, described how he had experimented with mental imagery while he was competing. One year, he had tried to be realistic, preparing himself for the possibility of failure. That year, he didn't achieve very much, so during the next season he consciously used positive mental imagery, imagining himself performing his hurdle races accurately and fast, and imagining himself winning as a result. That was the year that he won his gold medal. Not only that, but his practice times were significantly improved throughout the time that he was using the technique.

There are many other cases of athletes using positive mental imagery to good effect. Linford Christie is another classic example, who consciously used mental training to focus his mind and to prepare mentally for the sprint events at which he was so successful. Other players who rely on accuracy of performance, such as snooker players, also use it to good effect. Sport psychologists have developed a number of techniques for teaching sportspeople how to use positive mental imagery to enhance their performance, and many of them conduct workshops and training sessions with coaches and trainers in these methods.

Insight

Positive thinking has been shown to be the best thing to do in almost every situation, including sport. So why do we always insist on being so negative so much of the time?

There is, of course, far more to sport psychology than we have been able to cover here. But you can see from this, I hope, that psychology can contribute a great deal to our understanding of performance in sport, and how we can improve performance. Or, in the case of people who use sport as a hobby rather than a profession, to maximize our enjoyment as well as our sense of achievement. At a personal level, I have found it very useful indeed. As someone who only began to learn ice-skating at the age of 40, I found the insights offered by sport psychology to be tremendously valuable – not because I have any ambitions to be a star performer, but just in helping me to overcome some of the mundane tribulations presented by the new set of physical challenges.

10 THINGS TO REMEMBER

1 *Sport psychology is one of the oldest areas of applied psychology.*

2 *Motivation is an important topic in sport psychology. Need for achievement is relevant, but not the whole story.*

3 *Intrinsic motivation is more effective and lasting than extrinsic motivation.*

4 *Rewards and medals are not enough in themselves, but have value as signposts for goal achievement.*

5 *Sport psychologists have considerable expertise in skill acquisition.*

6 *All skill learning involves automatization, and this is only achieved through practice.*

7 *Skill learning often has breaks in improvement, known as 'plateaus'.*

8 *All skill learning needs feedback.*

9 *Good athletes make internal, controllable attributions for failure, rather than external ones.*

10 *Mental practising and positive visualization can help an athlete to achieve peak performance.*

17

Consumer psychology

In this chapter you will learn:

- *three areas in which consumer psychologists are active*
- *how cognitive psychology has helped advertising to become more effective*
- *the importance of 'heuristics' to our understanding of consumer decision making.*

Modern living in Western societies is all about consumerism. We are very rarely able to live on our own produce – instead, we buy what we need, and a lot that we don't need as well. What we buy depends on the lifestyle we have chosen to adopt, on the beliefs we have about diet and fashion, on the number of people involved in our household, and on many other factors. So perhaps it isn't surprising that consumer psychology has been an active part of applied psychology for a very long time.

Insight

Consumerism is so much a part of our lives that it has become part of our self-images. People who go to live in places where consumer goods are unavailable often feel very isolated as they adjust to being unable to define themselves through the consumer choices that they make.

Consumer psychology seems as if it is a new area, but oddly enough, it was one of the earliest forms of applied psychology. In the 1920s, the behaviourist J.B. Watson went into advertising when his career as an academic was abruptly terminated because his affair with his secretary came to light. Psychologists were already working in advertising, and Watson was very well known, so he was offered a job very quickly.

In those days, advertising was a relatively minor part of the US economy. During the subsequent century it grew dramatically throughout the Western world, and the massive explosion of consumerism in the 1960s gave it a prominence in society which is still going on. Consumer psychologists work in just about every area of the consumer industry. They work in advertising, bringing psychological knowledge to bear on the design, construction and placing of advertisements. They work in marketing research, identifying and analysing trends and patterns in what people are buying and when. They work in product appraisal, conducting research projects studying people's responses to new products; and they conduct research into consumer behaviour, looking at how people actually go about spending their money.

Insight

The explosion of advertising in the 1960s made a radical difference to society. Because of the novelty of the slogans and jingles, many are still remembered today where later ones have been forgotten.

Some consumer psychologists go into the area as a result of having undertaken a recognized degree in psychology and then carrying out research into the area, so that it has become seen as their specialism. Some are employed directly as graduates, and extend their specialist knowledge while they are pursuing careers in the marketing or advertising industries. Most consumer psychologists, however, undertake specialized training – several universities run Masters' degrees in consumer psychology – and people wanting to make a career in this area will often take one of those.

Figure 17.1 illustrates a model of consumer psychology. As you can see from the model, there are five different areas. The heart of the model consists of the decisions which the consumer makes, and the other parts identify just how those decisions are influenced. They are influenced, for example, by the individual person's own personality – factors such as our beliefs, our attitudes and values, and our motivation all make a difference to what we buy. They are also influenced by what we do and don't remember – and as we saw in Chapter 9, human memory can be pretty fallible! So this is another area where psychological knowledge contributes a great deal to the consumer process.

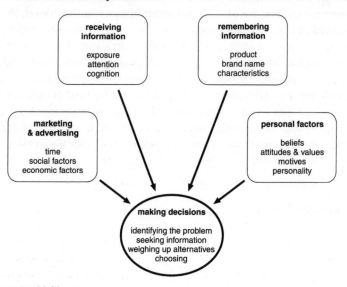

Figure 17.1 A model of the consumer process.

One thing missing from the consumer model in Figure 17.1 is the idea of lifestyle. Lifestyle implies whole patterns of consumerism, rather than the purchase of single objects, and it is all focused around an idealized self-image. The concept of lifestyle allows advertisers to group together and classify various products. It works both by framing and directing choices, and by reinforcing the social images that people have of themselves.

Insight

Some new products are not targeted on a single lifestyle, but on many. The iPhone and its range of apps, for example, was marketed in an extremely successful series of advertising campaigns which could relate to a vast range of lifestyles – not by going for a common market, but by emphasizing diversity and choice.

Another important area of psychology which contributes a lot to the work of consumer psychologists is their knowledge of how we receive information – how we notice things, how our attention works, and how we process information at a cognitive level. We looked at how applied cognitive psychologists have explored attention in Chapter 2, and a great deal of this work has relevance for understanding the consumer process. And, of course, the other area which influences the decisions which consumers make is how particular products are marketed and advertised. In this chapter, we obviously can't look at all of these, but we will look briefly at three areas in which consumer psychologists are active: in advertising, in marketing research and in the analysis of consumer behaviour.

The psychology of advertising

We are surrounded by advertising, in just about every section of our day-to-day lives, from the speaking clock to the designer emblems on knitwear. Advertisements are aimed at specific groups in the population, and carefully placed where members of those groups are most likely to encounter them. And they are carefully worked out so that they will attract attention, and encourage the person to be aware of the product concerned.

COGNITIVE FACTORS IN ADVERTISING

We have already seen how applied psychologists have investigated attention – what attracts our attention, and how long it can keep on doing it. Advertisers face a particularly strong challenge in this regard, because there are simply so many advertisements around. If they want to make their own advertisement stand out, they need something special, which will attract our attention and make us interested.

There are many ways that advertisers do this. Perhaps the oldest approach, but one which is still occasionally effective, is to use bright colours and catchy tunes to attract our attention. There is a great deal of research into the psychology of colour – not just how people respond to different colours, but also what different colours symbolize in everyday living. I mentioned in Chapter 14 how toothpaste packaging always tends to use white with blue or green, because those colours symbolize freshness. But there are more subtle symbols, too. The packaging for Italian foodstuffs, at least in the UK, generally includes green and red, because those colours symbolize Italy in the public mind, being the colours of the Italian flag, and also reminiscent of tomato and basil – distinctive ingredients of much Italian cooking.

Puzzles and problem solving are another way that advertisers put psychology to work. Most people enjoy seeing things which are problematic or unusual, and some particularly popular adverts are those which organize whole sequences of actions as a challenge or puzzle. This keeps the audience interested, and the mental 'work' involved in solving puzzles or identifying how things work helps people to remember the product far better than simple repetition would.

Insight

Music is one of the oldest but also one of the most effective ways of advertising a product. Musical jingles can stay in the head, and some classical tracks are now better known from their use in advertising than from their original contexts.

SOCIAL FACTORS

Another well-established technique is to use a celebrity, or someone who is well-known, to promote the product. Racing drivers, pop stars, quiz show presenters and other such people are all regularly asked to participate in various forms of advertising, and the product concerned is carefully matched to their likely audience. Pop stars, for example, tend to be asked to advertise fizzy drinks or other products associated with the teenage market, while racing drivers would be more likely to advertise watches, cars, or other products which suggested precision engineering.

Many advertisements draw heavily on the social representations of the society in which they are located. They are shared beliefs about how things happen or why things are like they are, and they form a firm set of assumptions which social knowledge is often based on. Television advertisements often draw on shared knowledge of this kind, involving their audience by making reference to things which they already know. Sometimes, this is based on things that have been in the news recently, but more often it will be a reference to a popular TV show or something of the sort. The comedian Harry Enfield, for example, found that the characters he had created for his television show were so widely recognized that they could, at that time, become the basis of a whole range of advertisements.

Insight

Humour has always been a popular way of attracting viewer attention in TV adverts, but it can backfire. Sometimes, what advertising executives think their target audience will find funny is very different from what that audience actually does think. Interestingly, such adverts don't fail because they are too clever. They fail because the target audience finds them either patronizing or insulting.

APPEARANCE AND PERCEPTION

Magazine and poster advertisements also draw heavily on shared knowledge, but they put into effect a great deal of research into design, layout and everyday symbolism too. This brings in knowledge from a wide area of psychology, including the study of perception, ergonomics and even brain functioning. It is known, for example, that the right side of the brain is slightly better at processing visual images, while the left side of the brain is better at processing text. So magazine advertisements often have the words on the right side of the advert (so the image of those words will fall on the left side of the retina in the eye and be passed to the left side of the brain), and the pictures on the left.

Not all adverts do this, of course, because advertisers also have to guard against their biggest enemy, which is boredom and predictability. But arranging the advert in this way means that its message is more likely to be noticed if someone is just idly leafing through a magazine. Contrast, colour and lettering are also carefully chosen to convey clear messages, and sometimes also a particular social meaning. A style of lettering which looks like attractive handwriting, for example, takes longer to read but may be used in an advertisement to convey an impression of style and quality.

Applied psychology has been put to use in just about every area of advertising, ranging from the design of the advertisement itself to the placing and time of the advert. The main TV channels, for example, broadcast very different advertisements at different times of day. Daytime television advertisements often emphasize domestic products, while advertisements broadcast during children's peak viewing time deal with toys and other child-oriented products. The afternoon 'teatime' programmes are surrounded by advertisements for products designed to help elderly people cope with day-to-day living – stairlifts, orthopaedic beds, bath supports and the like – while evening advertisements frequently emphasize cars, alcoholic products and internet services.

AVOIDING HABITUATION

I mentioned before that boredom is the main enemy of advertisers. If we are exposed to the same stimulus – any stimulus – continually, we tend to habituate to it, which means that we don't notice it any more. You may have come across this in the case of a humming fridge, for example. Generally speaking, you only notice the background noise it was making when it suddenly stops. Our nervous systems are geared to respond to changes in stimulation, not to continuous stimuli.

The same thing happens on a wider level too: we don't particularly notice the things we come across every day, unless they suddenly change or someone draws our attention to them. So advertisers need to make sure that we actually notice the product that they are trying to promote, and in order to do this they draw on psychological knowledge about how our cognitive processes operate. Novelty is important in this, as we have just seen, but it is also important to avoid overstimulation, because people respond to that by shutting off their attention, too.

One of the best ways that advertisers have found to get round this is to use humour. We remember things that amuse us, and so an entertaining advertisement is more likely to fix the name of the product into our minds. Nobody expects people to run out and buy something as soon as they see an advertisement for it. What advertisers actually aim for is that, next time we are buying something of that type, we should remember the name of their particular product and think about it positively. That can make all the difference between buying that particular product or a similar one.

Another way of fixing a product name in our minds can seem rather strange, but it is often used by advertisers very effectively. That is, by not revealing it. Cognitive psychology, as we saw in Chapter 11, shows us that we remember things better if we have to do mental 'work' to receive them in the first place. The more mental processing involved, the more we are likely to remember. So an advertisement which attracts our attention, but which requires us to think quite hard to work out exactly which product it is promoting, can be very effective. Once we have worked out what the product is, its name is very likely to stick in the memory.

Insight

Leaving out important information would have horrified the early advertisers, but in today's advert-full society advertisements where people have to stop and wonder what is actually being advertised can be very effective.

Interestingly, this finding is exactly contradictory to what some of the early advertising psychologists would have predicted. Behaviourists such as J.B. Watson believed that all human learning was based on forming a strong association between a stimulus and a response. When they applied this to advertising, the stimulus was the product they were trying to sell, and the response was the consumer buying it. So many of the old 'hard sell' advertisements had strong repetitions of the brand name, together with repeated exhortations to buy it. It was an approach which may have worked quite well before advertising became so widespread, but modern consumers tend to be rather more sophisticated. There are still a few of the old-fashioned styles of advertisement around, though.

Marketing research

Marketing research is a significant industry in modern life, which employs very large numbers of people including consumer psychologists. Market researchers explore just about every aspect of the marketing process: they conduct research into product development and placement; they conduct research into sales – how the product is actually displayed or in other ways made available to the consumer; they conduct research into the customers who are buying the products, and what their distinctive characteristics might be; and they conduct research into promotions of various kinds, ranging from 'two for the price of one' supermarket promotions, to the selective advertising of a luxury product to a small group of people.

Research as varied as this requires effective research skills, and many psychologists become involved in the field because of their expertise in this area. All recognized psychological degrees give students a very thorough training in research skills, and in different ways of analysing data. So psychology graduates often end up in marketing research because they are familiar with different ways of obtaining information from people – and with the problems and challenges that involves.

GATHERING INFORMATION

The process of gathering information about what people do may seem straightforward, but as anyone with any psychological training knows, that is an illusion. People act in all sorts of different ways, and even though they don't mean to, they can often mislead researchers. Market researchers gather data indirectly, through information about product sales and retail reports; but they also carry out research with people directly. These research projects mainly take the form of observational studies, interviews, questionnaires and field experiments. But each of these ways of collecting information has its challenges.

One problem with observational studies, for example, is that people behave differently when they know they are being watched. So observations of consumers need to be either covert – that is, where the observer is hidden from the consumer – or set up artificially, in simulations where people are trying deliberately to act in the ways that they would normally act. Some market researchers are able to use closed-circuit TV records for analysis; sometimes, too, they may carry out research on telephone sales by tape-recording the conversations salespeople have with customers.

There are ethical problems raised by covert observation, of course. Both the Marketing Research Organization and the British Psychological Society operate very strict ethical guidelines, which cover deception and covert observation as well as other aspects of ethical practice. What these amount to is that consumers have a right to be informed when they are in situations where they might be observed, so that they can choose whether to participate in that research or not.

There are problems with questionnaires, too. Questionnaires are very difficult to design well and a badly designed questionnaire can give entirely misleading information. But often, the person who has designed the questionnaire and is analysing the results from it doesn't realize just how misleading the information is. That happens because of a problem known as the **questionnaire fallacy** – the belief that the choice of answers provided in a questionnaire actually reflects what the person does. But people will always try to tick the boxes available. Even if there is a separate 'other' box provided, they will avoid using it because it is easier just to tick the main categories given. As a result, the answers people give in questionnaires rarely reflect their true behaviour. Instead, they reflect how good people are at responding to the options that the questionnaire designer has provided.

> **Insight**
>
> The best marketing information is that which reflects what people actually do. Records of sales are good, and so are diary methods and open-ended accounts. So it is surprising that market researchers still rely so much on questionnaires.

Designing a good questionnaire is a complex skill, involving lots of stages, such as piloting it on a test group and formatting the questions. Experimental studies have their problems too, and interviews present challenges when it comes to analysing open-ended data. If you want to know more about this type of thing, you could look in my book on research methods (*Doing Psychological Research*), which goes into them in some detail. But most applied psychologists are familiar with these kinds of problem and how to overcome them.

> **Insight**
>
> Marketing research has always suffered badly from the questionnaire fallacy. The best way to find out what people do is to ask them, and let them answer in their own way. This is more costly than using questionnaires, but giving people preset choices means that they give answers which fit those choices, and don't necessarily reflect what they actually do.

Consumer decision making

The other area in which consumer psychologists are particularly active is that of analysing consumer behaviour – that is, how people act. This includes looking at the decisions that they make, the patterns of behaviour which they show when shopping or making purchasing decisions, and how they respond to various types of consumer demands or initiatives. In the rest of this chapter we will look briefly at how psychology has enhanced our understanding of consumer decision making.

Decision making has been a major area of research for cognitive psychologists, and consumer psychologists have put to good use many of their findings. We make decisions all the time, ranging from trivial ones such as what type of sandwich we are going to have for lunch, to important ones which can affect our whole lives, such as which career path to choose, or whether to take up a job in a different part of the country.

When we make decisions, we very rarely use all of the information available to us. Instead, we use a set of shortcuts, known as **heuristics**, which help us to streamline the amount of information we need, and how we will use it. There are quite a lot of minor heuristics which people use, but the three main ones which are used in consumer psychology are availability, anchoring and decision frames.

AVAILABILITY

Availability relates to the way that some information is more readily available to us at any given time. We might have been reminded of something recently, or have just seen an advert about a particular product, and that means that we will bring it more easily to mind than other, equivalent products.

There are a number of factors which can influence availability. One of them is vividness – if the image of a product is particularly striking or different, it will stand out by comparison with others. The iMac computer, for example, is very distinctive. It has a distinctive shape which is very different from other computers, it is much easier to set up and to use, and it lends itself particularly well to 3D games and designs. Factors like that mean that for many people, the iMac comes most readily to mind when they are thinking about stylish home computers, which contributes a great deal to its enormous commercial popularity.

Another factor in availability has to do with the everyday social scripts which affect how we live our lives. Most social interaction falls into fairly predictable patterns, so we know what to expect from one moment to the next. This too affects consumer behaviour. Someone moving into a new home, for example, may make the purchase of a jar of instant coffee a priority even if they don't normally drink it, because offering visitors a cup of coffee is an established social script when visitors arrive.

Insight

Availability is the goal that all advertisers strive for – to be the brand that comes immediately to mind when people think of a particular product. In the early days of consumerism, that was quite easy, and a lot of brand names entered everyday language – Hoover, Biro and so on. But nowadays, availability is much more temporary. There are some examples, such as the iPod, but not many.

ANCHORING

Anchoring relates to how we use established information as the baseline for making comparisons. It is used in consumer psychology in many ways, but one of the main ones is in pricing policies. People have ideas about how much certain things should cost, and they use these ideas to make judgements about whether something is a 'good buy' or whether it is too expensive. House prices are a good example of this. Someone moving into an area where house prices are lower than where they used to live is likely to regard the price expected for a particular house as reasonable, if not cheap. Someone coming from another area, where house prices are even lower, might regard the same house as expensive. They use their previous knowledge as anchoring for their judgements about the current situation.

Another aspect of anchoring which catches us more often than we would like is known as **entrapment**. This is where we feel obliged to continue with a losing situation, because we have already invested a great deal of time, effort or money in it, which would be wasted if we stopped. Someone who buys a second-hand car always runs the risk of entrapment. A car might seem to be a good buy, but then develops a whole host of small problems, each of which costs money to fix. After the consumer has put a certain amount of money into fixing one problem after another, they are often reluctant to get rid of the car and get a new one, even if that would be the sensible thing to do, because that would mean that the money they had already paid out had effectively been thrown away.

Being trapped in that sort of situation is familiar to most people, and consumer psychologists have given a lot of attention to where people will draw the line. At what point do we say 'enough is enough', and what are the decisive factors which can influence someone in doing that? Researchers have also investigated the type of precaution consumers will take to avoid that happening, and some consumer products, such as the RAC pre-purchase car-checking package, have been established on the basis of just that kind of research.

Insight

It is in the advertiser's interest to ensure that we avoid entrapment and buy newer products. But drawing the line between when to repair and when to replace can be tricky. Many everyday items can be repaired surprisingly cheaply, but it is more common for people to throw them away than to repair them.

DECISION FRAMES

Decision frames are another factor in the way that we make decisions. These are all to do with the way that the question is being asked, and the background context in which it is located. These factors act as a kind of 'frame', which shapes the decisions that, people make. For example: a decision to shift from buying vegetables through a supermarket to subscribing to an organic vegebag delivery scheme would involve a number of factors. Availability and anchoring are involved, of course, but the framing of the decision is also relevant.

For example, it is likely that a person making this type of decision already has a commitment to eating organic produce, so that affects how the whole question of obtaining vegetables is perceived, and cuts out a lot of other consumer options. Similarly, the type of organic provision provided by the local supermarket sets the context of the decision, and the person's beliefs about supporting smaller business may also be a factor, as will the amount of time they have available for the preparation of fresh vegetables.

Research into decision-making, then, is one small part of the way that consumer psychologists study how people behave in various consumer situations. Like other areas of applied psychology, consumer psychology is a complex field, and one which offers a great many challenges to the psychologists who are involved in it.

10 THINGS TO REMEMBER

1 *Consumer psychology has existed for a long time. It is concerned with the decisions that consumers make.*

2 *Advertising uses many symbols and conventions, such as colours, for their psychological effects.*

3 *Celebrity endorsement draws on social representations and identity processes for its effects.*

4 *Consumer psychologists have shown how fonts and layout make an impact on information transmission.*

5 *Many advertisements aim to stimulate surprise or interest, to challenge habituation or boredom.*

6 *Old ideas about advertising involved repeating the brand name many times. But modern adverts are more sophisticated.*

7 *Marketing research is about gathering data from consumers about their marketing practices.*

8 *Some marketing research practices have been questioned on ethical grounds, such as those involving invasion of privacy.*

9 *Consumer decision making involves mental shortcuts like availability, anchoring and decision frames.*

10 *Entrapment is a process whereby people feel unable to change something that is failing because they have already invested so much in trying to make it work.*

Environmental psychology

In this chapter you will learn:
- *about three types of territory*
- *how psychological mechanisms are involved in 'green living'*
- *different ways in which our environment might cause us stress.*

In this chapter, we will be looking at the branch of applied psychology which is concerned with human beings in their environment – the many different ways in which the environment can affect human behaviour. These can range from studies of human reactions to urban overcrowding, to research into how redesigning living spaces can change the ways that people act.

Insight

The word 'environment' has come to mean a lot of different things. It may relate to green issues, to animal habitats, to people's everyday surroundings, to air temperature and quality, or to whether a place is natural or built-up.

The environmental psychologist Tony Cassidy described environmental psychology as having a long history, but a short past. Psychologists have been interested in how the environment influences people for almost the whole time that psychology has existed, and some major schools of thought in psychology have been based on the idea that environmental influences of one sort or another are the complete cause of everything we do. At the same time, environmental psychology as a specialist branch of the profession is relatively new, and although interest in the area is growing very fast, there are still relatively few people who are specifically employed as environmental psychologists.

There are some, though, and at present they tend to work mainly as independent consultants. They are increasingly asked to contribute to the planning of large-scale environments, or to housing projects or leisure facilities. They work with architects and planners on urban design, and with countryside trusts and sometimes local councils on recreational land-use projects. They also work with large commercial organizations in the planning of commercial ventures, such as large shopping malls and leisure complexes, and sometimes they work on a small scale, investigating specific problems such as a high incidence of traffic accidents in a particular area.

As with many of the newer areas of applied psychology, there is no single, systematic way of becoming an environmental psychologist. It is important to have a recognized degree in psychology, of course, and some people specialize in that area during their degree course and then pursue their interest in the field afterwards. A few are employed directly as graduates, usually on a project which will require extensive evaluation skills. Some go into the area as a result of pursuing a specialized training course, such as a Masters' degree in environmental psychology or a relevant doctorate. And others are academic psychologists who pursue research into the area in their university and consultancy in the field.

People and territories

People, as you may have noticed, have quite strong notions about the spaces that they live in. This ranges from the personal space we like to keep around ourselves, to the preferred areas of living space which we occupy, to the area we regard as being our own 'territory'. Some people compare this to animal territoriality, but it isn't really the same. Territoriality in animals is almost always seasonal, to do with mating and bringing up young, while human beings just seem to like to have their own personal bases which they can use as 'home' while they are in that area.

Our sensitivity to the spaces around us goes deeper than that, too. Even our memories are powerfully linked to how we move around our environments. You may have had the experience of trying to remember something, and finding that if you think back to the place you were in when you heard about it, it comes back to you. People who are forced to remain in one place without moving for long periods of time – perhaps because of a broken leg or a back injury – often find that their memories are strongly affected as a result. By losing the ability to move around in their environments, they lose the indexing system which lets them know what happened when. As a result, memories become much harder to store. A lot of the memory loss suffered by infirm older people has to do with the way that they can no longer move around at will.

In fact, our memories are so strongly linked with locations that one of the oldest mnemonics – memory aids – involves taking an imaginary walk and placing special images at particular locations on that walk. This is known as the **method of loci**, and it works because going over the route mentally provides the context to remember the images, and that provides us with the cues to the information which we need to remember.

Insight

Some people have argued that people are naturally territorial and that therefore wars are inevitable. But this has two problems – firstly, that people often share territories willingly; and secondly, because there is a world of difference between the immediate territories which we experience, and the abstract concept of territory involved in ideas like nationhood.

FORMS OF TERRITORY

In *Understand Psychology*, we looked at the idea of personal space, and the kind of 'comfort zone' within which we feel comfortable having a conversation with someone. But we have other types of personal space, too. Back in 1975, Altman said that we have three types of territory: primary, secondary and public. These are described in Table 18.1. As you can see, our territories can range from having our own bedroom to having a favourite chair in the living room or a particular table in the pub or café. Bars in Germany generally have a 'Stammtisch' – a special table where the regulars sit, and which strangers are expected to leave alone. Many other countries have similar traditions; and that is another form of territoriality. We also like to define our living space carefully, as is evidenced by the large domestic industry based around selling and maintaining fences and walls.

Table 18.1 Forms of territory

Primary territories	Territories which are private and carefully guarded against intruders, e.g. someone's home or, within a household, their bedroom.
Secondary territories	These are more open to other people, but are still not entirely available to all, e.g. a classroom or a local youth club.
Public territories	Territories which are open to just about anyone for temporary occupation, e.g. phone boxes, bus seats or park benches.

Source: Altman, 1975

People protect their territory in all sorts of ways. We use boundary markers such as coats or bags when we are in libraries or food bars; we use posture and disapproving facial expressions if we feel that people are coming too close; we use locks and fasteners on doors and lockers; and we use physical obstacles such as fences or other barriers to stop people entering an area where we don't consider that they are entitled to be. We define such spaces as 'private', and use that concept to limit other people's access to them.

CROWDING

Modern living often brings us into contact with crowds: when we are shopping, while we are engaging in spectator sports, when we are travelling, and in many other situations. Crowds are not always unpleasant. Indeed, they can sometimes be a very positive experience. Most football supporters, for example, find that the experience of being part of the crowd is an essential part of their enjoyment of the match, and many people enjoy wandering around the shops in busy town centres or cities on a Saturday afternoon.

So crowds can be stimulating – but as with any other form of stimulation, they can also become stressful. Part of this is because of the way that we react to strangers. We have already seen, and will be seeing again in the next chapter, how we naturally tend to see the world is in terms of 'them-and-us' groups, and we usually feel more comfortable with people we regard as 'us'. In the case of the football supporters, total strangers are connected by a common sense of unity of team support. But most of the time, 'us' means people that we know and recognize.

Our nervous system reacts differently to strangers than it does to people we recognize. We are more alert, more wary, and sometimes – depending on the culture we are in and our own personal experiences – more suspicious. Even when we live in cultures in which people are friendly towards strangers, they are still noticeable, and our attention is drawn to them. It is a natural part of our evolution as social animals, and one which is built in to our nervous systems.

The problem with urban living, though, is that we come across strangers all the time. In small, rural communities, the people we meet during the course of daily life are usually well known and familiar and strangers are unusual. But in modern urban contexts meeting someone we know is the more noticeable event. We can encounter hundreds of strangers in the course of a single day, and that puts quite a strain on the human nervous system.

PRIVACY

That means, of course, that we place even more value on the idea of privacy, and on having areas of our lives where we can restrict access to all but known people. Private living space, personal work spaces and recreational clubs are all an important part of urban life, because they represent areas where strangers are less common – and as a result, we find them more relaxing and easier places to be. They act as coping mechanisms which enable us to deal with the stress of crowding and urban life.

Like territoriality, privacy is an important concept in environmental psychology. The problem is, though, that actually defining what privacy means is pretty tricky, because it varies so much from one person to another. For some people it means being left alone by all other people. For some it means associating with others, but still retaining the ability to shut out strangers or the general public. And for some, it means having a private area that they can retreat into, where nobody else can go unless by personal invitation.

This variation suggests that there isn't any particular 'inbuilt' desire for privacy shared by all people. Indeed, if we look at the very different ways that people live around the world, we can see that the whole concept of privacy varies so much from one culture to another that it isn't necessarily the same thing at all. It seems to be mainly to do with how we live, and how we respond to the stresses on our particular lifestyles and in our own environments.

Insight

Some psychiatric diagnoses have more to do with crowding and lack of privacy than with physical disorder. What may be seen as eccentricity in a family with plenty of room for people to pursue hobbies in private, may become extremely stressful in a small house with limited living space. The social tensions can build up so much that they result in mental illness.

EXTREME CROWDING

Extreme crowding, which doesn't permit us to use those coping mechanisms, can have tremendously damaging effects. As we saw in Chapter 15, even in the design of the Mir space station it was important that the astronauts should have a little bit of private space.

Nobody can be with other people all of the time, and the psychological effects if they are forced to be can be profound. People experience changes in mood, leading to heightened levels of aggression and sometimes also depression; they become more irritable and far less tolerant of other people's idiosyncrasies; and they become much more likely to regard all the other aspects of their lives negatively. Some of the animal studies on overcrowding carried out in the 1960s, when they did research like that (it wouldn't be allowed now), showed massively increased levels of violence, and even cannibalism and infanticide when animals became seriously overcrowded.

Human adaptability means that human behaviour doesn't get that bad. But stress from crowding can damage relationships at all levels – both friendships, partnerships and families. Learning to cope with overcrowding means finding ways of adjusting our environment so that it can offer some kind of privacy or personal space, and allow the individual concerned to establish appropriate coping mechanisms.

There are, of course, enormous cultural and individual differences in this. The kind of privacy common in the prototypical suburban US home is actually quite extreme, and uncommon in most human cultures. Many people share their living space with several others – family members, friends, or other members of their particular community. But although they are well adapted to living with others, that adaptation also involves establishing their own privacy in some way – by spending some part of the day away from the home, or by cultural practices which establish periods without everyday conversation or without eye-contact with other people.

Crowding in urban environments correlates with crime, too. In one study of 175 US cities, the researchers found that the more people there were living in a given area, the higher the crime rate. This included murders and rapes as well as car thefts and robberies, and it didn't matter what type of residential area it was. Moreover, increasing the population density in an area resulted in an increase in crime rate, while decreasing it produced less.

Other factors are involved too, of course. One of them is poverty, which is always the single most significant factor influencing the crime rate in any country. Densely populated areas, for the most part, tend to be areas in which people are quite poor, and that is part of the answer. But increased crowding also leads people to a sense of anonymity, or deindividuation, and that too can make a difference to whether people are likely to commit crimes or not. Put that together with the emotional and cognitive intolerance produced by urban stress, and the sense of injustice from constant comparisons with lifestyles portrayed by the advertising industry, and the result is a situation in which urban crime becomes far more likely. The social scripts in TV and films which portray violence and crime as everyday occurrences don't help much, either.

HELPFULNESS

At the same time, people have a powerful tendency to co-operate with one another. Studies of bystander intervention show that people are far more likely to be helpful to strangers than not. Researchers have investigated why people don't help sometimes, but that has often caused them to overlook the fact that their data show how most people actually do help others. And there are numerous other instances of people helping one another out, and working to improve their environments and develop community living. The challenge for the environmental psychologist is to show how all of these processes can be put to good effect, to enrich the ways that the environment influences day-to-day living.

Green living

In recent years, another aspect of environmental psychology has been developing, which is all to do with the relationship between human activity and the wider environment, reaching as far as the whole planet. The realization of the damage which human activities have done to the ecosphere has shifted from a minority concern to a widely held social representation. As a result of this, people in the

Western world are being asked to adjust many of their habitually wasteful ways of living, and adopt a more eco-friendly lifestyle.

Psychologists have been involved in helping to manage these changes. In many cases, their role has been to mediate between the autocratic demands of governments and large organizations, and the comprehension and sometimes suspicion on the part of the general public. Behaviour can be changed, but it doesn't change easily – and ordering someone to change their behaviour is just about the least successful way of getting them to do it!

Insight

In science, it is the general consensus of evidence which matters, not the findings of single individuals. Environmental research has several examples where the views of single scientists or small groups have been taken by the press or politicians as much more of a challenge to the general scientific consensus than they really were. But the overall consensus is that the typical Western lifestyle is too wasteful, and needs to change.

In one study on water management, for example, Sefton (2008) discussed how people are very willing to become involved in community water projects which make sense to them. But they will refuse to change everyday habits or other aspects of their water use simply because of advertising campaigns or directives produced by the local water authority. This is partly because people need good reasons to change their behaviour – reasons which fit with their own personal constructs and social representations of such matters – and partly because of a well-established suspicion that the water authority is acting in the interest of shareholder profits rather than in the interest of society as a whole.

Insight

One recent 'green' change concerns the use of polythene carrier bags. Until about 2007 in the UK, they were seen as commonplace, but although they are still in use, there is a much greater acceptance of the value of reusable shopping bags, which have now become more popular.

WASTE AWARENESS

Having said that, people do change their behaviour over time, and the way that we treat household waste is a clear example. This is partly because of a growing awareness and acceptance of environmental concerns, but also because the actual process of recycling has become a great deal more manageable. For decades, the UK maintained the somewhat ironic position that only car drivers were able to recycle their household waste, because only they were able to transport it to recycling points. During the 2000s, however, recyclable waste collections from households became commonplace, which made recycling a manageable goal for most of the population.

The key to introducing these changes has to do with the psychological concepts of self-efficacy and manageable goals. If people feel that their actions can be effective, they are more likely to continue to make the effort to maintain those actions. We all need positive self-efficacy beliefs to maintain our motivation – it is difficult to keep up our efforts if we don't think that what we are doing is effective.

We also need to be able to take practical steps towards achieving our goals. As psychologists have shown in many contexts, having manageable goals is also a key motivator. Large-scale dramatic goals like 'save the planet' are fine as a general direction, but they tend to leave people feeling rather helpless in the face of such a big task. Having smaller, practical goals that people can achieve, which contribute to the larger goal but are not so very different from what they already do, is much more effective. And each small step can provide a stepping stone for the next one.

CONSUMER POWER

The ecological problems being caused by human activity have been identified since the 1970s and even before, but green campaigners made little impact on society for several decades. It was often asserted that people were apathetic about these issues, but some psychologists believe that it wasn't apathy, but learned helplessness which was the problem. People felt ineffective and helpless, and found it difficult to see what effective action they could take. Conflicting messages from different groups of experts, combined with 'doom and gloom' or extreme puritanism from many ecological campaigners, all acted to reinforce the sense of helplessness.

One example which supports this view was what happened on the one occasion when a clear and unequivocal connection was made between everyday consumer activity and damage to the planet. When the damage which CFCs were doing to the ozone layer became widely known, products containing CFCs vanished from the supermarket shelves overnight. This wasn't because of the foresight of supermarket managers – it was because ordinary people simply stopped buying those products. When they had something concrete they could do, which would really help, they acted straight away.

Insight

Consumer pressure can act rapidly, like the CFC example, but it can also grow more slowly, such as the demand for organic foods which has increased slowly but steadily since the 1980s.

The psychological mechanisms of self-efficacy and agency, as we have seen, are significant motivators from 'green living' activity. In 2008, *New Scientist* reported how a consumer-based initiative in Germany had significantly reduced electrical consumption, and also contributed a significant amount of 'clean' power to the national grid. Not only that, but it had stimulated relevant industries and contributed to the overall economy.

What had happened was that the government had agreed to buy electricity produced by micro-generation – small domestic sources such as solar panels or domestic wind turbines – at a fair and slightly above market price. This gave people an economic incentive to install such things, which eventually made a significant contribution to the national electricity supply. But those people became more aware of the electricity they were using as well as the electricity they were generating, and many shifted to a less wasteful use of power. The economic incentive had empowered people and allowed them to take greater control of their lifestyles, and the consequences both in terms of power generation and in the economics of the country as a whole more than covered the cost of the economic incentive itself.

THE 'CARBON FOOTPRINT'

Other aspects of consumer power, such as the increasing demand for locally sourced food, all demonstrate the general willingness of the public to act in ecologically responsible ways. In this context, the concept of the 'carbon footprint' has become the social representation which links all the different ideas about green living together, and gives people a framework within which they can see their actions becoming more effective. By encompassing so many everyday activities – food, transport, energy use, waste, etc. – it allows people to set their own manageable goals and encourages a sense of self-efficacy. As many psychologists have shown, intentions are not enough to change behaviour on their own. Being able to take practical action relatively easily is just as important.

Insight

The carbon footprint may be the greatest environmental gimmick ever. It allows people to make comparisons between one aspect of their lifestyle and others (did you know that keeping a dog and feeding it on proprietary dog food has a bigger carbon footprint than running a four-wheel drive car?). Expect more of these comparisons as the concept becomes ever more popular.

Environmental stress

The environment can affect us in all sorts of ways. A visit to the seaside or a particularly beautiful part of the country can help us to feel uplifted and serene. Moving around in a crowded city might leave us feeling tense and anxious. Socializing in a pub or at home with friends might leave us feeling relaxed and cheerful. But the environment can also be a major source of stress – particularly in urban, built-up locations.

Urban stress can take many forms, and is an ever-present factor in most people's lives – so much so, that many people often don't even notice it until they go on holiday or move to a quieter location. Even if we are not noticing it, though, the stress is still there, and we are only just beginning to acknowledge the damaging effects that it can have – ranging from ulcers, heart attacks and diabetes to asthma and migraines.

Insight

Human beings are so good at adapting that it is difficult to quantify the effects of environmental stress. We can acclimatize and continue to function in very unpleasant circumstances, and the harmful effects of that acclimatization may not show up for many years.

NOISE

Environmental stress can come from a number of sources. Crowding, which we have already looked at, is one source. Noise is another. In urban environments, for example, there is a constant background noise, which the people who live there become adapted to, but which is nonetheless stressful for the body as a whole. That noise usually comes from traffic, but it can also come from the maintenance machinery for the large buildings which characterize cities. Constant background noise has increasingly become recognized as a stressor for human beings – so much so, that it is often referred to nowadays as 'noise pollution'.

There are other types of noise pollution too – most notably the very loud noises caused by aircraft and other types of industry. Aviation authorities operating airports often put local people in touch with special sources of funding so that they can get their houses soundproofed; but they still have to cope with the noise when they go out into the garden. People can adapt to this type of noise pollution too, so that they hardly notice it; but it is still stressful.

Insight

We are often completely unaware of how much background noise there is around us. What frequently surprises people when they holiday in remote areas is just how deep the silence is. Sometimes, city people even find it hard to sleep at first because it is so quiet!

Many firms have found it useful to employ an environmental psychologist to analyse how the effects of noise pollution at work can be reduced. Their proposals may be relatively straightforward, such as the installation of sound-absorbing barriers, or they may involve a complete redesign of the working space. Sometimes, too, they work with occupational psychologists in a job redesign which will also help to reduce the problem.

TEMPERATURE AND POLLUTION

Temperature can also have a strong effect. Several studies have shown that there is a correlation between weather patterns and cases of riots or civil disturbance, and some have argued that the increased likelihood of civil disturbance during hot periods is a direct outcome of the stress induced by unusually hot weather. Others see the connection as arising from more social factors, such as the way that people in urban environments spend more time out on the streets during hot weather, and so are more likely to notice what is going on. If what is happening is socially unjust, such as particularly heavy-handed policing, then public reaction is more likely simply because there are more people around to hear about it.

Insight

Urban riots have been blamed on any number of factors, including temperature, lead in petrol, and diet. But every time
(Contd)

that riots are investigated, it is poverty and perceived injustice which have acted as the mainspring. Looking for other causes just distracts attention from the underlying social problems.

The human body reacts to pollutants in many subtle ways – they can produce specific disorders, such as asthma and allergies or heart disorders, for example, or they can have a more general effect on our general health. Dealing with pollution places a significant strain on the body's resources, and that in itself is enough to lower people's resistance to other illnesses, making them very likely to catch colds and other ailments in overcrowded environments.

Pollution affects people psychologically, too. Rotton *et al.* (1978) showed that there is a strong connection between moods and air pollution. When air pollution is lower, people feel happier and more relaxed, and they also rate other people and the things in their environment more positively. High levels of air pollution have a bad effect on both our own moods, and on how we see the world around us.

There are ways that these stressors can be reduced, and environmental psychologists often work closely with other specialists to identify ways that urban environments can be improved. Some trees, for example, have a cleansing effect, absorbing pollution from the atmosphere and raising the level of free oxygen. They also have a positive effect on people's sense of well-being, in that people find areas with growing things to be more relaxing. So many city development areas, and particularly traffic redesign projects, have tree planting built into the proposals. As the trees mature, they help to make the environment slightly cleaner.

Similarly, redevelopments in city areas often build in other features which are more relaxing for people, and will help them to dissipate stress. Herzog *et al.* (1982) showed that the areas in cities which people found most pleasant were the places that included natural features, such as trees, grass and water. People also like architecture which is distinctive and in harmony with its surroundings. Old, untidy and dirty settings such as factories and alleyways are generally regarded as the most unpleasant features of cities – along with the traffic pollution, of course. So city redevelopments often include open spaces for pedestrians. Shopping malls, too, generally include areas with waterfalls and plants, because of the way that they help people to relax.

We can see, then, that environmental psychology is another rich area of applied psychology. It brings together psychological knowledge from many different levels: from our physiological responses to sensory stimulation, to our sense of community and belonging. And, as ever, there is far more to this area of applied psychology than we have been able to deal with here.

10 THINGS TO REMEMBER

1 *Environmental psychology has only recently been widely recognized.*

2 *People are very sensitive to the spaces they move around in.*

3 *There are different forms of personal territory, involving different degrees of privacy.*

4 *Crowding can be stressful because of the constant contact with strangers.*

5 *Green living involves people adjusting their lifestyles to minimize damage to the planet.*

6 *The key to environmentally-friendly lifestyle change is manageable goals.*

7 *Self-efficacy beliefs are important to motivate people to take effective action in environmental issues.*

8 *The carbon footprint idea allows people to assess the impact their lives make on the Earth, and act to minimize it.*

9 *Noise, temperature and pollution can all contribute to environmental stress.*

10 *Many people are unaware of the stressors present in their environment until they go somewhere more peaceful.*

19

Political psychology

In this chapter you will learn:
- *how the fundamental attribution error applies in conflicts*
- *how multiple social identifications can help people to see their enemy as similar to themselves*
- *why the perception of social justice is so important to the resolution of conflict.*

The final area of applied psychology we will look at is also one of the most recent: political psychology. Psychologists are involved in many aspects of the political process, including contributing to **psephology** – the study of voting patterns in elections, the form and content of political choices, reconciliation of industrial disputes, and the use of diplomacy. In this chapter we will look at how psychology can contribute to some of the most important political events affecting us – major internal and international conflicts.

In the period since World War II, internal conflicts within nations have escalated, and accounts of genocide, ethnic cleansing and other extremes have become distressingly frequent. In some of these situations, the differences between religious, ethnic and other social groupings have become exaggerated, and hostility between the various group members has become so acute that the conflict has eventually become so extreme as to require diplomatic intervention from the United Nations.

Yet at the same time, in most countries of the world, people from different ethnic and religious groups live side by side and in peace. Amicable co-operation between groups is far more common than conflict, and most modern nations manage to establish multi-ethnic, multi-religious communities without obvious tensions. These don't hit the news, of course, and so we often gain the impression that conflict is more common, but that really isn't the case.

> ### Insight
> A growing movement in modern psychology holds that psychologists have a social duty to use their knowledge to promote world peace.

Information and propaganda

Large-scale conflicts don't just come out of nowhere. As a general rule, they have economic roots, but the underlying economic factors tend to be quite well hidden. It is other, social factors which are used to convince politicians and the public that war is necessary and justified. This is where the psychological understanding of propaganda becomes significant.

> ### Insight
> In wartime, particularly, we are much less ready to give the other side the benefit of the doubt. So just about anything which suggests how bad they are is accepted as probably true; while any information which suggests they may not be that bad after all tends to be disregarded. Until it is time to make peace.

As we all know from our everyday lives, the same action can look very different if done by a friend or if done by someone we dislike. There are several psychological mechanisms involved in this, and one of them is known as the **fundamental attribution error.** It is our basic tendency to judge other people's actions differently from the way we judge our own. For example, if we do something unpleasant, we will usually believe that we did it because we had to – the situation that we were in made it unavoidable to do anything else. That is a situational attribution – we see the reason as being because of the situation. But if someone else does the same thing, we almost always judge it as being because they are like that – they have a disposition which makes such unpleasant actions typical, or to be expected. That is a dispositional attribution.

The fundamental attribution error, then, is that we make situational attributions for our own behaviour, but dispositional attributions for other people's. And we do this for groups of people too. So actions taken by an opposing government are seen as sinister, while the same actions if they are taken by our own government are seen as justified.

Language comes into play here as well. The choice of words that we make, like government / regime, or terrorist / freedom fighter, can transform our understanding of what is going on. Emotively loaded words like these build a picture in our minds, and that picture then frames important decisions, so that only one set of outcomes can be seen as justified. That means that they restrict our understanding of the situation, making it harder to see possible alternative courses of action. In doing so, too, they make it very difficult for mediators to act effectively to promote peaceful alternatives between the two sides. Eventually, they can build up tensions to the point where war is seen as inevitable.

Insight

Try listening to the TV news and spotting all the emotively loaded words. Even on an ordinary day, you'll be surprised at just how many there are.

The aphorism 'the first casualty of war is truth' is in itself very true. While the population's support is being sought for any given war, just about any stories, no matter how implausible, can be used to convince the population of how necessary the war is. In the UK, Tony Blair's famous assertion that Iraq had weapons of mass destruction which could be set off within 45 minutes is one clear example. Although it turned out to be entirely untrue, it fitted with the mood of the time, and convinced a large number of UK MPs to vote in favour of the invasion of Iraq in 2003.

While a war is taking place, this type of propaganda can become even more extreme. During the Iraqi invasion of Kuwait in the 1990s, for example, most of the UK population believed the story that the Iraqis had taken premature babies from their hospital incubators in order to take the incubators back to Iraq. The story was completely fabricated – it had been made up by a tabloid journalist – and in peacetime it would have been unlikely to have got past the editor's desk. But because of the general anti-Iraqi feeling being generated at that time, it was published as if it were true, and widely believed.

EXACERBATING ETHNIC PREJUDICE

This kind of process doesn't just apply between nations. It can also produce civil wars, as it did in the Balkans where prejudice between different ethnic groups was systematically manipulated by politicians until eventually hostility between the ethnic groups became so extreme that the UN had to intervene.

Insight

Studies of social identification show that groups can co-exist quite happily until they are in competition for resources, or think that they are. At that point, inter-group competition develops. It works just as powerfully in real life as it does in the psychological laboratory.

Allport (1954) identified five distinct stages of social prejudice. The first is what he called anti-locution: that is, hostile talk and verbal denigration which targets a particular social group, such as the anti-Jewish propaganda which was common in pre-war Germany. The second is avoidance: that is, creating social distance between members of that group and others in society. At this stage there may not be any particular harm occurring, but inter-group differences are exaggerated, so that members of that group are made to seem more different from other people than they really are.

The third stage which Allport identified is discrimination, in which members of the group become excluded from civil rights, employment, housing and the like. This doesn't have to be official – it became a matter of state policy in Nazi Germany and South Africa – but it can also happen unofficially, in things such as preferential treatment for jobs, or in the ways that members of a particular social group find it difficult to obtain accommodation in some areas of a town or city.

The fourth stage of prejudice which Allport identified is when the tensions between the groups have become so strong that physical attacks begin to happen. Racially or religiously motivated attacks may be carried out by extreme individuals, but they exacerbate the conflict and make it more extreme than it already is. And the final stage of prejudice which Allport identified is that of extermination – indiscriminate violence against the entire group of people, which results in what has become known as 'ethnic cleansing', or genocide.

Allport's work was based on an analysis of what happened in Germany in the 1930s and 1940s, but it holds true for the Balkans and many other extreme conflicts. Social identity theory shows us how ordinary people become drawn into these conflicts, and become manipulated by politicians and propagandists. What also happens is that the social representations held by the various groups in the society are manipulated to change or refocus people's beliefs about their history and economic relationships with the other group. Social representations are closely linked to social identity (Wagner & Hayes 2005), and each reinforces the other.

Hewstone (2000) discussed how the key issues in this process are the apparent threats to social identity. They might be perceived threats to how a group acts and to its beliefs, perceived threats to its resources, or threats which result from the other group having more power or strength and using it to its own advantage. But they all have the same effect, which is to exaggerate the sense of difference, bringing social identity 'us and them' mechanisms into place to make those differences seem even more extreme.

CHALLENGING CONFLICTS

Information which challenges the prevailing mood at such times
is often dismissed or censored. It is notable, for example, that
political satire or comment shows tend to disappear from TV
screens when the country is in the throes of an intensive war –
unless it continues for too long, that is. But the much more open
access to information represented by the internet offers a challenge
in that respect. During the US/UK invasion of Iraq from 2003, for
example, John Sloboda and other psychologists began keeping and
making public detailed statistics of civilian Iraqi deaths resulting
from the invading troop actions. The information they gathered
directly challenged official statistics, but more importantly, it was
open to anyone with internet access, so the information could no
longer be kept under wraps.

Research into the psychology of minority influence suggests
that minorities are most effective and influential when they are
insistent, persistent and consistent. They need to make sure that
they are noticed and heard (being insistent); they need to make
their case repeatedly so that people can see its continued relevance
(being persistent); and they need to give a clear message which
doesn't change its nature over time (being consistent). Major
social changes, such as the abolition of slavery, began with the
vocal influence of just a few people, but as they stuck with these
principles more and more people became convinced by their
arguments, until eventually social change was able to happen.

In the case of national wars, these minority influences may take
considerable time to have an effect, but over time they link with
other social issues such as the attrition rate, and begin to challenge

the generally held belief that the war is justified. It took several years, for example, for the minority groups opposed to the US war in Vietnam to have an effect, but eventually they were able to convince enough people of their case that the US government perceived a political need to end the conflict.

In Chapter 17, I talked about the psychological process known as **entrapment** – the way that, for example, we may become trapped into spending more and more money on an old car, simply because we have already invested so much in it and that would all be lost if we scrapped the car and bought another. Entrapment doesn't just apply to buying cars. It works with bigger decisions too, and particularly the question of when or whether a nation should pull out of a war that it is demonstrably losing. The argument that the nation should not do so because then the lives of servicemen killed in that war have been wasted for nothing, is a classic example of entrapment. As Vietnam and other wars showed, it doesn't make a good argument for continuing, but it makes it more difficult for the politicians to make a case for withdrawing from the conflict.

It has been said that the general popularity of the Falklands War in the UK was because the war itself was of such short duration, so there was little time for the influence of minority dissenters to build up.

We can see, therefore, that the role of public information is a major factor both in initiating wars and in maintaining and ending them. Modern electronic sources of information mean that people have access to a greater diversity of sources than ever before. It remains to be seen how much this eventually changes modern warfare.

Psychology and diplomacy

At the World Congress of Psychology held in Stockholm in 2000, the diplomat Jan Eliasson discussed various ways that psychology could contribute to diplomatic attempts to deal with these problems.

One of these is in the area of conflict prevention: psychology can identify the early warning signals of developing conflicts, and also ways of preventing existing conflicts from escalating into all-out civil wars. Another is in the area of conflict resolution, and in particular effective mediation. Psychology can show how to build trust and co-operation between participants in the conflicts and those who are attempting to mediate between them. And a third area is in the negotiation of peace – in a better understanding of reconciliation processes and principles, and how to prevent conflicts from re-erupting at a later stage.

CONFLICT PREVENTION

Hewstone (2000) discussed the various types of conflict that psychologists working in this area have identified. One useful distinction is the difference between objective and subjective conflicts. **Objective conflicts** are those which concern issues like the power, wealth or territory possessed by various groups, and they are backed up by social, economic, political and historical structures. **Subjective conflicts,** on the other hand, concern the distinctions between different groups and the positive values which are associated with belonging to one group or another. They begin by being closely interwoven with objective differences between the groups, but they can continue long after those differences have actually been resolved.

Psychology has a great deal to offer to our understanding of how to prevent conflicts, and how to identify the early-warning signs. One of the most useful theories in this respect is social identity theory, which, as we have seen, explains how easily people can form into 'us' and 'them' groups. All of us have several social identities, and they are an important part of the self-concept. Social identities encompass the various social roles that we play in life: that is, how we act with other people. But they go a little deeper than that, because our membership of a particular social category can also affect how we receive and understand information. The approach used in social identification gives us a good way of understanding just how and why belonging to a group is so important to people (see also *Understand Psychology*).

That importance also means that people will react if they feel that the status or social standing of their group is threatened. And this makes them very vulnerable to manipulations from politicians and others who want to exaggerate the differences between groups and manipulate social conflicts for their own ends. It's not uncommon, for example, for politicians to stir up inter-group conflicts as a way of diverting social attention from the poor ways that their government is performing.

Psychological understanding of these issues can help us in preventing conflicts from escalating until they become extreme. One of the problems faced by diplomats is that this type of problem often isn't recognized until it has become acute and has exploded into violence – and at that point, it is far more difficult to resolve.

Establishing good early-warning systems can help to pick up the symptoms of such conflicts at an early stage, and with luck prevent them from escalating. So Eliasson (2000) identified the importance of having 'eyes and ears' in countries – people who are aware of the indicators of escalating conflicts, and who can alert the UN or other peacekeeping agencies to a developing problem. Fact-finding missions and third-party interventions can often do a great deal of good in the early stages of conflicts.

Part of what they can do involves going to the root causes of problems. I mentioned the distinction between objective and subjective conflict earlier, and many extreme social conflicts have their roots in social causes: poverty, repression, one group's lack of access to the society's resources, violations of human rights, or a simple lack of diplomacy between the various groups. External bodies can sometimes contribute towards effective treatment of these issues. The Social Charter of the European Community and its various Community Action Plans concerning human rights and equal opportunities are examples of attempts to address extreme inter-group disparities before they escalate into social conflicts.

When the conflict has become apparent, there are some other steps which third parties may be able to take before it becomes extreme. Article 33 of the United Nations Charter concerns the 'Pacific Settlement of Disputes', and discusses various approaches, including mediation, arbitration, negotiation between parties, enquiry into social conditions, and conciliation between groups, as some of the types of action which can be taken. The use of economic sanctions is also a possibility, although Eliasson (2000) expressed some concerns that these would be effective only if they were carefully analysed and designed to hit the leadership, rather than the ordinary people who have been caught up in the situation.

It is apparent, then, that psychology has a great deal to contribute in the area of conflict prevention. There is other psychological research into the symptoms of inter-group conflict, and how tensions between groups can be made more extreme or can be minimized by different types of action. Our understanding of this area grows all the time.

Conflict resolution

Once a conflict has actually become extreme, the challenges become rather different. The problem then is not how to prevent it from escalating, but rather how to stop it. Many politicians have discovered to their cost that it is easy to stir up inter-group conflict, but not so easy to bring it under control again. Once it has begun, the participating groups develop their own understandings, histories and sense of injustice, and bringing them back together becomes extremely difficult.

One of the psychological processes closely involved in this is the formation of **social representations**. Social representations are the shared beliefs held by members of a particular group, which are used to legitimize social actions. They are passed on from one group member to another, and are often powerful factors in holding the group together and maintaining social identification with the group. Sometimes they can be stated simply, but often they operate through an unspoken understanding, which members of the group understand implicitly and which are expressed by metaphors, anecdotes and illustrations rather than stated directly.

Insight

Social representations are intimately bound up with people's perceived history. Historical experiences are retold, edited and reshaped by conversations within families and social groups. These ideas become worked into powerful social representations which justify inter-group conflict or other social practices.

Finn (1997) conducted an analysis of the murals in the conflict areas of Belfast, in Northern Ireland. These murals are huge wall paintings by the various groups involved in the dispute, and they use symbols and slogans to express the social representations concerned. As a result, they help to create and maintain social pride and ideas about the sources of its sense of injustice. Images like this are used to bring together sections of the community, and to strengthen their shared understanding of what the conflict is all about – an understanding which may be very different from that shared by members of the other side.

Getting groups with opposing views to communicate with one another is the first step in resolving conflict. But when hostilities are high, that almost always has to take place through a third party, who will mediate and act as a go-between. In recent years, UN representatives have adopted a key role in mediation of many extreme conflicts, but other organizations, and sometimes even individuals, have also been involved at various times. Eliasson (2000) identified three key issues in the question of mediation, which can be summed up as 'who, when and how'.

The 'who' concerns who will actually be doing the mediation. What is important here is the build-up of trust, so that all of the parties involved in the conflict will be prepared to listen to the mediator, and to hear what they have to say without suspecting a hidden agenda. So it is important that the mediator comes from an agency or body which is unbiased, and doesn't have an interest in siding with one group rather than another.

It is also important that the mediator continues to act in such a way as to continue to build up confidence and trust. Their reception in the initial stages of a negotiation is likely to be guarded, but research into the psychology of mediation in conflicts shows that a mediator's effectiveness can increase over time, as the mediator becomes better known and their personal qualities become respected by the participants.

Eliasson argued that a good knowledge of culture and history is often just as important for a mediator as a knowledge of what the dispute was actually about. When Terry Waite was acting as a mediator in the Middle East, his knowledge of and respect for religious issues gave him more credibility than many other mediators had experienced. Being an avowed Christian could have been a hindrance, but it became an advantage in view of his open-mindedness and willingness to respect other viewpoints. It helped to establish him as a representative of a group which was not directly involved in the conflict, so he could avoid being placed on either side of the 'them-and-us' divisions in that society.

Insight

Psychologists are particularly useful in mediating conflicts because of the way that their training allows them to understand all the different sides of a problem. In any conflict, all the participants believe that their own side is justified, and it often takes considerable expertise to take all these viewpoints fully into account.

The 'when' comes in because the timing of the intervention is also important. Ideally, mediation needs to happen earlier rather than later in the conflict – it can save many lives that way. But sadly, sometimes conflicts need to reach a certain point before the groups concerned perceive a need for mediation. If a proposal is put forward too early it can be entirely ignored, and that makes it difficult for a mediator to put forward the same proposal again. Eliasson proposed this as one of the challenges for psychologists: to identify the psychological dimensions of timing in mediation.

How a conflict is mediated is also a crucial factor. Mikula (2000) discussed a number of different aspects of mediation, including the need for any resolution of conflict to be perceived as fair by both sides. Perceived social justice is perhaps the most important issue for internal disputes – it can't be a question of 'winner takes all', because that breeds resentments which can flare up at a later date. So the mediator needs to find a solution which will provide something for everyone – and also, which the leaders of the different factions can present to their own people without losing face.

Mediating a conflict can be about how ideas are expressed, as well as about the practicalities of an area. There is a considerable amount of research in psychology which deals with how social discourse is framed, and what gives it credibility. Social representations can be active in this, in terms of the way that they place interpretations of particular metaphors, but often it is more general issues of phrasing and metaphor which are involved. Eliasson gave an example of a difficult situation in which it was necessary to establish a localized ceasefire so that important humanitarian supplies could get through. The groups in conflict had little time for the idea of a localized ceasefire, perceiving it as a political manoeuvre, so attempts to negotiate this were unsuccessful. However, when it was called a 'humanitarian corridor' instead of a 'localized ceasefire', both sides agreed to co-operate. The new name emphasized it as an unbiased, humanitarian move rather than as a political compromise, and that made it much more acceptable.

Insight

One of the secrets of successful mediation is not allowing the established, emotively loaded words to dominate discussion. Rephrasing accounts into neutral language allows both sides to take a fresh look at them.

Political psychology, then, can also contribute to the processes of mediation. Psychological knowledge can give us insights into effective mediation and the build-up of trust and confidence in the mediator, and it can give insights into how language and knowledge of culture and social representations may be shaping the dispute. Although there is a need for more research in this area, there is already a great deal of psychological knowledge which has relevance for our understanding of mediation.

RECONCILIATION

Once a solution to a conflict has been successfully mediated, there is still a great deal of work to be done. As we've already seen, conflicts have their own history, and the psychological aspects of them can remain until long after objective unfairnesses have been sorted out. Each side in the conflict will have developed its own social representations of the dispute, and will have its own stories and anecdotes which favour their own group and make the other side appear to be the ones who were acting unreasonably. These accounts of what happened have their own momentum and their own psychological reality, and if a conflict is not fully resolved and the two sides reconciled with one another, it can arise again and again on later occasions.

A violent conflict causes psychological damage to all of those involved. That damage needs time to heal, but it also needs the opportunity. Addressing the emotional issues raised during the conflict is important, since, like other forms of abuse and psychological damage, these do not go away on their own. Psychologists studying the effects of child abuse, and also those studying post-traumatic stress disorder, are well aware of how ineffective simply burying the memories are. They can have lasting effects many decades after the event, and they need to be brought to the surface and dealt with if the person is to recover from the damage.

The same applies in the case of inter-group conflicts. Atrocities and perceived injustices need to be opened up and addressed, even if this is a painful process for all concerned. That isn't for revenge, which is of questionable value when it comes to psychological healing, but in order to get at what really happened. Truth commissions and tribunals have an important role to play in this. By allowing people to bring out their experiences, and to be heard openly, they help the society as a whole to come to terms with what has happened. Without that opportunity, the people concerned will still discuss their experiences, but only in families and friendship networks, keeping alive their resentments towards the other group. As a result, the conflict can re-emerge several decades, or even generations, later. So public enquiries, giving people the opportunity to be heard, are a vital part of the reconciliation process.

Insight

Truth commissions are vital because people need to express what has happened to them and how they see it. That's not only important for the society, but also for the individual and their personal recovery – for example, those who have been encouraged to speak freely about their experiences and express their anger tend to experience less severe post-traumatic stress disorder than those who have not had that opportunity.

The other important aspect of reconciliation is finding ways of reducing the strength of the 'us-and-them' distinctions which have resulted from the conflict. Hewstone (2000) identified two issues which can be helpful in this respect. The first of these is improving the opportunities for contact between the two groups. Contact has been identified for a long time as an important factor in reducing prejudice, and there has been a considerable amount of psychological research into how this happens. Some contacts are more effective than others, and it is important that contacts between members of the two groups are of high quality and likely to encourage the reduction of prejudice.

Contact on its own is not enough, of course. In the former Yugoslavia, for example, there was a great deal of positive contact between Serbs and Croats, but this was not proof against the deliberate machinations of politicians (Biro, 1995). Nevertheless, as long as objective injustices are addressed, contact is an important factor in the breaking down of prejudice and in-group favouritism. Applied psychologists working in this area need to explore how the quality and quantity of contact between members of previously opposing groups can be made most effective.

The second type of intervention which Hewstone identified is that which targets social categorization – how people classify themselves and each other as either 'one of us' or 'one of them'. He identified four ways of doing this, which are summarized in Table 19.1. Effectively, what each of these strategies does is to make the distinction between members of the opposing groups less important in some way or other – by changing the nature of the distinction, or by putting some other category in its place. This makes it more likely that the people from the different groups are going to be able to interact with one another positively, instead of always seeing the other as the 'enemy'.

Table 19.1 Challenging social categorization	
Decategorization	Working to remove the old categories which were producing the problems.
Recategorization	Changing the important categories from ones which generated a sense of 'us' versus 'them', to ones in which all participants can be seen as 'we': that is, as part of the same group.
Subcategorization	Establishing or emphasizing dual identities within the same overall categories.
Crossed categorization	Emphasizing how different categorizations overlap with one another, and how people often share categories on at least one dimension.

Source: Hewstone, 2000

The reason why this can work lies in the psychological processes underpinning social identification. As I said earlier, we all have several different social identities, and these become important at different times. If I am at an interdisciplinary workshop discussing cognitive systems, then my social identity as a psychologist becomes salient – that is, relevant to the situation – and that will affect how I discuss issues and answer questions. But if I am in a discussion of educational systems with lecturers from other European countries, then being a psychologist isn't particularly relevant in that situation, but being an educationalist, and British, is.

Social identities come to the fore when they are **salient** to the situation. In an inter-group conflict, membership of the various groups can become regarded as so important that it colours all of the interactions between the people concerned. But that doesn't have to be the case. There are numerous cases of people belonging to opposing sides in armed conflicts being able to co-operate and interact together as a result of a special situation – from accounts of soldiers in World War I giving Christmas presents to one another, to guerrillas being prepared to help people in serious distress even if they have come from the other side. The capacity for co-operation and helping doesn't entirely disappear in anyone, and it can be brought out by rendering the hostile 'us-and-them' boundaries far less important.

The challenge, then, is to replace the conflicting social identities with other social identifications which make it easier for positive contacts between people to happen. Shared experiences, shared identifications, and fair allocations of resources are all factors which have been shown to contribute to this, and there are many more. Psychologists don't have the answer to all of these questions, of course – there are economic, political and cultural issues involved as well. But they can contribute a great deal to the understanding and resolution of armed conflicts.

Insight

Encouraging people to become proud of unifying social identities is important. But it is important that such identities are not seen as in conflict with existing ones. One can be proud of being British, *and* being European, *and* being English, all at the same time. The three identities don't need to conflict – they can work together, complementing and helping to define one another.

What political psychology aims for is to develop better ways of aiding the diplomatic process, and contributing psychological knowledge to the resolution of conflicts. This includes identifying the early-warning signals of such conflicts, and working with diplomats to find ways of translating those warnings into effective early action. It includes identifying the optimal psychological conditions for conflict resolution and reconciliation. And it involves contributing psychological knowledge to help diplomats and others involved in the peace process to negotiate effectively, and work towards positive multi-ethnic and multi-cultural co-existence within different societies and cultures. Applied psychologists are only just beginning to become involved systematically in this area, but they have a great deal to contribute to it.

10 THINGS TO REMEMBER

1 *Applied psychology has a great deal to bring to our understanding of political processes.*

2 *The fundamental attribution error applies to judgements about other nations as well as about other people.*

3 *Political propaganda involves manipulating social representations through emotive words and phrases.*

4 *Untrue accounts may be used to enhance social representations.*

5 *Social prejudice can exist in many degrees, from mild to extremely severe.*

6 *Politicians can easily become trapped in costly and futile wars as they are unable to face admitting that they have lost.*

7 *Mediating conflicts can involve exploring the root causes of inter-group disputes.*

8 *Conflict mediators need to be trusted by both sides, so it is important that they are seen to be neutral.*

9 *Truth commissions are important for the healing of psychological wounds once conflicts have been resolved.*

10 *Successful reconciliation involves forging new inclusive 'us and them' social identifications.*

20

Applied psychology as a profession

In this chapter you will learn:
- *about the interaction between 'pure' and 'applied' psychology*
- *how the psychological profession is regulated*
- *what qualifications are needed to become an applied psychologist.*

Applied psychology, as you will have discovered if you have read this far, is a diverse and variable subject. There isn't just one kind of applied psychology. As we've seen, psychology can be applied in any number of different fields, and applied psychologists use any number of different methods, depending on the problem that they are dealing with at the time.

That flexibility is mainly possible because psychology itself, as a discipline, is so rich. It's been a specific area of study for over 140 years now, and during that time psychologists have gathered a tremendous amount of knowledge about how people work. There's still a great deal that we don't know, of course, and plenty of scope for future research, but what we have learned, as we've seen, is already extremely useful.

This is the second book that I have written for the 'Teach Yourself' series. The first one, *Understand Psychology*, dealt mainly with psychology as a subject in its own right, and only looked very briefly at some of the ways that it has been applied. This book, on the other hand, has focused much more strongly on how psychology has been put to practical use, and hasn't dealt very much with the academic side of psychology.

That may be a false distinction, though. Actually, pure and applied psychology interact with one another all of the time. There is a continual exchange of knowledge between that acquired in the field by applied psychologists putting psychology into practice, and researchers who work in universities (usually) exploring psychological knowledge in a way that is slightly more distant from the messy realities of day-to-day life. Academic psychologists applying for a research grant are always expected to indicate how they believe their research would be useful in the field, and applied psychologists conducting research in real-world settings as part of their work publish it in academic journals, as well as reporting it in their professional newsletters.

Insight

Many professional psychologists didn't start out intending to go into their particular branch of the profession. They began studying psychology from interest, and then found that they were drawn to a particular specialism over time.

Sometimes, the distinctions are very hard to pin down. Health psychology, for example, is an area of applied psychology which first developed in academic departments, as university psychologists with an interest in this area began to develop research projects to investigate real-world problems. As that field of knowledge developed, and its relevance became increasingly apparent, people became more and more interested in employing health psychologists, until eventually specific qualifications were established and that area of applied psychology became formally established as part of the range of professional psychology.

Psychology has relevance to just about any area of everyday life. Anything relating to people has something to do with psychology, in one way or another. This is partly because psychology is such a broad discipline, covering so many areas of knowledge, and partly because human beings are so very complex that just about everything they do involves several different sets of processes.

A simple example such as eating a meal can draw in psychological knowledge at the biochemical level, in the ways that different foodstuffs can affect our brain functioning; at the behavioural level in terms of the associations we make between food, caring, comfort and other stimuli; at the cognitive level in terms of how we perceive the food and whether it looks attractive enough to eat; at the social level in terms of who we eat it with or who prepares it for us; and at the cultural level in terms of what, when and how we eat it.

Insight

It isn't necessary to be a qualified psychologist to benefit from psychological knowledge. Many people who work in the 'people' professions have psychology degrees, and find that these have helped them in numerous small ways to carry out their work.

That's just one example, but as I said, just about every aspect of day-to-day living involves psychological knowledge of one sort or another. As our psychological knowledge grows, so the range of applied psychology grows too: it's constantly changing and developing. Like psychology itself, applied psychology learns, changes, accumulates knowledge, and reflects the interests and concerns of its time.

Professional standards in applied psychology

Applied psychology, though, involves a lot more than just learning a bit about how human beings work and then going out and putting it into practice. Like any other area of scientific knowledge, psychology can be used or it can be misused. It is all too easy for people with only a limited amount of psychological knowledge to mislead the public, or to put that psychological knowledge into practice in a way which is manipulative and deceptive.

Ethical issues are such a fundamental part of psychological research that all significant research projects now have to be approved by an ethics committee before they can be carried out.

This is why psychologists have such rigid professional standards. All professional psychologists have to abide by a Code of Conduct, which establishes ethical practice and what they may and may not do. Someone who breaks that Code of Conduct is likely to be brought before a disciplinary tribunal, and may be struck off the professional register. The ethical guidelines which psychologists have to follow are very strict, and are aimed to protect the clients and other people with whom the psychologist is dealing. So if you see someone misusing their psychological knowledge for manipulative or deceptive purposes, you can be pretty sure that person isn't a fully accredited professional psychologist. Or if they are, you can report them to their professional association.

Insight

Many of the early studies in psychology wouldn't have passed an ethics board. Some psychologists say that therefore we should not use their findings, but others say it is important to learn from our history and some of those insights are invaluable.

As we've seen in various places in this book, becoming a formally qualified applied psychologist involves several years of quite rigorous training. It begins with a first degree in psychology which, in the UK and USA and increasingly in other countries too, has to have been approved by the professional association. In the UK, this approval is given the name of the Graduate Basis for Registration, or GBR for short. What it means is that the degree in question has been checked to make sure that it will provide someone who takes it with a good broad knowledge of the various areas of psychology. Other countries have similar systems, but they all have different names.

That degree forms the basic knowledge that they need, and some people go on from there to pursue research degrees or other courses which will lead them into one of the newer areas of applied psychology. To get into one of the more established areas, though, such as clinical or occupational psychology, it is then necessary to take a higher, specialist degree. Usually, someone who wants to do this will have to get a couple of years' relevant work experience too, so that they have some practical knowledge of reality in the field that they want to go into. Their higher degree includes a period of supervised professional practice, and that is followed by a couple of probationary years when they are newly qualified. It's a complex business, but not that much different from other professions such as law or medicine.

Insight

Psychology doesn't provide simple one-word answers to questions about people, because explaining human beings inevitably draws on several levels of explanation. Perhaps that's why it's so under-used in the kind of social discussions where people are looking for single causes and solutions. The trouble is, though, that simple solutions don't often work.

If you want to know more about psychology, there are several other places you can look. *Understand Psychology* would be the one to start with, if you haven't read it already. I have also written some textbooks about psychology which you might find interesting, including *Foundations of Psychology*, and a book on research methods.

I personally have always found psychology to be a fascinating subject, always giving me something new to explore or to learn. So it has been a pleasure for me to introduce you to some of it. If you do go on to find out more about it, I hope you will enjoy it as much as I have. If not, I hope you have enjoyed this book anyway.

THINGS TO REMEMBER

▶ *It is very difficult to draw a hard-and-fast line between 'pure' and 'applied' psychology.*

▶ *Psychology is involved in all aspects of our lives, to some extent.*

▶ *Professional psychologists must abide by strict codes of conduct and ethical standards.*

▶ *Psychological training begins with a recognized first degree in psychology, but can involve many more years of study before final qualification.*

▶ *All professional psychology training involves some supervised practice. It is not possible to learn everything from books.*

▶ *There is more about psychology in the sister book to this one:* Understand Psychology.

Index

Credits

Notes